NOBBY STILES
AFTER THE BALL

My Autobiography

About the Author

Nobby Stiles was brought up in Collyhurst, Manchester and dreamed of playing football from an early age. He played for Manchester schoolboys and signed for Manchester United in 1956 at the age of 15. His full English debut was against Scotland at Wembley; then came his role in the 1966 World Cup. United's European Cup victory followed, making him one of only two Englishmen ever to win both the World Cup and the European Cup.

Nobby Stiles lives in Manchester.

NOBBY STILES
AFTER THE BALL

My Autobiography

NOBBY STILES

with

James Lawton

CORONET BOOKS

Hodder & Stoughton

Copyright © 2003 Nobby Stiles

First published in Great Britain in 2003 by Hodder and Stoughton
A division of Hodder Headline

The right of Nobby Stiles to be identified as the Author of this Work has been
asserted by him in accordance with the Copyright, Designs and Patents Act 1988.

A Coronet paperback

3 5 7 9 10 8 6 4

A CIP catalogue record for this title is available from the British Library

ISBN 0 340 82888 9

Typeset in Galliard by Servis Filmsetting Ltd, Manchester
Printed and bound in Great Britain by Mackays of Chatham Ltd, Chatham, Kent

Hodder Headline's policy is to use papers that are natural, renewable and
recyclable products and made from wood grown in sustainable forests. The
logging and manufacturing processes are expected to conform to the
environmental regulations of the country of origin.

Hodder and Stoughton
A division of Hodder Headline
338 Euston Road
London NW1 3BH

To Kay, Shay and the families

CONTENTS

ACKNOWLEDGEMENTS

I resisted the idea for a long time but I'm glad now that I finally got round to telling my story. I've always been grateful for the affection that has been shown to me in all parts of the country and I hope this is reflected in the book. Certainly, I have tried to give an honest account of my life in and out of football. The process of writing it was less painful than I had imagined – indeed, the hours spent with sportswriter and friend Jim Lawton gave us both the chance to wallow, most happily, in the past. I have many debts to the game and all the people who inhabit it, and to all those who coloured my youth in Manchester, and I hope these are properly discharged in the following pages. I'm particularly grateful to my son John who organised the project on my behalf and gave me much encouragement as, inevitably, did the rest of my family led by my wife Kay. I must also say I've been very fortunate to have a publisher of the quality of Roddy Bloomfield. His support and insights have been tremendous.

Photographic acknowledgements

The author and publisher would like to thank the following for permission to reproduce photographs:

Associated Press, Colorsport, Empics, Evening Gazette Media Co. Middlesbrough, Getty Images/Hulton Archive, *Manchester Evening News*, Mirrorpix, Popperfoto.com, Press Association, Thames Television/Jack Crawshaw, Topham Picturepoint.

All other photographs are from private collections.

PROLOGUE

I KNOW now there is not much to recommend a heart-attack. It hits you with pain and terrible anxiety and for a little while you wonder if you will ever feel whole again. You fear you will never get back the strengths and the certainties of those convictions about yourself that made you what you were – in my case, a basically cocky little bastard who always believed he would finish up a winner. But if you come through it, and maybe learn from it, it does bring one great benefit. It makes you think deeply about your place in the world, and what is most important in it, in a way that you may never have done before.

If you are very lucky, there is another bonus. It is a surge of exhilaration that you have survived to put a new value on your one and only life, and the people who have shaped it, and it was this sensation, I think, that took me on a damp and misty Manchester morning back to my deepest roots.

I went to the old burial ground in Collyhurst where as a six and seven year old I played football with my mates on the upturned gravestones. It was a little difficult to find. There were some barred gates and I had to find my way through some workshops that I didn't easily recall. Hedges and bushes were overgrown. But then, magically, it was there – the old place with the gravestones

1

dating back to the eighteenth century, stretching out and providing the pitch for the ghosts of my past; and the ghosts came alive again, racing for the ball, shoving you into the wet grass and the shale, and crying 'twat' and other endearments when you nicked it away from them and kept your feet on the greasy stones and dribbled over the memorial lines to some long-gone beloved husband or wife or, tragically common, some darling infant.

We never thought we were violating anyone's memory. We were just enjoying being young, and, anyway, my dad was an undertaker and once, after my brother Charlie and I saw a body in an open coffin while we were playing hide-and-seek in the funeral parlour, my mother Kitty told me, 'Norbert, it's not the dead ones you have to worry about.' It was strange that we never felt a touch of dread at the old burial ground. It could be a little spooky going down some of the cuts and alleyways in Collyhurst before first light or at night – you always looked over your shoulder for fear of a bogeyman – but we never had any fear when we played on the gravestones. There was a big factory works nearby and you could hear the hooter going and see people standing outside the gates having a fag. You could see them pushing coal and coke in prams in the street and you could smell the tobacco from the Gallagher's factory. Just around the corner there was a charity shop where the poor people went and you could get a free cup of hot cocoa. We played on the gravestones but there was life teeming around us.

It all came back on that post-heart-attack morning. I could hear the old workhorses snorting in their stables beneath the arches of the railway line that ran along the River Irk. The horses had gone but the sound of them remained. Below the burial ground the buildings of the Charter Street Ragged School and Home for Working Girls have long been used for other purposes, but the signs are still up, speaking of another world. I saw so many things in my mind's eye that morning. I saw my father playing his last game of football, as hard as ever even though when he took off his boots I could see his feet were covered in blood from the stud nails coming through. I saw all the good players of my youth, including the really talented ones who some said were unlucky not to go as far as me in the game, to which I responded, occasionally, that we all started off on the same terms, playing on the Red Rec at Monsal and the Loco ground where Manchester United started their existence. I saw the banners of my church, St Patrick's, unfurling on the Catholic walk on Whit Friday, and the shining white shirts and scrubbed faces of my schoolmates, and heard my mother saying when the sun shone for our march, 'God looks after his own,' and then when it rained, 'God waters his own.' There were 35,000 in the parish of St Patrick's then. Now there are barely 4,000. They moved many of the people – including Doreen Bracegirdle, the girl who caused me to blush whenever I saw her and gave me the first hint there was more to life than football, and whose big sister Barbara beat me up when I gave her some cheek – out to such places as the Langley estate in Middleton and Wythenshawe on the edge of the city, and they knocked down the little houses. But as I walked over the old gravestones again, the people and the houses were back in place. The Bowery Boys were playing at the Osborne Cinema a little way up Rochdale Road. I could smell the pea soup that warmed me in the café before we called in at Yates's Tavern on the way to Old Trafford where my uncle Peter, tall and still thin from the Burma campaign, held me up on his shoulders, when the world was a place that offered so much you sometimes felt you were in danger of bursting. I could hear the rattle of the trams and the roar of a place that now has stretches of green parkland and trendy townhouses where before there was just a sea of close-built bricks and mortar and human life.

As I heard all those old sounds and saw all those old things, I performed a brief little dance. It was nothing so elaborate or as wild as the Wembley jig on the pitch when the World Cup trophy passed from Bobby Moore's hands into mine. For reasons I will explain later in some quite painful detail, the origins of that famous celebration, for which I suppose I will be remembered more easily than for any tackle I made, will always be a blur. After receiving my World Cup medal from the Queen (which I don't remember doing) and passionately kissing my team-mate George Cohen (which I do), I danced on a tide of joy and adrenaline, but I cannot tell you what was going through my mind.

It was different at the old burial ground. It wasn't, perhaps, the work of Zorba the Greek. The choreography was impromptu but the feelings ran deeply and precisely. Maybe it was a small state-ment of survival, of acceptance that if the heart-attack, which came ironically at the start of the 2002 World Cup, had been a terrible shock – I denied its very existence, despite the pain tearing from my back into my chest, until my wife Kay, as she has done so often in our life together, took control and ordered me to the hos-pital, holding my hand as I sweated and groaned in the back of a neighbour's car – it was also maybe a signal for the enjoyment of the rest of my days. A man couldn't have had a better wife or sons or friends, or memories of the one thing that had coloured all his days, the game of football, the great passion of the blood in my part of town.

It was, probably more than anything, recognition that my life, despite some pain and disillusionment and some days that could only be described as desperate, had been a ball – and that, even now at this late hour and with the trauma of the heart-attack still so fresh in my memory, the music played on.

1

NICE ONE, FRITZ

O N the night of 18 May 1942, the Germans flew along the
River Mersey, found the line of the Manchester Ship Canal
and made several direct hits on Baxendale's, a building goods
factory situated a few hundred yards from our two-up, two-down
terraced house at 263 Rochdale Road. My mother remembered
the occasion vividly for two reasons. One was that the sound of
the explosions was terrifying. The other was that at the time she
was giving birth to me in the cellar with the help of some neighbours. There was a shelter a little way down the road but the
bombs were falling and she was frightened to go into the night.
In her labour she also wanted some privacy.

The neighbours naturally provided the midwifery. The people
were always in and out of each other's houses. One of my
mother's duties as an undertaker's wife was to lay out the dead. I
suppose the bombs were just bringing a little extra drama to the
cycle of life and death. I never took the bombing incident and its
threat to my existence personally. If I reflected on it at all, it was
only to celebrate the accuracy of the German bomb-aimer.

In Collyhurst the trick was always to get on with life. No one
ever said it was going to be easy – as I was reminded eighteen
months after the bombs fell when I was hit on the head by a tram

after toddling out of a baker's shop and into the street. Neither the Luftwaffe nor the Manchester Corporation transport department were able seriously to damage the gift of natural aggression that served me well in the neighbouring streets and then later on the football fields of the world. The tram, which left a permanent scar on my forehead, may have contributed to, or perhaps even caused, my chronically bad eyesight, but it was only much later when the problem threatened my professional career that there was any serious investigation. In the meantime, I squinted through smarting, watering eyes for most of my schoolife. In Collyhurst, spectacles were only for cissies.

I made a noisy arrival in the cellar of 263 and my father later observed in his dry but not unfond way, 'He's a tough little bugger.' That proved true enough, but I was also a happy kid, and never more so than when I went across the main road to St Patrick's School on Livesey Street, where Sister Veronica gave me some of my first lessons in the game – and put me on the roster of altar boys serving mass at the Convent Chapel. My mother sent me off to school with great confidence. One day she waved me goodbye, turned to my father and said, 'Norbert Peter Patrick Paul goes off to Livesey Street to play football – and beat them all.'

The game, as it was for so many families in those Collyhurst streets, was deeply interwoven in our lives. My father and his friend Jim Barlow ran the St Patrick's senior team. In their hard-working time they made two pitches, one out of a tip, bulldozing them as flat as they could and marking out the touchlines with sawdust. I was an eager helper. I carried my bag of sawdust proudly. The St Pat's senior team played on Saturday. The boozers played on Sunday, their supporters spilling out of the pub and shouting the odds. That wasn't my father's style. He never smoked and rarely had a drink. He was a serious man – serious about life and his business of death and, above all it seemed at times, football. Once he took me to a house where there had been a death and soon enough I discovered the reason why I had been taken along. The bereaved family were related to Jimmy Delaney, the fine Manchester United winger, and one of his shirts was hanging on the wall. At an appropriate moment my father explained how passionate I was about football and how Jimmy Delaney was one of my heroes. Would it, he asked, be possible for me to put on the shirt for a moment or two? The lady of the house, who was Jimmy Delaney's niece, took the shirt down from the wall, put it on me and patted my head.

Later, I liked to think of the little ritual as a rite of passage – the transfer of the warrior robes of my tribe from one generation to another. Certainly by then I had formed the unshakeable belief that I would one day wear such a shirt in my own right. As a five year old I caused great confusion in the parlour at 263 when I managed to get my head stuck down the sofa during the excitement of the 1948 FA Cup final between United and Blackpool. My father, my brother Charlie and I had been crowding around the radio when Blackpool went into a 2–1 lead. In my grief, I buried my head in the furniture, quite literally. My father rescued me, a little impatiently, but he was rewarded soon enough with two goals from the electric Jack Rowley and one from Stan Pearson. I danced around the parlour without any further mishap. On another occasion, when United fell behind in a Cup-tie at Wolves, I ran into the backyard in despair and kicked the wall, very painfully.

Then, Manchester United was the fantasy, the dream that would one day turn into reality. In the meantime, I had the day-to-day glory of St Pat's senior team. I recall, as vividly as any big game at Old Trafford, a Bank Holiday Church Cup final match at Newton Heath Loco with my uncle Tommy Byrne playing in front of 8,000. The playing surface was cinder. The tackles were ferocious.

Many years later I was shown an old grainy picture of the St Pat's team standing proudly in the schoolyard, their spiritual home. That was the place where the values that would last a lifetime were imposed, and where I was tutored in the game, and life, by first Sister Veronica and then John Mulligan, a man who would prove as influential as my father. Mr Mulligan was a passionate teacher and football enthusiast whose father had played for Ireland. He had wavy dark hair and a club foot, which never impeded his flying progress across the schoolyard or Monsal Rec, where he refereed and coached us with a tremendous eye for detail. He taught me all about competing and the necessity to win.

During one school game I was standing behind the goal at Monsal Rec, holding Mr Mulligan's heavy overcoat. As always, I got very caught up in the game. My brother Charlie was playing and whenever he was in possession I yelled advice along the lines of 'Go by him, Charlie, for fuck's sake' – things you could say only out of the earshot of your parents and the nuns. Charlie had lovely skill but I always thought he held something back. It used to drive me mad. Suddenly, our goalkeeper was caught out of his ground and an opposing player lobbed in the ball. Without thinking, I threw down the coat and kicked the ball away just as it was about to cross the line. Mr Mulligan shouted, 'Norbert, was that ball going in?' I replied, 'Definitely not, Sir.' Mr Mulligan waved play on after shouting, 'No goal.' Naturally, the opposing team went crackers.

I thought of incidents like that when I looked at the old photograph of the team and the fierce expressions of the players – grown men still immersed in the game of the schoolyard. In the background, sitting on a wall and peering down with an expression of awe, was a kid in short pants. Without surprise, I recognised him easily enough. It was me.

The first pitch made by my father and Jim Barlow, who owned

a grocer's shop and whose son Colin went on to play for Manchester City, was on the side of a hill that ran down to the River Irk. My job was to stand at the foot of the slope and grab the ball before it splashed into the water. If it did that, you could forget it. It was reckoned you could catch at least six terrible diseases if you set foot in the Irk. So I scampered to catch the ball as it came bouncing down the hill, then I carried it back to the field before returning to my station. At the end of the game, my dad or Jim Barlow gave me a tanner – a sixpenny piece (2½p).

Later, they had to give up the 'tip' ground. The owners, Wilson's Brewery, who had made beer barrels in a workshop on a corner of the site, had sold the land and now it was needed for more practical purposes than football. It was a small crisis for such determined pitch-makers. A new field was fashioned out of wasteland that stretched out on a high promontory on the other side of the river. The new site was beside a brickworks and a great pool of stagnant water, but Jim Barlow and my dad just got down to the work. We crossed the Irk like a rag-tag football expeditionary force, climbing up over an iron bridge which had thirty-nine steps. I remember each of them.

Many years later the artist Harold Riley presented me with a beautiful set of drawings that covered the landscape of my young life, including the thirty-nine steps and the old burial ground, and the Red Bank, which had some of Collyhurst's poorest housing. I'm told that the Red Bank now fits the estate agent's demand of 'location, location, location' being a smart little area of expensive apartments, but back then, for those of us a step or two further up the survival ladder, it seemed like the local version of hell.

My mother washed and ironed the team's shirts. It is the strongest memory of my childhood, seeing the shirts all hung out to dry in our little parlour. I can smell them now. They would often be caked with mud and sopping wet when they were handed to her. She would bundle them up and take them along to the washhouse, which was next door to the Osborne swimming baths. I would go along in the belief that there could be no more glamorous work. Recently I saw a television documentary on the old working-class life and the narrator talked of washhouses as if somehow they were places that should be remembered with shame. I thought, 'Bollocks – there's nowt wrong with washhouses.' There were plenty of laughs at the washhouse.

Our house was filled with candles and other paraphernalia of the funeral business – and, it seemed, always football shirts. In the little parlour, Mam would hang them up to dry on dollyhorses suspended from the ceiling. They filled the room with the smell of cleanliness. I dreamed of wearing one of those green shirts – later, they acquired a flash of gold along the sleeve – and when I did so, the thrill of it remained with me always. In the future there would be the red of United and the white of England, but first there was the green and gold of St Pat's, and I always knew that whatever happened to me, they would be colours that would never fade. St Pat's was more than a football team. It was a point of identity, a statement, like the Whit walks, about who you were and from where you drew so much of your strength.

One of my father's team-mates was my mother's brother, Uncle Tommy, the hero of the Loco. He was a good, hard wing-half-back playing in front of my dad, a full-back who tried to model himself on the great Johnny Carey of Manchester United and Ireland. 'Look at Carey,' he once told me, 'at half-time and the final whistle. Look at his shorts. On the muddiest day, they will be shining white. He has such balance he always stays on his feet. You cannot make a tackle while you're sitting on your arse.' It was through football and the friendship of Tommy Byrne, the wing-half, and Charlie Stiles, the full-back, that my parents met. So for us it really was the game of life.

But, of course, if you lived for it, you couldn't live by it. It was the release, the means of expression, that was a vital need in lives that were dominated by the demands of paying the rent and putting food on the table. Because my father was part of the big Stiles undertaking family, it was assumed that we were on easy street, but it was never so. We lived in that pokey house with an outside toilet and our bath was a tin tub. We used to bathe in front of the fire and a hob leaded black. Apart from laying out bodies, taking the bookings of the bereaved and having to be by the phone on a Saturday night when my father was called out on business, my mother also worked as a machinist. If she could, she liked to take Charlie and me to the pictures on Saturday night, but when it wasn't possible she would walk us up to the cinema and ask somebody to take us in. It is hard to imagine such trust now, but then it was something that wouldn't even raise an eyebrow.

My mother was a gentle woman in many respects, and later she would worry obsessively about the need to pay tax – a state of mind that came as a result of the tangled affairs of the undertaking empire – but whenever it was needed she could produce a touch of steel. Charlie and I used to laugh when she put on her posh phone voice. She would phone through death notices to the *Manchester Evening News*, carefully spelling out the names – A for apple, B for Bertie, C for Charlie – and when someone called to give details of a death, she would pick up her pencil, lick the end of it, and put on her best professional tone. Sometimes Charlie and I would go the public phone box, call home and get Mum to take down some information on a bogus death. Then in the middle of it we would shout, 'Hiya, Mum.'

The patriarch of the family was my grandfather, Herbert. He was a bigwig at St Patrick's, familiar with the priests, and always given a prominent position in the Whit walk contingent. He walked with the roll of a sailor and every stride announced his belief that he was a man of substance. I was proud to have such a high-profile relative on such an important day. For weeks before the walk, you would hear your parents discussing the savings required to buy you a new suit, and hear Mum praying for good weather.

There was great rivalry with the Protestant families up in Abbot Street. In the winter we would have snowball fights, but there was no badness. Really, we had similar lives and, deep down, I always thought of us as all pals together. Of course, we were always keen to take the piss out of each other. We marched on Friday with our saints, our virgins and our bagpipes. They responded on Monday with their bugles and trumpets. We used to say, 'Hey up, here comes the hurdy gurdy band.' It seemed more like fun than anything else, and the bonus was that grown-ups would come up to you and give you a tanner.

Later on, I learned that grandfather Herbert was quite a bit of a character and he certainly liked a bet. Unfortunately, the way he ran the business meant that my mother and father didn't enjoy much benefit beyond a very basic income. The eldest son, Herbert, had the business in Oldham. My father was number two, and we lived just a few yards from the Rochdale Road branch, where there was a shop, a garage and the place where they made the coffins. A third brother, Cliff, operated in Ardwick, and my great uncle, Norbert, had the business in Moss Side. It should have been a rich living, and perhaps it was for my grandfather, who had a big house to go along with his lofty status on the Whit walk, but not much cream trickled down to number 263. Much later, it ended badly for my parents. The short version of the story is that Uncle Norbert did what amounted to a bunk to Canada, leaving unpaid bills from the tax authorities and coffin-makers. My parents just about recovered from the consequences, but it was very hard for them to achieve much comfort.

In all our time,we had just one family holiday – a trip to Bray, the seaside resort south of Dublin, which was odd because later I found my wife and a whole new dimension of my life in Dublin. Kay is the sister of my greatest friend and former team-mate, John Giles.

We were seven hours on the boat from Holyhead and it was absolutely brilliant. My dad, who was not much of a gambler, had come up on the horses and for a few days we lived like toffs in a guest house overlooking the sea. After Collyhurst, the air was so fresh it made you feel giddy. In one of the hotels, a pianist was making an attempt on the world marathon playing record.

But that was a rare taste of the high life, and for my parents a point of rebellion was maybe inevitable. When it came, it was not surprising that it was my mother who took a stand. One of her many duties was to make lunch each day for grandfather Herbert, his sons, his brothers and a couple of drivers. My mother would make the food in her little scullery and Charlie and I would wait around as the men in the black suits ate and talked. One day she just snapped. She said, 'Get out all of you. I'm sick of this. Charlie gets £8 a week and I have to feed you lot.' My grandfather's mouth dropped open. My father shuffled his feet in embarrass- ment, but there was no going back, and he supported my mother. For two years he went beyond the pale of the family empire. He got a job in the Cleansing Department of Manchester Corporation, driving a street-sweeping wagon. It may not sound much of a job but I was dead proud of him. He and my mother had grafted so hard and in the end there was so little to show for it; together they would go their own way. In those days it must have been a hard decision; you did what you were born to do, what circumstances dictated, but my parents were saying, for once in their lives and however briefly, that they just didn't have to take without question what was being handed down to them.

Charlie and I didn't suffer. We had wholesome food on the table – our favourite came on Saturday lunchtime before we went off to the match, chicken and dumplings. When things were particularly tough, Mum would send me down to Barlow's for something on the 'knock' – she would settle it when she could. Everybody did it. It was how you got by. I loved the way they would wire-cut you half a pound of butter out of a big churn and wrap it in greaseproof paper. It was a bit like receiving a sacrament and it didn't seem to matter that it was on the knock. No, we didn't really suffer at all. We had the pictures and we had football and boxing and – this may come as a little bit of a surprise – I also had Collyhurst's version of the 'Black and White Minstrel Show'. When I joined the Hugh Oldham Boys' Club, which was sponsored by Manchester Grammar School for the 'cultural and recreational' development of working-class lads, I volunteered for all the activities, including the entertainment of old people. I couldn't dance a step or sing a note but I was already a devoted fan of Al Jolson, and I eagerly 'blacked up' for my audition. Logic told me I didn't have a chance, but in some crazy part of my head I saw and heard what I should have looked and sounded like. The producer was at least impressed by my gameness. 'Thank you, Norbert,' he said. 'I think we can find a place for you in the chorus.' My chief duty was throwing up my hands and cheering at the jokes delivered by our three comedians. One of them, Mr Interlocutor, stood in the middle of the stage. He was the big boss. I loved every minute of it.

For a little while I showed promise as a boxer. My father told me about all the great Manchester fighters who had performed at Belle Vue – Johnny King, Jock McAvoy and our own local hero, Jackie Brown. Jackie was a superb flyweight champion and he was revered in the neighbourhood. He lived around the corner from us with his sister, Mary, a lovely, refined lady, and kids like me would shout 'Hiya, champ' from a respectful distance when he ran by in the street in his training gear. He was long finished as a fighter and now worked as a car-park attendant. His aura lingered on, however, and no one wanted to dwell on the fact that the ring had taken its toll on the great man. Maybe Jackie Brown was punchy from the eleven knockdowns administered by the ferocious Scotsman Benny Lynch at Belle Vue, but in our mind's eye he was still a star. When he went by, we all felt bigger and more accomplished than before, and proud of who we were and where we came from. I would have liked to have spoken to him, told him how much he was respected by me and my mates, but I never got up the nerve. It was enough to feel his presence among us. I'd worn Jimmy Delaney's shirt and Jackie Brown came running by my front door. It meant that I could beat anyone, on the field and in the boxing ring.

Unfortunately, this didn't include Michael Sutton, who beat me in my second fight at the Boys' Club. I won my first fight in the big ring in the gym, where spectators perched on ladders running up the walls to the ceiling. I liked the feeling that came with that first fight, which seemed so easy. I was tougher, quicker than the other kid and I thought that if I couldn't be Al Jolson maybe I would be the next Randy Turpin. My father allowed me to stay up late to hear the Turpin–Sugar Ray Robinson fight on the radio, and after the excitement of that, and the thrill of hearing him declared 'the new middleweight champi-ON of the world', I wore myself out shadow-boxing for days. I hoped my father would be proud of me because, despite being such a quiet and basically gentle man, he had a great feeling for the ring and the men who went into it for a living.

In its own way, his own living was very hard, and I always thought he showed great character in not turning to drink. From an early age, I noted that so many undertakers were hard drinkers. I supposed it got them away from all the pain and the sadness. My father talked of fighters with the same reverence he applied to great footballers, but somehow there was a difference. Football could be as hard or as easy as you made it, but fighting cut down your options.

Michael Sutton was smaller than me but he was very hard. There was a big crowd of people from Manchester Grammar School watching the fight; it was our annual show for our sponsors, 'the toffs', and we got plenty of cheers for our efforts. That made me a little uncomfortable. I had a sense that we were there for somebody else's amusement, which I knew was also partly true when you played football, but then you didn't taste blood in your mouth or hear howls in your ears keeping pace with the pain in your head. I hit Michael Sutton a lot of times but I couldn't keep him off. He just kept coming through my punches and landing his own. They left me hurt and beaten – and a former boxer.

I still loved boxing but Michael Sutton taught me a quick, sharp lesson. He showed me that I wasn't good enough, but I was glad I had tried. It was another rule of Collyhurst: if you didn't push open all the doors you could, you might never find a way out. Not that I was ever dissatisfied with what life had given me in those days. If anyone had told me I lived on the wrong side of the railway, I would have said they were mad. Collyhurst wasn't a ghetto. It was my playground, and on Saturday night it was also a profitable workplace. I would go with a pal to a newsagent's shop on Queen's Road and collect a quire – twenty-five copies – of the early edition of the old *Empire News* and we would sell them in every pub along Cheetham Hill Road. As the evening wore on – and the beer flowed – the profit margins would increase. The plan was to put on your pathetic little urchin's face, straight out of Charles Dickens, and more often than not it worked nicely. It was not unusual to get a shilling – at least four times the cover price. Sometimes I used to imagine what my mother would have thought about the performance, but neither she nor my father knew about this business enterprise. I raised the capital by taking back pop bottles. The profits usually went on sweets, which is probably the reason why I scarcely had a tooth of my own when I did my dance at Wembley not so many years later.

Canon Early, the parish priest, was not so indulgent as the boozers along Cheetham Hill. He was one of the celebrants of early morning mass at the convent chapel that adjoined St Patrick's, and he demanded strict punctuality from the altar boys. The younger priests – Fathers Ryan, O'Leary and O'Clary – were much more tolerant when I arrived a little late for duty after dragging myself from a warm bed on a winter's morning for 7 a.m. mass. That was my duty, from Monday to Sunday. I would pull on my cassock and slip in by the altar as mass proceeded, suffering no more than a frown from Sister Veronica and Sister Monica, who was in charge of the altar boys' roster. But the first time it happened with the Canon there I suffered a great humiliation. I still shudder at the memory of it. When he turned and saw me, kneeling as piously as I could, he clicked his fingers and dismissed me with a sweeping gesture of great contempt, saying, with a terrible finality, 'Off.' According to him, I was guilty of a terrible insult.

I retreated from the altar, returned my cassock to its peg in the little vestry, and raced down the stairs. I could feel my face smarting. When I reached the bottom, Sister Monica was waiting for me. She was not unkind. She said, 'In future, Nobby, when you are late and see that the Canon is saying mass, don't come on to the altar – just go home.'

I never served the Canon after that. The days when I was late were invariably when he was on duty. Many years later, when I returned to St Patrick's to receive an award, I confessed to Sister

Monica that it had never been a coincidence. I deliberately arrived late when I thought the Canon would be saying mass, then raced home down the dark street for an extra half-hour in bed. 'I know, Norbert,' sighed Sister Monica. 'I always knew.'

It was a pity because, in its way, the ritual of the mass had become a big part of my life, and my identity. The nuns adopted me to a certain extent. I think they recognised certain demands I made of myself. I think they saw that I was eager to do well, and the truth was I was quite an efficient altar boy. It was just that the Canon put me off. I could easily imagine dropping a cruet of wine or water while operating under his stern eye. Certainly, I was fascinated by the trappings of the old religion, the incense, the hush of the chapel, the way you felt you were being let into a secret world when you were there to see the nuns take the veil, and replace the white one with the dark. I saw all that. I saw them prostrate themselves at the altar as they gave up all worldly things. I also noted that Sister Monica was smashing looking. She would have made a great girlfriend.

At home, death was a business, a commonplace you learned to accept as just another part of life. That was fine until my Uncle Peter died. It was the end of my boyhood in a way, and the really painful thing was that there were two deaths – a little one when I waited on Rochdale Road for him to pick me up and take me on his delivery round, and then saw his truck turn down a sidestreet never to reappear, and then when I heard that he had died, partly from the strain on his system caused by being a prisoner of war in the Far East. He lived in Moston, a few miles away, and in the summer holidays I was his constant companion when he delivered provisions around the district. He was my mother's young brother, a quiet man who had obviously been hurt by his experiences but was still very kind. I loved him very much. I loved it waiting for the bus on Saturdays when he was taking me to the

United ground. He would just lean from the platform of the double-decker and scoop me up.

What happened on that day when I waited on Rochdale Road, I understood later, was that he wasn't strong enough to deal with some trouble in my mother's family. There had been a bit of a split-up and he had to choose between one side and the other. My mother was furious when he didn't pick me up. The arrangement had been made at a family funeral, when, after some time not seeing him, he said to me, 'How would you like to come on the wagon next week?' My mother was pleased – she had a great soft spot for Peter – and I was overjoyed. But when it came to it, I suppose he lost his nerve.

For a while, Uncle Peter's passing left a hole in my life as real as those that were appearing in the neighbouring streets as the wrecking ball came and so many of the people were moved out to neat new houses with inside toilets and their own gardens. In the wake of Doreen Bracegirdle, I wondered what was so great about a garden. We had the Red Rec and the old burial ground. We had each other. But Collyhurst, anyone could see, was changing. However, we didn't move to Wythenshawe or Blackley. We had to stay behind to bury the dead of the dwindling population. It was, I have often thought, a bloody good job I had my big brother Charlie.

2

FOR THE LOVE OF CHARLIE

'YOU should have looked after me, Charlie. I could have been a contender. You're my brother, Charlie.'

Maybe you remember those words. I recall them so well they might have cut through to my bones. They are from the film 'On the Waterfront'. They were spoken by the failed young fighter Terry Malloy, played by Marlon Brando, to his elder brother, a racketeer portrayed by Rod Steiger. My first thought when I heard them – in the cinema where I had sneaked for a free viewing – was that this was a speech I could never have made to my brother Charlie. Had I done so, for some wind-up reason, he would have been entitled to take me into the backyard and hang me on a hook next to our tin bathtub.

I was Charlie's burden. In those teenage years when everything is changing and you want to break away from the things of childhood, he always had me at his heels. Four years older than me, Charlie found that whatever he tried to do he could never shake me off. With both our parents working, he had to take me everywhere, even on some of the biggest days of his life when he played trials for the Manchester Schoolboys team.

This was the gateway to the football big-time, and while his pals Billy Gormley and Terry Beckett, a very talented player who, in

21

company with the great Duncan Edwards, made it to the Manchester United A team, showed up for the trials with a swagger that said they were ready to take on the world, Charlie had to have half an eye on his snotty kid brother. Often I think now how much he must have hated it, but back then Charlie's discomfort didn't cross my mind for a second. I was just chuffed to be with him, shouting advice from the touchline, which was usually something like, 'Get stuck in Charlie, you're better than this lot . . .' or, 'Charlie, stick it to the bastard.' Sometimes he would glower at me and say, 'Shut it,' but mostly he suffered in silence. I was so proud of him, and before I wanted it for myself, I wanted it for him. I wanted him to beat the world.

His most embarrassing experience was probably when he had to take me to Heaton Park, a lovely field where he was playing for the school Under-15 team. Because someone failed to turn up, John Mulligan put me in the team. 'Just do your best,' he said, 'and help out the lads where you can.' I was ten years old and I could see on the faces of Charlie and his mates Gormley and Beckett that they were disgusted at having to play with this kid with running eyes who ran on to the field wearing short pants and street shoes. Naturally, I saw this as my great chance to make an impact. They stuck me out on the left wing but I refused to be isolated. I tore around calling for the ball and I was never discouraged, not even when I lost it on the rare occasion it was passed to me, or when one team-mate looked up from the ball and told me to 'fuck off, you stupid little sod.'

There are many examples of the care Charlie gave to me when we were not fighting on the furniture, or when he wasn't chasing me down in the backyard for some piece of cheek I had given him. We'd go back into the house and clear up the mess we had made and put the dinner in the oven before Mum came back from her sewing machine and my dad from burying the dead. But for the time I remember best, and most strongly and clearly, when my football career hit such peaks as the World and European Cup finals, we have to jump forward a few years. I had made it to the groundstaff of United. I was on my way, and because of the success I had enjoyed at an early age, playing with boys two, three, even four years older than me, I was accepted into the company of bigger lads who were beginning to go into pubs and dancehalls. It was the rock'n'roll time of Elvis Presley and Bill Haley, teddy boys and girls in trooped skirts, and you didn't hear Bing Crosby or Frank Sinatra on the radio so much.

In Collyhurst, most of my football mates had put aside their dreams of going professional, for one reason or another, and were instead embarking on their own build-up to the swinging sixties. Their faces, framed by greased hair and sideburns, took on tough expressions over foaming pints of bitter. Jackie Doyle, Billy Gormley, Terry Beckett, Anthony 'Dixie' Dean and Bernard 'Sugar' Poole were all talented players. Before me, Sugar had become attached to and then detached from United. But somewhere along the line there is a point where you can go one of two ways. You can decide you are going to fight for that dream of being a professional, or you can have a good time with the boys and, maybe, the girls. That latter prospect, anyway, was my half-baked ambition one Saturday night when Sugar Poole invited me to go on a pub crawl with the boys along Oldham Road, concluding with a visit to the Palladium dancehall in Newton Heath. I was fifteen. I had never been in a pub for any other reason than to sell the *Empire News* and I was enjoying this exciting new and grown-up world until Charlie, with a few pals, came into the place where we happened to be.

Charlie was laughing with his friends but the moment he saw me at the bar clutching my pint his face changed.

'Get out of here, Nobby, get home straightaway – or you're in

23

big trouble,' he told me. Sugar pushed between us and said to Charlie, 'Leave him alone, the kid's having a good time. You can't boss him around any more. He's one of the lads now, don't you know?'

Charlie looked at Sugar quite coldly and said, 'No, he isn't one of the lads, Sugar – he's different from you and me and the rest of the lads here. We've all had our chances and I think we know we're not going to make it. The kid's got a chance, and I'm not going to stand here and see him pissing it away like the rest of us. If he doesn't get his arse out of here now, I will tell Dad. If he doesn't make it, he can spend a lifetime pubbing, if that's what he wants. We all have a choice, but Nobby's too young to make his – and he's not going to make it at his age, on the piss.'

There was no doubting that Charlie meant what he said and, deep down, I knew he was right. It hurt me to leave the lads that night. It was another occasion when I believed I was having a ball. But there was a bigger picture, I knew that, and Charlie painted it for me very clearly amid the noise and the thick cigarette smoke of that pub. So I slunk off home. I knew I had to break away from these lads who had promised me a night of booze and who knew, just possibly, birds. Some of the lads were still my heroes but I couldn't stand the idea of disappointing my dad. I didn't want to let him down – or myself or, now, Charlie.

It was a short speech from my brother but it said a lot of things and brought a lot of thoughts up to the surface. A lot of people had given me a lot of time and a lot of love. And I knew something else was true. I really did have a chance – and it was quite a big one.

In one huge way, Charlie gave me more of an insight into how I needed to tackle my future than he could ever know, and it was something that ran deeper than his brilliant stand on my behalf in the Saturday night pub somewhere along Oldham Road. It was more than all those times he had to drag me along to stand on the touchline of his big games, and into the company of his mates. It was something in himself, in his talent and that part of his nature that held him back from exploiting football gifts that were at least as good as mine when it came to basic skills such as controlling the ball and running with it. The truth was that the brother who looked after me, who did so much to make sure I didn't waste my chances, should also have been a contender.

I don't suppose I'll ever know quite what held Charlie back. As I said, it was nothing to do with his ability. During his first trial match, I remember thinking, 'Why isn't Charlie sticking it to them? Why isn't he going past his full-back?' He had two good feet and plenty of pace. He could go past his man either side, yet so often when he had the chance to make some impression, he would just pass the ball. I would stamp my feet on the touchline and shout, 'For fuck's sake, Charlie, go for it.' He played well enough to draw the attention of Manchester United, who had him playing junior games, but then someone said that maybe they were using Charlie to get to me. I didn't think anything of it at the time, but I know now it is the kind of thing football clubs do.

Maybe Charlie was too anxious to do well; maybe he wanted it just as much as I did. After all, he was my father's son and he too had grown up with the smell of the shirts and all the talk of Johnny Carey and Jack Rowley. But for some reason, when it came to the trials for Manchester Boys, Charlie did not grab at his chances. I always felt that, at the very least, Charlie should have played for Manchester Boys. When I got my opportunities, I never forgot how it had gone for my brother. He was a good player with two good feet and I had just one foot, a right one, but I put it to a lot of use. Watching Charlie, I told myself, 'If I get a chance like this, I won't care – I'll just go for it. I'll want the ball every second of the game. I'll fucking demand it.'

I suppose I always believed I could play the game, and maybe that was the greatest gift I received. In the same way that I auditioned for the 'Black and White Minstrel Show', and put my name down for every activity at the boys' club – even the Boy Scouts, which was a big mistake that lasted just one meeting – I threw myself into football in the belief that I would be good.

I still remember the time when I made my first overhead kick. I was about six years old playing with Tony Lucas, who was four years older than me, in the street outside St Patrick's. There was a little doorway into the school that served as our goal and we attacked and defended it alternately and very fiercely, and when the ball flew into the air and over my shoulder, I suddenly realised I could kick it perfectly. I did it, and it was such a feeling of fulfilment. For a split second, there was no fear of a crash landing on the street; there was just the ball and the angle I had to make with my body to get the proper contact, and when I did that, and saw the ball, which had been lobbed over my head – and made me think, 'He's a good player' – flying to safety, and the look of surprise on Tony's face, I flung up my arms in triumph. I said to myself, 'I've got a chance here. I like this game. I can play it.' Tony could play, that was for sure, but he died young. He lives in my mind, however. We shared fleeting moments in the street, which were in most ways like a thousand others, but this one, because of the overhead kick and the look of surprise and approval on the face of an older kid whom I respected, will always be frozen in my memory.

More significant than my own self-assessment, however, was the fact that John Mulligan thought I was showing signs of being maybe a little bit more than useful. He put me into the St Pat's Under-11 team a year early, and after my first game he wrote in his report, 'Stiles will do better.' Mulligan was excellent at bringing on a kid. Physically, he was not a huge man, but he towered in my life. When I think of him now, I always place him at the Red Rec, where we changed beside the wall, in rain and sleet and ice and snow. He filled the place with his enthusiasm and his authority. When, a few years ago, the BBC dragged me kicking and screaming into a studio as the subject of 'This is Your Life', John appeared and paid me a great tribute. He said, 'They don't make 'em like Nobby any more.' I was very touched, but I couldn't help thinking that whatever I was, at least as a footballer, he carried great responsibility. He was determined to get the best out of me, and it is my suspicion, a sad one for generations who have come after me and my mates, that they don't make too many school-teachers like John Mulligan any more; people who live their jobs every hour of the day, who give the impression they like and value the kids they teach and want to help them make the most of any talent they have.

I'm sure there are teachers today who have the same instincts as John Mulligan, but just as it would be unthinkable now to ask a stranger to take your young son or daughter into the dark of a cinema, how wise is it for today's teacher to get close to individual pupils? Because of the way the world seems to have changed, I have to believe that Mr Mulligan, racing across a field or school-yard unhindered by his club foot and with his whistle in his mouth, was indeed the last of a breed. Stern both in the classroom and on the football field, he had the knack of helping you to learn things for yourself.

My father, in his quiet way, also had a lot of serious input. He had played the game passionately at his own level, and anything he had learned on the field had been conditioned by his observation of the great players who appeared at Old Trafford. Yes, he was a passionate fan – as he proved that night in the parlour when he shouted at me, 'Nobby, United are losing a Cup final and you've got your bloody head stuck in the sofa.' But, however impatiently, he did free my head, and from time to time he tried to put something sensible into it.

Before my final trial match for Manchester Boys, my father, maybe out of his hurt at what had happened to Charlie, said I should not forget the need to attract some attention to myself. My father knew I had been well educated in the game, that I understood what was most important – making your tackles, covering the ground, always having the needs of the team foremost in your mind. He also knew that schoolboy football was a less than perfect world, that sometimes the good kid, the one who, like my brother, always tried to do the right thing, sometimes got lost in the rush for the eye of the selectors.

'Stop trying to lay everything on for everybody else,' said my father. 'If you get the chance, go and have a pop yourself. People sometimes notice that more than if you're doing the right thing all the time.' I thought about what he said, and, bearing in mind what had happened to Charlie, I could see his point. But I also thought that there was a right and wrong way to play the game, and what I had wanted to see from Charlie was not the abandonment of all that he had been taught by John Mulligan, but a little more devil, a bit more belief that he was every bit as good as Billy Gormley and Terry Beckett.

As it happened, I scored a goal in the trial, but I knew I had played poorly. On the way to the match my bus had broken down and I'd had to run the last mile to the ground. I was hot and anxious and the confidence I had become noted for on the field disappeared when I needed it most. Although I had scored a lot of goals in school football – I broke the record at St Pat's and I'm proud to say it held up to the challenge of Brian Kidd, who arrived at the school a few years after me – my best position, I believed, was right-half. That is where I was playing the trial, and where I intended to display my understanding that football is a two-way game, and the really good players know instinctively when to go and when to stay. I prided myself on my ability to understand the rhythm of a game, and how a player with the right approach could shape it. But it didn't work out that way – at least, not to my satisfaction. I scored a good goal, but it came after too many lapses in what I had hoped would be a perfect performance.

However, my father, who was naturally pessimistic – maybe it came with his job – was proved right and I won my place in the Manchester Boys team – a vital stepping stone for anyone who wanted to play for Manchester United. But I couldn't kid myself that I had played well; nor had I convinced Mulligan. As soon as I arrived at school on the following Monday, he asked me, 'How did you think you played?' I said I was pleased I had scored but that I didn't think I'd had a great game. I explained the problems I'd had getting to the ground, and how my state of mind wasn't so good. He listened with a fixed expression on his face – a bit like a priest hearing confession – and then he said, 'No, you didn't play well, Nobby, and it's no good making excuses. You didn't play your real game. You didn't play for the team. You forgot what has made you such a good little player. You went poaching. Let's hope you got away with it.' I did, but not without learning a lesson I would try never to forget. It was that football, like boxing, was something you had to respect. You couldn't just take it how you liked, how it suited you at the time. You had to know the real point of playing. You had to understand how you fitted into the team and what your best contribution could be. In my case, it was to read the play, to get dug in and make the tackles, and look up when I had the ball to see who among my team-mates was in the best position to receive it.

Looking back, I see that I had a lot of advantages as a potential professional footballer. I had that strict education from Mulligan, the interest of my father, which I discovered from time to time ran far deeper than I had ever imagined, and there was always Charlie. My Mum? She washed the shirts and I knew she was always proud of me, but she couldn't bear to watch me play. The first time she came to see me in a school game I was carried off injured and she never came again.

I played at every level for St Pat's, captained Manchester Boys and played five times for England Schoolboys. At Wembley, before a match with Wales, I was introduced to Field Marshal Montgomery. Many years later, the widow of the great Joe Mercer sent me a photograph of the moment. Monty and I are standing in a beam of a sunlight. The beauty of it all was that my football career unfolded within a brilliant boyhood. I did almost everything I wanted to do, experienced everything I thought the world could offer, and at no cost to the football. I went to Old Trafford to watch my heroes Cyril Washbrook, Brian Statham and Roy Tattersall playing cricket for Lancashire. Charlie took me, of course, and we ate soggy tomato sandwiches and drank water from a bottle which became filled with breadcrumbs as the long day progressed. I slurped it down, anyway. I loved every minute of it.

'On the Waterfront' wasn't the only great film I saw free at the old Essoldo cinema up Rochdale Road. Avoiding the need to buy a ticket was a fairly simple operation. We would club together and one of the lads would pay for his ticket. Then, in the dark, he would pretend to go to the toilets only to stop at the emergency exit, which was hidden behind some curtains, and nudge open the push-door. We would sneak in and crawl our way to the back seats. You had to be a little streetwise. If it was a windy night, you had to make sure that the curtains didn't blow. If they did, there was a chance that an usherette would realise what was going on and come charging down, grab hold of us and call the manager.

Maybe I should say that I didn't get quite everything I wanted in my eager boyhood. I wanted to go to St Gregory's, a big Catholic grammar school where they played on grass. I worked very hard in a class of forty-odd pupils at St Pat's junior school. Some days it was hard to concentrate on the books because my eyes were hurting so much, but I was determined to prove that I wasn't thick, and to a certain extent I think I managed that. The first two in the class went through to St Greg's. I came third. My great rival was John Creme, both in the classroom and on the football field. He was a talented player and a clever lad, and when the results came in I had to accept that he deserved to go through. I told myself that I wasn't the brainiest kid along Rochdale Road, but I hadn't let myself down; and it did mean that I could be out playing, and watching, football when John was carrying home a bag full of books.

My football education moved forward strongly and towards the end of my time at St Pat's it had more or less taken over my life. Cricket, the pictures, the Wythenshawe-based Doreen Bracegirdle, had all tumbled down my list of priorities. Right at the bottom was woodwork and this created one unforgettably painful episode in the wind-down of my schooldays.

In my last two years at St Pat's I had to attend a session at a technical studies centre on Oldham Road once a week. The place was known as 'the manual', presumably because it was meant for those destined to work with their hands. This was a fancy thought in my case. I finished just one assignment – an ironing board – and presented it proudly to Mum. Unfortunately, it fell apart the first time she used it. Quite a bit of the time at the manual was spent playing football in an underground playground, a big cellar. Everyone joined in and there was hardly any supervision. When England were playing – on a Wednesday afternoon at Wembley – a few of us used to slip away with one of our classmates, Anthony Roddy, who lived a few streets away. He was always very popular around the time of an international – his family had a television. What usually happened was that we would watch the first half and get back to the manual before classes were dismissed. But on this occasion we found the entrance door locked and the woodwork master shouting from a window, 'You boys go straight back to St Patrick's. Mr Ridley will be waiting for you.' Joe Ridley was the headmaster and he was tough.

We were called into his study and he asked us what we thought we had been doing.

'Watching the match, Sir,' I chirped. 'We really wanted to see England play and that's why we left school.' I thought that most rational people would understand the lure of England and Tom Finney, Nat Lofthouse, our own Roger Byrne and Tommy Taylor, but he didn't look at all impressed. He told me to go across the room and bring the cane, which was hanging from a ledge. We then bent over and received six of the very best.

Naturally, we didn't show the effects of the pain. In Collyhurst that would have been seen as evidence of an unforgivable flaw in our characters. Walking down the stairs we agreed that at least we'd seen the match and who cared about six strokes of the cane. We thanked Anthony for his kindness and strutted into the playground. When some of the kids asked us how many strokes we had been given, and how painful they were, we stuck out our chests and said, 'It was nowt.'

Our second misfortune of the day was that Ridley was watching our gritted-teeth hard-men performance through his study window. He opened the window and called down, 'Would you now return to your woodwork class. The teacher is waiting for you.' You can imagine the chill that this particular phrase brought. We trudged up to Oldham Road with heavy hearts and extremely sore bottoms, and, as you might have guessed, our worst fears were realised. We got six more lashes, which of course hurt at least

ten times more than the first lot. It may be true that corporal punishment is barbaric, but it does make you think.

John Mulligan was never reluctant to use the cane but he didn't
rely on it. First, he asked us what we wanted from our schooldays
and our lives, and he said that if he could help us achieve our ambitions he would. He never once said, 'This is going to hurt me
more than it hurts you,' but if he had so done, I would have
believed him. He was on our side, like Sister Veronica, Sister
Monica and Miss Skirston.

Miss Skirston looked after us the year before we went into big
school. She seemed to realise it could be a tough life both inside
and outside the school walls, and she tried to soften it for us.
When we had the school pantomime she was in charge of the
make-up. She was very gentle, unlike Miss Morgan, who was quite
often referred to as the Witch from Hell, particularly when she was
lashing the backs of your legs with her strap. Miss Morgan's strap,
like Joe Ridley's cane on Bad Day at the manual, may just have
had a little more value than the pleasure that some people get
from inflicting pain. At least it put a permanent question mark in
my mind about the dangers of being macho for its own sake. If
you want to strut, you'd better be aware of the possible consequences, which is a lesson that doesn't seem to be applied quite
so vigorously these days as in the time when I first had to step on
to a field against characters such as Dave Mackay of Spurs,
Norman Hunter of Leeds and Tommy Smith of Liverpool – not
to mention my dear brother-in-law John Giles.

Michael Sutton in the boxing ring, various kids in the street,
the discipline of my teachers, and Canon Early with his contempt
for my lateness at the altar, all helped to toughen me up in the
knowledge of what I could do, and what I couldn't. And Charlie
was always there for me to measure myself against. At first, when
I snapped at his heels for the ball in the backyard, or on the croft,

or, I remember, one day on the beach at Blackpool, he held me off easily. I was like a little terrier but he just shielded the ball and let me yap away in frustration. Slowly but surely, the gap began to close. He was finding it harder to hold me off; I just kept gnawing and yapping at him, and then I began to nick the odd ball off him. Suddenly, it was his turn to struggle to win the ball back.

For me, it was the same feeling I had when I responded to Tony Lucas's lob with my first overhead kick. Maybe I really did have something. Charlie was a good footballer, a star among the lads, and he got a call from United, but by the age of ten or eleven I was beginning to compete with him quite genuinely. The confidence I got from this could be quite amazing. In the schoolyard I could go through a bunch of lads, knocking the ball against the wall, controlling it again and charging on. It meant that when I arrived at Old Trafford as a fifteen year old, playing a one-two was automatic. Play a one-two, give it and go, it was the most natural thing in the world. It was easy-peasy. It was all deep down, especially the tackling.

Apart from my father making the point about Johnny Carey's balance and the important explanation for his immaculate shorts, no one ever taught me to tackle. It was just something that welled up in me, although no doubt any natural ability I had in this vital part of the game was enhanced by the years of playing on the black cinder of Newton Loco and the red shale of Monsal Rec. It made me an instinctive student of the bounce of the ball, and very early in my schoolboy career I realised the big advantage we held over the grammar school toffs when we played them on cinder or shale. For them, it was a dangerously uncharted journey when they came to play on such alien surfaces. They always assumed football was played on grass.

Jimmy Murphy, Sir Matt Busby's right-hand man and a brilliant enforcer of the fundamentals of the game, and then Sir Alf Ramsey constantly re-stated the message I first received from John Mulligan at the Rec and the Loco – be first to the ball and get your tackle in; that dictates the play. I knew it well enough because I had always got to the pitch of the ball to stop it bouncing, got it down under control and into play. It was like eating soggy tomato sandwiches – I just got it done. It was necessary and, for me, enjoyable work.

I fully accepted my father's point about Carey's balance. I always knew you had to time a tackle, and that you couldn't sell yourself. I never tackled stupidly, and I learned soon enough that to do it properly you had to be at least a little brave. The tackling became just a natural part of your will to win.

The whole football environment of Collyhurst was a gift to boys like me and young Brian Kidd. There was the edge imparted by the conditions on the Loco and the Rec, and it was something we would always have. Like me, Brian had the game in his blood. Also like me, he was a bit of a tiddler in his early years, but he had a growth surge. Whatever the state of his physical development, you could see he had it, that mysterious quality that separates just a few kids from all the good ones who will always lack the little touch, the little understanding of what you have to do to make it as a professional.

Brian was seven years younger than me, and I didn't get to know him well until we played together at Old Trafford. Even then, and much later when I worked with him on the coaching staff and the old days seemed to have happened in another life-time, I couldn't say I really got to know him. I don't think many people have. He is one of those people who don't seem to be able to give you a straightforward answer to any question you ask. You could ask him something quite simple and he would go all around the houses, leaving you saying, 'Kiddo, what are you going on about?' But then I've always liked Kiddo – he had a brightness and a humour about him, and you could see he understood the game. It helped that, like me, he had a good family background. The Kidds, like the Stiles, had a passion for sport.

I played with Brian's elder brother Jimmy in the St Pat's team. He was a good centre-forward, strong and skilled, and he also showed a lot of promise as a boxer. Bernard was the middle brother, less competitive than the other two, a lovely gentle lad who was particularly attracted to the more sedate rhythm of cricket. They lived just a couple of streets away from us across Rochdale Road, and I would always be bumping into them, at the boys' club, which was just across the street from them, where Jimmy did his boxing and where Michael Sutton discouraged me, and at all kinds of football matches, including watching the boozers on the field next to the church. Sometimes we had casual games against the boozers who could play a bit – senior St Pat's players including Jack Collins and Tommy Hardiman, a big centre-half who was known (don't ask me why) as the Colonel. If they were too drunk, they would curse us as we played the ball through their legs and performed other cheekiness. There was a lot of bellowing and laughter. My father didn't really approve. He thought I should save myself for serious football, and when I told him I wanted to play for the boys' club he shook his head in a way that told me I shouldn't pursue it. Boys' club football just wasn't serious enough; it was a recreation, not a real test of your ability.

My father didn't always let you know how he was thinking, but we could guarantee he would take a pessimistic view of possibilities. Sometimes when I told him how I had got on in a game, I would say we had been well beaten, and he would sigh and say, 'Yes, I didn't expect too much – I didn't think you would win,' and then, trying to hide a grin, I would say, 'As a matter of fact, Dad, we won 4–0.'

There was no saving his feelings, however, when St Pat's seniors, with Charlie in the team, played Christ the King in the Cassidy Cup final at the Loco. The game loomed huge in our minds in the days leading up to the bank holiday Monday. On the day, some of my pals and I marched up Oldham Road chanting 'Two four six eight, who do we appreciate? ST PAT'S.' It was impossible to see us losing the Cassidy Cup final. The Cup belonged to us – it was named after one of our own, Lawrence Cassidy. Lawrie was headmaster at St Pat's and the first of our old boys to play for Manchester United, launching the tradition followed by Wilf McGuinness, me and Kiddo. We were convinced we couldn't lose as we made our noisy way along the long road leading to the Loco. What we didn't know, however, was that on the night before the game, the lads, including Charlie, had been doing a little bit of premature celebration. Quite a few pints had been taken. They had taken victory for granted and they paid the inevitable price. Christ the King kicked the arses of Charlie and his talented team-mates Billy Gormley and Jackie Doyle. The score was 6–1 and I've never allowed my brother to forget it.

When he visited my hospital bedside after I'd had my heart-attack, I said, 'Remember that game at the Loco?' Before I'd finished the sentence he groaned and said, 'For God's sake, will you ever forget that bloody match?' There were so many games at the Loco, but he knew the one I meant. He will always know the one I mean.

Quite how closely our father watched over Charlie and me became apparent only by degrees. Two great examples came when I made two of my five appearances for England Schoolboys, one in Plymouth, against the Republic of Ireland, and the other against Northern Ireland in Belfast. He took our wins and losses to heart. He stored them up, analysed them, and then gave us his opinion on what we had done right and where we had gone wrong.

He never made much of a show of his feelings, and sometimes you wouldn't know he was there – except in church, and we always knew when he had arrived by the sound of his distinctive cough. Whenever Charlie or I heard the cough coming from one of the back pews, one of us would nudge the other and say, 'Hey up, behave yourself, Dad's in church.'

I didn't hear the cough, though, on the nine-hour train journey to Plymouth, or on the ferry boat to Belfast. On both occasions, I had a schoolteacher chaperone and I didn't even know Dad was making the trips. He stayed well away from me. He didn't want to fuss around me, which he knew would be an embarrassment for a young kid trying to exert himself on a big new stage. Maybe, also, he didn't want to load me up with too much awareness of how much he wanted me to succeed. But that didn't stop him following me wherever he could.

He was at Plymouth when we beat the Irish lads 9–1, and at Wembley when we played Wales the day I met Monty and got involved in a goal that came in the first thirteen seconds. When that goal went in, when I realised I felt so at home in the stadium that had always seemed like a distant temple of the game, and which previously I had seen only on Anthony's flickering little telly round the corner from the manual, I knew I had a special reason to thank my father. Before the game, he had given me a piece of advice, which stayed vivid in my mind. It is something I never forgot for a second when I walked out into the roar of a crowd waiting for a big game.

Dad had been to Wembley twice before to see Cup finals, and on one of the occasions, when he had got hold of two tickets, he took Charlie along to see the Arsenal team of Jimmy Logie, Joe Mercer and Denis Compton beat Liverpool 2–0 in 1950. I was told I couldn't go because I was too young. I was so sick. I listened to the game on the radio, and festered. My father didn't waste his ticket. When he heard I would be playing at Wembley, he told me, 'One big thing I've noticed at that place, son, is that the players who keep their heads down when they walk out of the tunnel just don't perform. The ones who are looking up, taking it all in, always seem to get stuck right into the game. It's like they're saying, "This kind of day may never come again, and I'm not going to waste it." So I want to see you with your head up and I want you to be saying, "I'm here to play."'

He didn't swear. He spoke quietly, but every word went home. Down the years, I've seen how true his words were. For some players, however talented, it is all too much. You see them dwindling before your eyes. What might have been the day of their football lives becomes a blur.

Dad couldn't come to Stuttgart when we played Germany in a curtain-raiser before Scotland, with Tommy Docherty and Bobby Collins, and beat the reigning world champions. I met the great Scottish players before the game and they patted me on the head and wished me well. It was as though I was walking on air. Then, in a German restaurant, I was given soup with a raw egg floating in it and that brought me down to earth. The point was that the egg cooked gently in the hot soup, but at that stage of my travels there was only so much I could absorb. Later, Bobby Charlton guided me through the mysteries of foreign cuisine. Bobby would eat more or less anything and really enjoy most of it.

A whole, vast new world was opening up for me. Before the Wembley game, we stayed at a little hotel near Euston Station. At the time, I thought it was the last word in luxury. You could have a bath without getting out the tin tub. I was moving on, I knew for sure. The word was strong that I would join my heroes at Old Trafford. I had been to London and Belfast, Sheffield and Plymouth, and now Stuttgart. I had worn Jimmy Delaney's shirt and hobnobbed with Tommy Doc and Bobby Collins. Where would it end? I had the highest hopes of going forward in football but I knew I would always be part of the life that had shaped me, and I would never be able to forget all the people who had given me so much.

Our house and the life we lived hadn't been perfect. There were hard times and some unhappy ones, but I don't suppose the sound of my parents rowing after Sunday morning mass would have been considered remarkable in most of the houses that stretched so densely along Rochdale Road before the wrecking balls began to do their systematic work. If we knew a bit of strife, we also knew a lot of love.

Before I travelled to Plymouth to join the other England schoolboys – including Bob Wilson, the Arsenal goalkeeper, who later decided to switch to Scotland, the land of his fathers, after many years of operating in the shadow of Gordon Banks – my mother announced that I had to join her on a rare trip to town. She bought me a duffle coat, a blazer and a gleaming white shirt. When we got home, she sewed my Lancashire Schools badge on to the blazer. She had always stressed the need to be smart. She said wearing the St Pat's blazer separated you from the riff-raff.

When it was time to go, I hugged my parents and Charlie and I said I would do my best. I got on the train to Plymouth feeling as good as anyone in the world.

3
ON THE RUN

THE dream was fulfilled but, before I could enjoy it, there was a nightmare that for some terrible weeks wouldn't go away; first, though, the dream.

Manchester United's chief scout Joe Armstrong came calling at 263 Rochdale Road. United wanted to sign me as an apprentice professional. I would get to play for the Reds, and, before that, I would do the next best thing – I would clean Eddie Colman's boots. 'Snakehips' Colman was my hero of heroes.

Born a few miles away across the city in Salford, he was just six years older than me, but it was as though he belonged to a different and superior species. It is amazing to look back now and remember how huge he had grown in my imagination by the time I got the call from Old Trafford. When I stood in the corner of the ground with Charlie or my father, I always gave a special roar when Colman's name was announced before the game – 'No. 4 Colman.' For me, it wasn't a team detail – it was the whole glorious show. I played in his position, right-half, and I fantasised that one day I would wear his shirt. Part of me said it was a cheeky ambition, but then I did recognise the need for patience. 'Coly' was the young master and the most exciting of the Busby Babes.

Of course, Duncan Edwards was a young giant, plainly heading

41

towards the status of a master of the game. Roger Byrne, the captain of the club and the country, was wonderfully sure and smooth in his play, and he carried the natural arrogance of a great player. Tommy Taylor was full of thrilling dash, but it was Colman who touched me most deeply. He had a tremendous head on him and great, twinkling feet; he saw an opening in a flash and, though he played beautifully, there was nothing ornamental in what he did. Everything had a hard and proper purpose and the beauty was a bonus. Maybe it was easier for me to identify with him than the towering Edwards because he was a little fella too, and quite podgy. You don't expect elegance from such a figure, but Coly had elegance to burn. He had that instantly famous swivel of the hips. He could run with the ball while defying all challenges, and then when his marker was at the end of his tether, he could split the opposing team with one arrow of a ball. I saw him play brilliantly for United against Real Madrid in a European Cup semi-final game. I just marvelled at his touch and composure and I couldn't see any limits on his career. Ronnie Clayton of Blackburn Rovers was a good footballer and, I learned later when I played against him and met him off the field, an extremely nice man, but whenever he played for England with the No. 4 on his back, I thought he was an imposter. It was Coly's shirt, I insisted vehemently. Coly was my little home-town god.

And, yes, one of my duties would be to clean his boots. I wondered if he would ever know how it was that his boots would shine so much brighter than any others, how much passion had been involved. As I thought of this, I grappled with the idea that soon I would be exchanging the red and white scarf I wrapped round myself on all those trips to Old Trafford for an official red shirt and hobnobbing rights with the great men. It should have been the most uncomplicated time of my life, a time to go dancing down the street. The sparrows coughing in the scrawny hedgerows of the Red Rec should have turned into nightingales. But it wasn't quite like that. In fact, before the dream became reality I suffered the torment of waiting to see if the consequences of a stupid escapade would catch up with me. That they didn't has always left me in the debt of a pal of mine, Terry. But the waiting was terrible.

One moonless night, Terry fell into the hands of the law as he shimmied down the side of one of the derelict buildings – an old church – that had become increasingly common as so many Collyhurst people moved out to the edges of the city. An every night occurrence in my part of town, a little nicking of lead from an unused building, you might think – and you would be right. The trouble was that I was Terry's partner in crime. While Terry was collared, I slipped away – at first as stealthily as I could, then at a full clattering belt down the sidestreets and the cuts that separated me from the safety of 263. There wasn't much relief when I got home. I could still hear my heart thumping, and all night – and for many other nights – I sweated sleeplessly over the question that I knew could have a huge influence on the rest of my life. Would Terry split on me? Would the police bully and cajole from him the name of Norbert Stiles, England schoolboy football star, captain of Manchester Boys and a kid about to step into the charmed circle inhabited by anyone attached to Manchester United? I didn't seek out Terry – I just waited in horror for the knock at the door.

You might wonder how, and especially after Charlie's magnificent speech in the pub on Oldham Road, I could put all those dreams I had carried for so long at risk for a few bits of lead? It certainly wasn't the money. Even after we bent the lead around pieces of brick, to push up the weight when we took it to a local knacker's yard, we were talking about just a few bob. It was no doubt the excitement that appealed to us. Country kids would go scrumping apples but there weren't too many orchards in Collyhurst, so we went 'leading'. We nosed around the old buildings feeling smart and streetwise. It was, we decided, a little bit of adventure. The whole neighbourhood was being broken apart. So many buildings had been abandoned. Who could begrudge a couple of lads a thrill or two, and a few extra bob? The kids in the new suburbs had their backgardens and their newly planted trees and landscaped walkways. We had this old, crumbling playground, spiced with just a faint hint of risk.

But then suddenly the possibility that the rest of the world – and especially Old Trafford – wouldn't quite see it this way kicked in with great force. A criminal record would not endear me to Sir Matt Busby, who had a famous phrase when any of his players did something he considered unworthy of the club they represented. He would give the culprit a stony stare and say, 'That's not Manchester United.' I writhed about in a state of panic, saying to myself, 'If United find out, you're well and truly fucked.'

Now, I'm not so sure. Down the years, most football clubs have tended to set most store by what a player does on the field. Diego Maradona, Paul Gascoigne, Eric Cantona, Tony Adams and my team-mate George Best have all had their scrapes with the law without the roof automatically falling in on their careers. But they were big-name players when they got into trouble. I'd made a bit of a reputation for myself in schoolboy football, but United, like no other club before or since, could pick and choose and there were plenty more kids where I came from who would be willing to run through hell for a chance to inherit the shirt worn by Eddie Colman.

I also thought of the effect on my parents if Terry ratted on me. Their lives would have been shattered. I thought of how the headline would read in the *Manchester Evening News* and the *Chronicle*

– 'United boy star convicted of theft'. My blood ran cold when I imagined my mother, who had taken me down town for the blazer and the duffle coat and sewed on the badge, reading that headline after coming home from the rag-trade sweatshop. I couldn't bear to think of my dad with all his pessimism confirmed. What would Charlie think? And John Mulligan? And Sister Veronica and Sister Monica? I prayed that Terry would keep his silence, and I made extravagant promises about the perfection of my future behaviour.

Miraculously, I thought, Terry did keep quiet. I thanked God for that, and also for the fact that he wasn't carted off to some home for bad lads. He was basically a good lad; like me, he learned that today's bit of devilment can easily become tomorrow's disaster.

If the incident taught me anything apart from the need to remember that my life had changed, and suddenly I had such a lot to lose, it was that I had always been lucky with the great majority of my friends. Some of them were a bit wild and some of them never quite made the effort required to lift their heads above the streets where they lived, but there was little badness and you never went long without hearing the sound of laughter, even if sometimes it carried a touch of bitterness. Mostly they were great lads and they will always be my people. I grew away from most of them, including Terry, because of circumstances, but I've never lost my warm memories.

The friendship that stayed closest for the longest time was with John 'Wocka' Collins. He was a team-mate at St Pat's, a good, hard-tackling full-back, and when, after Charlie's ultimatum, I turned my back on the 'Saturday Night Fever' of pubs and the 'Pally', I often spent time in his house, listening to records and keeping out of trouble. We were pals right up to the time I met Kay, and when I got married he came to Dublin to represent so much of what I would always hold dear – the friendship and the fun that carried us through the hard times and all the scrapes.

My parents never knew about the tightrope I walked in those tense days before I reported to Old Trafford, scrubbed and pink and raring to go. But then it is also true that it was quite some time before I learned the degree of the sacrifice they made so that the triumphant moment would happen.

When it came to my possible future as a professional, my dad was always emphatic. 'You leave all that to me,' he said, 'and concentrate on your football. There will be lots of talk around you, but don't say anything to anybody – not to scouts who want to chat you up, not even to your team-mates. You've got enough to do learning the game. Just keep your head on your shoulders.'

There were times when it was quite difficult to follow my father's order. When I joined the England Schoolboys squad, there was always a lot of excited chatter about which scouts were keen on which players. Deep down, I knew my father was right. Most of it was probably a load of bollocks, but the talk was thrilling. You felt you had joined some inner circle where it was guaranteed that you would make a big career as a professional. Of course, there is a huge gap between playing schoolboy football, even at the highest level, and proving that you're a sure-fire pro, but back then you wanted to believe everything you heard. When Bob Charles, a big kid from Southampton who was a rival of Bob Wilson's for the goalkeeper's job, said to me, 'I suppose you'll wind up at United,' a thrill like an electric current ran through me. It was the matter-of-fact way he said it that persuaded me; well, I thought, that will probably happen.

I haven't seen Bob Charles, who played for a while with Southampton, since those faraway days, but, perhaps partly because he helped to create that feeling of excitement about what might be around the next corner, I remember him quite clearly, and affectionately. Recently someone gave me his telephone number, and when I put it in my pocket I realised with some surprise that I remembered his mother's address in Southampton – 52 Canada Road, Woolston.

As the rumours swirled around, and inside, my head, my father insisted again, 'That stuff will only distract you – leave it to me.' I now know the full story of how I came to go to Old Trafford and it confirms, completely, that first instinct that my career prospects could not have been in better hands.

I never met a scout before I shook hands with the great starmaker Armstrong upstairs at Old Trafford on that first day of my professional existence. My father saw all the scouts. The big three recruiters in those days, at least in my part of the world, were United, of course, Wolves, the great club led by the formidable and famous Stan Cullis, and Bolton Wanderers. Bolton were not in the same league of importance as United and Wolves. Under Cullis, and helped by such stars as little Johnny Hancocks and Bill Slater, Wolves had created a huge appetite for international club football with their epic games against Spartak of Moscow. But the Wanderers of Nat Lofthouse and Tommy Banks did have quite a bit of lustre, and their canny old manager Bill Ridding had a reputation for signing up some of the best kids, one notable coup being Francis Lee, who would become such a major force for Manchester City and England. Ridding could paint an alluring picture of a club with a great tradition, one that put a lot of care into the development of young footballers. Bolton also offered money – big money.

The Bolton scout offered my father £3,000 for my signature. That may not sound like a king's ransom today but then it was huge. It would have changed my parents' lives. About six years later, I bought a semi-detached house in Stretford, which was quite a few steps up the social ladder from Collyhurst, for around that amount. I can give my parents' decision to turn down Bolton another perspective. It is provided by the newspaper bill old Phil Burns delivered to our house a month or two after I'd joined United. Burns kept a dilapidated old corner shop and newsagent's just across Rochdale Road. Each night he delivered the *Evening News*, but he told my parents they had to pay up if he was to continue the service. The bill was for £2.50, a trifling amount today, less than half the cost of a packet of cigarettes. But no bill is small when you don't have any money. Mum and Dad, in those pre-television days, used to devour the *Evening News*, but they had to tell Phil Burns they couldn't pay.

The scout who made the biggest impression on my father was from Burnley. The East Lancashire club were acquiring a good reputation for finding and grooming excellent young footballers, a policy that excited such optimism across the Moors that a future manager, the former England wing-half Jimmy Adamson, went on to declare that Turf Moor would be the home of the 'team of the seventies'. That never happened although there was probably more chance of it doing so than of my joining Burnley, whatever the weight of my father's advice. He told me the Burnley scout was a lovely man, a soft-talking Scotsman. My father had told him that he would be kept informed of our thinking as we came to make the decision. I didn't tell my father what was going through my mind – 'Lovely man or not, I know where I want to go.'

My father knew well enough, and he told Joe Armstrong that my heart was in United and of course I would sign, with no money under the counter and for an apprentice's pay of £3 a week. It was all done very smoothly, very quietly – so quietly that one day, several weeks after I had signed, I was sitting on the lavatory at the back of the Old Trafford stand when I heard a couple of kids talking about something they had read about me in the *Evening Chronicle*. 'It's about time,' said one of them, 'they signed that bloody Stiles.'

My first month at the ground was mostly anti-climax. I didn't get to clean the great man's boots. Not only didn't I rub shoulders with Coly or big Duncan or Roger Byrne, I scarcely got a glimpse of them. I licked stamps in the front ticket office, which, when you think of today's slick computer systems, was incredibly primitive. Like today, they were selling around 65,000 tickets per game but it was slow work. Piles of money were everywhere, and when I heard that it was quite usual for the latest apprentice to serve a stint in the ticket office, I twigged straightaway that they didn't have me there to streamline the system. No, I had to lick the stamps and pass – or fail – an honesty test. The fact that United would deliberately put a kid in the way of temptation brought the lead-thieving flirtation with disaster roaring back into my mind.

Maybe I had been right to live in terror of a knock on the door. There is, of course, a big difference between scrambling along the roof of a derelict building in search of bits of lead, and whipping away a wad of pound notes from a place you have always thought of as the centre of the universe and which contains everything you have always most wanted. But the temptation was real enough for kids who would never see such amounts of money, even if they saved a couple of years' wage packets and opened them all at the same time. I wasn't too surprised to learn, a few months later, that one of my successors had been caught with his hand in the till. When I heard about this, it made me feel grateful to Terry all over again.

The feet of the boy who failed the honesty test hardly touched the ground when he was marched out of Old Trafford. For an entirely different reason, neither did mine when I had served my time in the office and walked into the start of my real education as a Manchester United player. I certainly knew the depth of my commitment to making good with United. They could have rolled the Kohinoor diamond on to my little patch of desktop in the ticket office without raising a single question in my mind. There was nowhere in the world I would have rather been. I learned soon enough, though, that signing forms and licking a few stamps didn't automatically bridge the vast gap between the gods in the first-team dressing room and the rest of humanity.

In those first weeks I had little or no contact with the top players. I got down to the dressing room in the afternoon after completing my office duties, but by then the first team had left the ground after morning training and a 'wholesome' lunch, or gone up to the snooker room. Eventually, when I finished my cleaning duties, I would go to the snooker room with a few of the other apprentices and gawp at the likes of Duncan Edwards and Tommy Taylor as they played their shots. We had no more presence than flies on the wall, until the stars returned their cues to the rack. Then, when they left, we swarmed around the table, little big men copying their heroes. There was a lot of role-playing and my part, naturally, was Coly – I wanted to be Snakehips. I wanted to be The Man.

In the meantime, my first duty on a Monday morning was to sweep the gym and then mop it. Then there would be general cleaning duties around the ground and in the dressing room. I did the boots, lingering over Colman's, and collected all the muddy, often sopping-wet shirts, shorts and socks and took them down to the two washing ladies, who were the mother and aunt of one of the assistant club secretaries, Ken Ramsden. I knew Ken as a kid in Collyhurst, which helped, along with that familiar smell of drying football shirts, to make me feel a little bit more at home in a place that might otherwise have been very intimidating. I spent a lot of time down in the washroom with the ladies. They were lovely – and you could get them to make you a cup of tea.

My first collision was with David Gaskell, a senior apprentice from Wigan who was two years older than me and already announcing that he would be a strong challenger for goalkeeper Ray Wood's first-team place, and then later, Harry Gregg's. Having said that he was a goalkeeper, it is probably unnecessary to add that Dave didn't always march in step with those around him. Brian Glanville, who wrote the book *Goalkeepers are Crazy*, probably had other models in mind, but Gaskell would have done nicely. He was a tremendously talented goalkeeper but from time to time the great saves were accompanied by touches of madness.

For some reason that amused only him, Dave would sometimes put spin on the ball when he threw it to you, and if it bounced the wrong way, which seemed to be his hope, he had the irritating habit of shouting, 'You missed the googly,' or 'It were a wrong 'un.' He had another alarming trick. If he considered a shot was going to hit the crossbar, he would drop his hands and shout, 'Bar.' Apart from being a bit eccentric, Dave could also be a bit arrogant. He certainly had reason to believe in himself. He had already tasted the big-time, playing in a Charity Shield match against Manchester City at Maine Road as a sixteen year old. It had left him very impatient with the chores of an apprentice.

On my second day in the job, as I walked into the dressing room, he shouted to me, 'Hey you, you know where the brush is – go and get it and sweep up the floor.' I replied, 'And what are you doing?' He said, 'I'm going up to have a game of snooker with the lads.' He hit me on the raw the way he spoke to me, and I also thought that maybe it was already time to stand up for myself. Old Trafford, I guessed, was not a place for kids too willing to doff their caps to anyone except those in genuine authority. So I said, 'So am fucking I.' In fact, I stood around, like him, as the stars monopolised the table.

Over the years, I came to learn that Dave was a great character as well as a brave and talented goalkeeper. He made 120 appearances for United and was good enough to keep Gregg out of the

1963 FA Cup final. On the other hand, I wouldn't always be sure exactly what was going through his head.

The nearest thing to intimacy with the first-teamers came in that snooker room when one of them would announce he was hungry and send one of the apprentices to the café over the bridge from Old Trafford for a box of bacon butties. Mark 'Pancho' Pearson and Alex Dawson, who were in their last year as apprentices and leading performers in the youth team, occasionally made the run, but more often it was me who got the job. Maybe the stars saw my eager little face and thought I was a little keener to please than some of the lads who had tasted a bit more of the flavour of the big-time. Soon it became a regular job, racing over the bridge and getting back before the bacon sandwiches were cold. My reward was to get one for myself. I would munch away happily on that first rung of the stairway to my particular heaven.

I couldn't get enough to eat at that time, and only recently the comedian Ivor Davies recalled, 'When you first showed up at Old Trafford you were a skinny little bugger, and after a few months you were a fat bastard.' But there was never much danger I would run to too much podge. I had too much energy, too much ambition, for that, and I quickly got back to my best playing weight, which, at 5ft 5ins, was between 10 stone 7 lbs and 11 stone.

The second challenge was Bobby English. Like Dave Gaskell, he had caused a bit of a stir on the field. He hadn't made the first team, but he had had some impact in the youth team. The youth team was the glittering shop window of Busby's peerless youth system, and at that time was showcasing the amazing talent of a quiet kid from the north east who would become one of my greatest friends – Bobby Charlton.

English was a stylish player but, unlike Charlton, he wasn't a quiet kid. He clearly believed he was on his way to the top, and I wasn't too keen on his attitude. The crunch came during one of the twice-a-week night sessions at the club's training ground, the Cliff, when the apprentices joined with all those talented amateurs fighting for a professional contract when they became seventeen. He treated me with a little contempt when he was on the ball. I thought he committed the unpardonable sin of showing off at the expense of a fellow player, and it didn't help that the Busby Babes, including my hero Colman, were walking past our game on their way to the dressing room. My response was a ferocious tackle. I went through the ball and into him with all the force I could produce. He jumped in the air and then, when he had recovered, he chased after me. But I told him that if he ever tried that approach on me again, he could expect similar treatment. He did, and I clattered him again. It didn't worry me a little bit that one of the senior players shouted, 'You dirty little bastard,' when English went down.

I took Bobby English's place in the youth team and a few years later he went off to Canada – unfortunately, not before he had involved my great friend and team-mate Shay Brennan in a business venture that cost him a lot of money and plenty of anguish.

What was becoming clear to me was that getting to Old Trafford had been one thing – staying there, and making a claim for a place in the first team might be quite another. Some kids blazed into early prominence and then slipped from sight. I felt at home, and thought I was learning and getting better, but I also thought that maybe I belonged in another category to such lads as Tommy Spratt, who came down from the north east with at least as much fanfare as Charlton. Spratt was banging in goals all over the place and catching a lot of people's attention.

The important achievement, I told myself in the face of this hot competition, would be to prove myself tough enough and patient enough to go the whole course. Tommy Spratt was the classic example of a kid who ran hard and fast in the early going but wasn't around when it came to time to perform in the big show. He and I were the same age and we would probably have played in the England Schoolboys team together if he hadn't suffered a cartilage injury. But if he didn't get to shake hands with Field Marshal Montgomery, he certainly had the knack of grabbing some notice for himself. Like me, he was a wing-half or an inside-forward, and, like English, he didn't seem to have many doubts about his chances of making it.

He jumped ahead of me and, to be honest, I think the club probably thought of him as a bigger signing than me. They had looked after him very carefully when he was in his last year as a schoolboy, arranging the operation on his cartilage and giving him plenty of push when he finally arrived at Old Trafford, eager to fight his way into the front rank of Busby Babes. He responded to United's faith in him with some quite spectacular progress which took him into the reserve team while I was still fighting to get beyond the A and the B teams.

I couldn't warm to the kid for the same reason I took umbrage with Bobby English. It seemed to me he believed in himself in a way that went beyond that self-confidence every competitor needs and without which there's not a lot of point in trying to be a professional in the first place. He was particularly pleased with himself when he scored fourteen goals in a 25–0 win in a junior game against a team who were plainly at that boys' club level my father had warned me against touching a few years earlier, back in Collyhurst. It was a match you got through and played as well as you could, without mistaking it for a real contest or any kind of proper test of your ability. But Tommy was banging in the goals and enjoying every minute of it. As it happened, I was making quite a lot of them and I wasn't surprised when my dad, who was on the touchline of the pitch in Chorlton-cum-Hardy, repeated that old point of his about the need sometimes to draw a bit of attention to yourself.

But my worries about the threat to my chances presented by Tommy, talented young player though he was, proved as groundless as the ones that had tortured me so much in the wake of Terry's arrest. Maybe United pushed him too hard too soon; maybe he did it to himself. Perhaps he was unlucky with injuries at vital times, but Tommy Spratt ran out of momentum. He didn't get anywhere, which was a pity for him, but, if I am honest, it didn't cause me too much mourning. It is a truth of the professional footballer's life that however warm – or cold – your feelings about your team-mates, ultimately you find yourself thinking of your own situation. Every player's career is filled with times when another man's misfortune is his opportunity, his lucky break. A club-mate who plays in your position goes down with injury and while you feel for him you are also thinking, 'How does this affect me?'

Spratt ran his race and I ran mine. On the long course, I happened to win but nobody needed to tell me that you don't get anywhere in football without enjoying a few of the right breaks. Yes, you make your luck, and quite often I talk to old rivals Tommy Smith and Norman Hunter about what we think separated us from all the other tough and talented kids who fought but failed to come out on top at Liverpool, Leeds United and Manchester United. We always agree that luck is part of it, but good fortune doesn't put you in the right frame of mind, or develop the instincts, to take advantage of any breaks you might get. When somebody comes up to me now at some St Pat's Old Boys do and says, perhaps with the inspiration of a few pints, that I was lucky to go so far beyond the achievements of some of my more talented schoolmates, I unashamedly fall back on an old line. 'You may be right,' I say, 'but all I know for sure is that the harder I worked the luckier I got.'

The more tackles I made and passes I read, the more running I did in training, the better I looked after myself and did all those hard things that you have to do if you want to last as a serious professional, the more my confidence increased. If you did all those things, if you made the required sacrifices, the self-belief that every player, however gifted, needs reached a level where you expected the good things to happen. You operated in your own aura. You believed that whatever target you set yourself there was a very good chance you would hit it.

The Busby Babes filled the Old Trafford dressing room with a sense of that confidence so strongly it touched you whenever you set foot in the place – something somebody like me wasn't encouraged to do except to fulfil some necessary function of an apprentice, some trivial chore that you were expected to complete without drawing any kind of attention to yourself. This was why I felt a rush of dread one day when Pancho Pearson handed me an autograph book and said, 'Get the first-teamers to put their names in this and don't take no for an answer. If you don't do it, I'll knock all your fucking teeth out.' I had no reason to be disbelieve Pancho. He was a tough kid from Derbyshire. He'd earned his nickname by growing thick bushy sideburns, which were supposed to be fashionable but made him look less like the pop star Tommy Steele than a Mexican bandit.

Trying to get autographs from Tommy Taylor, Roger Byrne, Duncan Edwards and the rest was a job that got tougher by the day. They had become legendary figures in the course of a year or two, and the demands of celebrity loomed new and heavy in their lives. I went into the dressing room with no great optimism and I was instantly proved right in my fears. I hadn't been treated with such contempt since being foisted on Charlie and his mates in that school game at Heaton Park. 'Fuck off, you little twat,' was the theme of the reaction to my nervous pleadings of 'Oh, go on, please, please.' I was pushed away by another volley of insults and I gave up the first attempt. Then I thought of Pancho and his threat and went back into the dressing room.

'They're not for me,' I told the great men. 'Please, just this once, sign the book.' It was then that *he* spoke.

'Aren't you the little kid,' he asked, 'who played for England Schoolboys the other day?'

Breathlessly, I said I was. He reached out for my book and signed it after writing 'Best wishes and good luck in your career', and then he turned to his team-mates and told them, 'Sign the kid's book – we may have a good one here.'

It would be nice to tell you that *he* was Eddie Colman, the man who had been at the centre of my dreams for so long, but it wasn't him although he did sign the little book along with Liam 'Billy' Whelan and Roger Byrne, David Pegg and Mark Jones, Ray Wood and Tommy Taylor.

Billy Whelan was tall and not particularly quick but he had wonderful skill and a tremendous certainty in front of goal. One year he scored 33 goals, including 26 in the First Division, and when in 1954 the Brazilian World Cup team saw him playing in a youth tournament in Switzerland, they wanted to take him home, so impressed were they with his touch and his goalscoring ability. Billy was a bit solemn and quite religious, and was friends with quite a few priests. He once told me off for swearing at someone during a five-a-side game in the gym – but his name glowed on the page of the autograph book.

Byrne was a master player, a little older than the rest and slightly set apart. David Pegg was a quick, skilful winger heading for a place in the England team. Wood was the veteran goalkeeper, one of the lads who was among the first to join any card school. Taylor was the dark, handsome Yorkshireman who cut a glamorous figure on the field, and knew it. Mark Jones, a tremendously sound centre-half from Barnsley, was one of the kindest of the great men. He always had time for the youngsters desperate to make their way in the game, and although his name was one of the easiest to get into a kid's autograph book, it didn't take away any of the value.

The names went into the book, one by one, and suddenly the threats of Pancho Pearson simply floated away. All the big names had followed into the pages the greatest prize signature of them all. *He* was Duncan Edwards, the young man who had dazzled the football world and who, in the normal way, wouldn't look twice at some little apprentice holding out his autograph book like Oliver Twist with the gruel bowl.

I left the dressing room in triumph, putting the book in my pocket and patting it down. That's where it would stay until I got it home to Rochdale Road. Pancho Pearson could do what he liked.

4

THE DAY THE SKY
FELL IN

MARK PEARSON, like a lot of young professional footballers, had some rough edges, but he had good instincts for the game. Behind the tough front, he was really just like me, desperate to do well. He was one of those kids who arrived at Old Trafford eager to watch, listen and learn. It meant that when he wasn't handing me impossible dares and threatening to knock out my teeth, he was able to give some good advice.

Physically mature for his age, he was a seasoned member of the most successful youth team in the history of English football, the breeding ground of the Babes and a side that had won the FA Youth Cup five straight times when I joined its ranks at the age of fifteen years and eight months. Despite my own good football education at St Pat's, there was still a danger of getting carried away in the footsteps of Edwards and Colman, Pegg and the new young sensation, Charlton, and when I did, Mark was at my side to give me a dig and a very hard word.

It happened in the quarter-final of the FA Youth Cup as we marched to what I assumed would be our sixth consecutive triumph in a competition that had become so prestigious that crowds of 20,000-plus regularly showed up at Old Trafford for the home legs. The big crowds happily played the game of picking the next Dunc or Coly. We were beating Newcastle 6–1. They couldn't really compete with us, physically or in skill or tactics. It was when they lost heart that I began to get a little fancy on the ball.

I do recall deigning to believe that Wolves, under the guidance and iron discipline of the great Stan Cullis, might be a threat in the semis or the final, but that was something for the future. In the meantime, I was doing a little of that thing I had so strongly disapproved of in Bobby English and Tommy Spratt – I was showing off. Pearson came alongside me and said, 'We don't do that stuff here. We keep it simple. We pass to a red shirt, we run, we try to make angles, we get on with our business. If somebody we want to pass to is marked, we're patient. We keep hold of the ball in the right way. We don't stage a cabaret. It's what we're taught to do. Showing off is no good – Manchester United don't do that.' I listened to what he said and acted upon it. I became a serious footballer again, and I helped in the scoring of two more goals. We won 8–1. The best little team in the land was marching on.

There were so many things you didn't do if you were Manchester United. Some of it I had worked out for myself. Some of it I was told. You didn't thieve lead. You didn't get seen in the pubs around town knocking back pints. You didn't dress scruffily. You didn't forget that you represented the greatest club in the world. And, most definitely, you didn't one day get into an aeroplane that had frozen wings and went hurtling down a runway, refusing to take off when that was the alternative to slewing into banks of snow.

You didn't die in a blizzard when you had an arrangement to conquer the world. That wasn't in anyone's script, and when Bill Inglis, the reserve-team trainer who helped with the youth team, came into the dressing room as we were towelling ourselves down after coming out of the big bath and told us that there was a problem with the first team in Munich, that their plane had crashed, we didn't think, we couldn't think, that he was talking about anything more than an inconvenience, a delay. Maybe the lads would have to wait while they repaired the plane, or sent for another one. Maybe, someone said with a laugh, we might get a chance to show what we could do – no worries, Duncan, Coly and Roger, we would look after business. It was quite a bit later on in that bone-cold day before any of us grasped that our world had slipped off its axis.

After all, 6 February 1958 was supposed to be just another shift at the football dream factory. It was a frosty morning, the kind that had so often kept me in bed for an extra half hour when I knew Canon Early would be saying mass. I took the usual 112 bus for the forty-five-minute journey from Collyhurst to Trafford Bar. There the bus crew changed for the final short leg that took me to the ground. Inevitably, much of the talk on the bus concerned United, particularly so that morning. The day before, the first team had qualified for the semi-finals of the European Cup, drawing 3–3 with the fine Red Star team in Belgrade, after taking a one-goal lead from the first leg at Old Trafford.

The team, despite its youth, was growing before everyone's eyes. On the previous Saturday they had won 5–4 at Arsenal in one of the most thrilling games ever played at Highbury. For so many people in Manchester they were young gods, and when I heard the talk on the buses and in the street I swelled with pride. I knew these gods. I ran for their bacon sarnies. I had successfully pleaded for their autographs. I cleaned their boots. I watched up close, enthralled, as they played in baseball boots on a stretch of concrete beside Old Trafford on Friday afternoons; twenty-two of them, first team and second string, shouting and joking and showing bits of skill and creating a world you couldn't wait to join.

But first you had to serve your time – 6 February 1958, another day on the apprentice's job. Same old brilliant routine. Mop the gym. Clean out the baths and showers. Clear some snow from the pitch. Maybe squeeze in a game of head tennis in the gym. Go for lunch at Mrs Rimmer's, who had a little house near the ground and cooked for the apprentices and some workers from the factories in Trafford Park. You could get steak and sausages and there was always a load of boiled potatoes. I was a growing lad. I could never get enough boiled potatoes. Train. Run round and round the ground and up the terraces. Dive into the bath. Then, something different. Bill Inglis in his white coat talking about a plane crash.

'We've got some bad news,' he said, his words sailing over our heads. Arthur Powell, a lovely gentle man who wore a brown coat, had come into the dressing room with Bill. He trained the A team and did all the odd jobs around the dressing room. He didn't say anything but he had an expression on his face that would only make sense later. 'What I advise you lads to do,' said Bill, 'is get your mums or dads to phone in to the ground in the morning and see what's happened.'

I found out what had happened when I changed buses in the centre of town. I went up to the newspaper seller and bought an *Evening Chronicle*. It was strange seeing the faces of Roger Byrne, Geoff Bent, Eddie Colman, Mark Jones, David Pegg, Tommy Taylor and Liam Whelan staring out of the front page. They belonged at the back of the paper. But they were dead. Coly was dead. He couldn't be dead. I cleaned his boots. None of them could be dead, but especially not Coly. But that's what the *Chronicle* was saying in big black headlines.

I felt sick. We'd been laughing about this crash back in the dressing room, saying maybe somebody had broken a leg, maybe the big chance for one of us had come. I got on the Collyhurst bus and

I didn't hear anything going on around me. Everything seemed normal enough. The streets and the shops looked just the same. The sun was presumably still up there behind the low leaden sky, and I guessed the moon would take its place in a few hours time.

I knew nobody would be at home. My mum and dad and Charlie would be working. I couldn't face an empty house. When I got off the bus I walked across Rochdale Road and down Livesey Street and into the church. You could just walk into a church in those days. They're all locked up now. I prayed and prayed. Prayed that the *Chronicle* had got it all wrong, had played the sickest practical joke in the history of newspapers. I prayed and I wept. I sat back in the pew for a long time. It could have been an hour or two, I don't really know. There was no one else in the church. Then I went home. The house, as I expected, was empty. The lads were dead, or so I had read, but people still had to work. I put the dinner in the oven.

The rest of that day and night is mostly a blur. I remember my dad calling Jimmy Murphy, Busby's right-hand man, who hadn't made the trip to Belgrade, hadn't sat on the runway while the plane was re-fuelled and the wings froze over, and telling him that he had a car at his disposal. My dad ran Jimmy to all the funerals.

That's all we seemed to be doing for weeks, going to funerals. I served on the altar for several requiem masses. Not Coly's. I went to his funeral, and I was surprised to learn that he wasn't a Catholic, not that it mattered. Coly was dead. It kept coming into my head, but it wouldn't stay there. For a long time it was a shock that greeted every new day – Coly was dead. It was devastation. I'd given his boots their last shine. I'd never again see him moving upfield so smoothly, so quickly, despite carrying a bit of podge. That was his body type, but it didn't affect his game. He could leave his marker with an easy change of pace and great control. He could really motor when he decided to go forward, and I tried to copy everything he did on the field. Later, when I scored my first goal for United – against Newcastle – I was proud for lots of reasons but the biggest one was that I thought it showed a touch of Coly. I broke quickly and sent the ball into the top corner of the net. It was a nice goal for a kid to dedicate to his hero.

For a while it seemed that the only thing that kept Manchester going was that Duncan Edwards was still alive. He fought for his life in the Munich hospital for fifteen days, and then his great heart gave out. At his funeral back in Worcestershire, the vicar said that we would see great talent, even genius, again, but there would always be only one Duncan Edwards. There are so many stories about the impact of big Duncan, how it was that by the time he died at the age of twenty-one he had already given notice that, beyond all doubt, he was going to be one of the great players. However, the tale that I think tells most about the sheer range of his ability concerns a Youth Cup game at Chelsea.

Jimmy Murphy ran the team and he was very conscious of the debt it owed to Edwards. If a match was under United's control, Duncan tended to play at centre-half. If we were not doing so well, Jimmy's standard instruction to any player who won the ball was simply, 'Give it to Duncan.' But on this occasion Murphy thought it was time for a change.

'I want you to do a bit of thinking for yourselves,' he said. 'When you get the ball, don't automatically pass it to Duncan. Try to express yourself a little bit. Go for another option if it's available.'

At half-time United were losing 1–0. Murphy was clearly upset when he came marching into the dressing room. United didn't lose Youth Cup-ties.

'Remember what I said about expressing yourselves,' said Murphy. 'Well, never mind about that – when you get the ball give it to Duncan.' They did and United won 2–1.

Such certainty of belief in a single player is the rarest thing in football, and on the fifteenth day after the Munich tragedy it was gone.

For a little while the fear was that everything would go with it. When the mourning was over, when the sky stopped weeping rain and tears, what would be left? Would all the brave speeches about a new United rising from the ashes of Munich sound so convincing next month, next year? Who would pick up the United flag? Would Bobby Charlton, who walked away from the plane unscathed, survive cleanly the mental trauma of losing so many of his team-mates? Would the fire inside him dwindle away? Would the club of destiny and dreams, which had staggered the football world with the brilliance and maturity of its young team, lose its way under the great weight of sadness?

It might have done but for two huge factors. Unlike Duncan's, Matt Busby's heart didn't give out. He came through, and if he looked like the ghost of himself when he eventually returned to Manchester with his body battered and a terrible grief in his eyes, he was still able to say that he would consider the challenge of building another great team. After months of hospital convalescence and the care of his family, he said yes, he would go on. He would try to build a new team that would one day be worthy of the names of the young men he had lost and would miss every day of the rest of his life.

Some said that in all Busby's pain there was a tinge of guilt. He had defied the Football League and pursued the challenge of Europe. He had crowded United's programme of League and Cup with the commitment to European football. But then, as he had said, the young team had swept to two straight league titles. It was a team that had to grow, and how could he know that so quickly it would be torn from the sky?

So Busby was the great symbol of hope and renewal, the prime factor in the rebirth of United. The other was Jimmy Murphy.

Busby fired United with the challenge of winning back horizons that had been so cruelly redrawn, but it was Murphy who kept the club on the road. It was Murphy who held the line against any submission to disaster. It was Murphy who reminded us of what we had been, and what we could be again. In the meantime, we had to fight for survival. We had to do the best we could.

In the aftermath of Munich, Murphy showed that he was a great manager in his own right. He was a dapper ex-army man who had a good career as a player with West Bromwich and Wales. Busby saw and admired his qualities as they served together in the Eighth Army during the war, and decided he was the ideal man to help him build a football empire. Looking back on his own career, Busby said that probably his shrewdest move was to sign Murphy.

Busby saw the big picture and, maybe like no manager before or since, he put his faith in players. He didn't load them up with tactics. He urged them to give expression to all their talent. Murphy had plenty of vision when it came to assessing the potential value of a player, but was more of a nut and bolts man. He certainly wanted a bolted defence, and down the years he used to scream at my friend Shay Brennan when he regularly ignored instructions to boot the ball into the stand and give his defensive colleagues time to re-group when the pressure was on. Shay knew Jimmy hated the way he would just knock it over the touchline rather than follow the order to put it in the 'fucking sixty-sixth row of the stand', but he kept doing it. It was a little quirk in Shay's nature, and it made him one of the few players ever to risk the anger of Jimmy Murphy.

Murphy managed Wales for twenty years and got them to the 1958 World Cup in Sweden. Some of his team-talks were ferocious, if not always politically correct. Allegedly, one of his most effective came when he sent Wales out to meet the reigning 1954 world champions West Germany at Ninian Park. The Welsh players were expecting the team-talk around two – an hour before kick-off – but there was no sign of Jimmy. As the clock ticked down, the players were in something near panic. They were talented and experienced, with such stars as Cliff Jones and Ivor Allchurch operating under the captaincy of the great John Charles, but Jimmy's team-talks had become legendary, and this was a big match. He had still to put in an appearance when, ten minutes before kick-off, the referee knocked on the dressing-room door and told the players it was time to come out. Charles shrugged his shoulders and said, 'We'd better go, boys.' As they were walking out, Jimmy walked in. His team-talk supposedly consisted of one sentence – 'Remember, lads,' he said, 'these German bastards tried to kill your mums and dads.' Recently, I was told the story is a myth. I had swallowed it whole because it was so believable.

Before a game with Wolves, Jimmy was concerned about the potential of their skilful inside-forward, Peter Broadbent, to do some serious damage. Broadbent's style always had the effect of winding up Jimmy. Wilf McGuinness, who was a formidable tackler, was taken to one side and told, 'Wilf, this prima donna Broadbent will be taking your bonus if you don't win. I say "fuck that".'

For a little while after Munich the Murphy style had to be gentler, but the iron hand was still apparent. He assembled all the players and said we had to fight as we had never done before. Seven of the team were dead and Duncan Edwards was fighting a losing battle for his life. Johnny Berry and Jackie Blanchflower had such serious injuries they would never play again. Busby, the man who made United, was hovering between life and death after being given the last rites. Everyone had mental wounds. We could submit to all of this – or we could fight.

Under Murphy the club fought so well it reached the FA Cup final, an amazing achievement that gathered its first momentum on the most extraordinary night any player or fan of Manchester

United would ever know – Wednesday, 19 February, thirteen days after the crash. Nearly 60,000 squeezed into Old Trafford for the FA Cup-tie with Sheffield Wednesday. I was in the ground and I was a fan again.

There were eleven blank names in the programme where the names of the Babes should have been. The only atmosphere I could compare it with was the second leg of the European Cup semi-final against Real Madrid the previous year, when, after losing 3–1 in the Bernabeu stadium, United drew 2–2 at Old Trafford. The Babes were eliminated but they played beautifully and they served notice on all of Europe that spring evening. Tommy Taylor scored, as he had in the first leg, and Coly played magnificently. He looked at home in the company of Di Stefano and the other Real legends, as of course he had every right. I rushed to Old Trafford that night from the Monsal Rec after playing one of my last games for St Pat's. I changed back into my street clothes in the usual Red Rec dressing room – beside the wall where we piled our gear in all weather. It was a wonderful night at Old Trafford, the crowd were excited, intensely involved in every touch of the ball – and there were so many beautiful touches. You had a sense of the start of something thrilling.

This night in February, less than a year later, could scarcely have been more different because whatever the result against Wednesday, it marked not a start but an end; the end of a stunningly bold football adventure, one that strongly suggested it would have huge meaning not just for Manchester but for all of English football.

It meant that the atmosphere in Old Trafford when we played Sheffield Wednesday was unlike any other anyone present could ever have known before. As I said, I bracketed it in my mind with that much happier night against Real Madrid, but if both occasions grabbed hard at the emotions, the Sheffield game took us far beyond any imaginable scale of a mere football match. It was as though the football was just a ritual, a vehicle for memories that were so brilliantly fresh, and at the same time a statement of how brief and fragile were all our lives. The Babes were youth, hope and artistry and had been snatched from us. So what could we do in the big stadium but feel hurt and very close to each other and, when my club-mate Shay, who would become one of my greatest friends, scored from a corner – something he would rarely do from any position in a fine career – there was maybe, suddenly, just a little reason to be optimistic about the future that that been so obscured by tears.

Murphy couldn't really think of the future. That would be for Busby when he healed, mentally and physically, to the point where he could see that there might just be a life for United after Munich that wasn't weighed down by pain and regrets. Murphy had to get by, and, by special dispensation from the football authorities, he was allowed to do something that flew against all of the club's recent tradition – he went into the market to sign some old professionals. Ernie Taylor, the little Wearsider inside-forward who had so relentlessly fed the genius of Stanley Matthews in the 1953 FA Cup final, arrived from Blackpool, and Stan Crowther, a craggy wing-half from Aston Villa who signed at Old Trafford just an hour and sixteen minutes before the start of the Wednesday game. In their different ways, they brought vital qualities to the transition fashioned so superbly by Murphy.

Taylor, who had served as a submariner in the war, stood just 5ft 4ins tall, wore size 4 boots and weighed less than 10 stone, but he was a great little craftsman. 'Tom Thumb' was always happy to talk to kids like me. As the pain of Munich ebbed, Taylor was someone who could take you back into the mainstream of football history. Over a cup of tea in the washroom, he could tell you how it was winning FA Cup medals for Newcastle in 1951, when two goals from Jackie Milburn beat the Blackpool team he joined a few months later – and then, two years after that first triumph, what it was like to be such a crucial figure in the Matthews final, when Bolton were so unforgettably defeated. Just three months after arriving at Old Trafford, he could also tell you about the shifts of football fortune as he walked off Wembley, having so remarkably helped our broken club to the final, beaten now by an avenging Bolton and the scoring power of Nat Lofthouse.

Crowther was a less amiable figure than Taylor, but he had his reasons. He came from the Black Country, where he had been orphaned at the age of fifteen. Murphy saw in him the edge of a true competitor. My first impression of Stan was that he was a bit of a 'narky sod', but he had plenty of time for me, and he was another old pro who could pass on little secrets.

Stan Crowther playing amid the Babes would have been an oddity, a stylistic sore thumb; but when the Babes were gone, he was for a little while an important element. He hated to lose, and he was making an even swifter return to Wembley, having been in the Villa side that had beaten United twelve months earlier after their Irish winger Peter McParland had collided with Ray Wood's head. Stan left the following December for Chelsea, for whom he made fifty appearances before making his way down through the leagues with Brighton, Rugby Town and Hednesford Town. Eventually, he became a senior foreman in the Armitage Shanks factory back home in Staffordshire. His distinction was to win England Under-23 caps, play for the Football League and three famous First Division clubs. He also played a part in maybe the greatest drama English football will ever know.

In Manchester, we didn't really share the tragedy with the rest of England, although we knew there were great waves of sympathy across the land. It was our pain, our hurt, and it was only later that anyone could really measure the devastating effect of Munich not just on United but also England.

Nearly half the England team – Edwards, Taylor, Colman, Byrne and Pegg – died in Munich. Imagine those names as the nucleus of an England challenge for the 1958 World Cup in Sweden and the 1962 World Cup in Chile. Imagine, also, the early effect on Bobby Charlton's game if it had been allowed to develop in the optimum circumstances of playing week in, week out, in the company of such extraordinary talent. As it was, Bobby had to work through years of struggle before Denis Law was called back from Italy and George Best emerged so sensationally from the streets of Belfast.

What I knew as a young footballer, and fan, riding the 112 bus home to Collyhurst after that draining night at Old Trafford, when Wednesday were defeated 3–0 by Jimmy Murphy's ragtag army of raw troops, a couple of veteran mercenaries and a wall of emotion that couldn't have been penetrated by a scud missile, was that I, along with contemporaries including Pancho Pearson and Alex Dawson was the inheritor of a short but amazing tradition. Bestowed upon us had been pain and glory in unprecedented amounts.

We were obliged to grow up faster than any footballers before or since, and not just as players but as young men who had been stripped of all the illusions of youth. We had plenty of those on the day when Bill Inglis, with his soft Scottish voice, tentatively broke the news of disaster, but they were gone now. We knew pretty much the full story. Now, when I look from the distance of an intervening life and career as a player, a coach, a manager and – most stunning of all to me when I occasionally stop to think about it – a public speaker dealing in the insatiable appetite for memories of football, I see as vividly as ever the sheer weight of that inheritance.

The first echo of what Manchester United meant to me came in the wake of the World Cup success in 1966. Like it or not, I had become something of a celebrity after my toothless, disjointed jig on the Wembley pitch, and on a flight to Dublin to see Kay's family I was drawing quite a bit of attention. More so, in fact, than one of the men who had done so much to make United's name synonymous with football of the highest class and who happened to be travelling on the same plane.

It was Johnny Carey, whose immaculate tackling was such a key element in the football education handed down to me by my father. I told him how much I had admired the play and the leadership he gave to United when they won the Cup so memorably in 1948 and, four years later, swept so brilliantly to the league championship. I said a special memory was the goal he scored against Chelsea, which gave their excellent international keeper Reg Matthews no chance, when the campaign was crowned by tremendous victories over both Chelsea and a still formidable Arsenal team. Carey was then playing at right-half, a position from which he wielded vast influence. I told him how I'd been watching with my brother Charlie while sitting on the wall above the scoreboard when he picked up the ball and moved with it so gracefully.

'I'll tell you how I did it, Nobby,' he said. 'I dragged it inside the defender and then, after dropping my shoulder and going the other way, got away from him at the halfway line, took it on and then shot with my right foot into the top corner.'

'That's exactly how I remember it, Mr Carey,' I said. But then you wouldn't forget something like that, would you?

You wouldn't forget that the younger Roger Byrne, who would be the old man of the Babes, played outside-left that day. You wouldn't forget Carey's goal and you wouldn't forget anything. You wouldn't forget embracing Charlie, a little precariously, while you sat on the wall. You wouldn't forget another delirious journey home.

Down the years, as we fought to re-establish the name of United, we came to learn that what happened at Munich was not in fact the end of something. It was a terrible punctuation mark; something that brought a long and agonising pause. We would get past it, all right, but anyone who loved Manchester United would not forget the cost. The young men who died at Munich paid the supreme price, but there were other degrees of pain.

I know, for example, that my friend Bobby Charlton can never forget that night of blizzard and horror when his world could so easily have ended. I knew that for sure when Shay Brennan and I sat alongside Bobby on a flight from Los Angeles to Hawaii in 1967, nearly ten years after Munich. We had a twelve-hour stop-over in Los Angeles and, as this was a summer tour, we had a few drinks. Unusually, Bobby, I noticed, had a few more than Shay or me. When we got on to the plane Shay and I immediately started playing cards. Bobby fell fast asleep. You wouldn't have thought an earthquake could disturb him, but the moment the plane started to move away from its blocks he was wide awake. Shay and I were asleep before the plane levelled out into its flight altitude, but when we were nudged awake by the stewardess as we descended into Honolulu airport, we saw that Bobby was still wide awake. He had the same expression on his face as he had when we roared down the runway in LA. It wasn't so much an expression as a mask. I would never know what went on behind that mask on the long flight across a massive stretch of the Pacific. But then how could I?

5

A BOLT OF LIGHTNING

FOR a while I thought I was lost in the aftermath of Munich. A wave of young players was rushed to the front line and, although I was still so short of experience, I felt I should have been part of the big squad Jimmy Murphy took to the Norbreck Hydro Hotel in Blackpool for a week of preparation for the sixth-round Cup-tie against West Bromwich. I had felt very much involved in the effort to make United live again, clearing snow from the pitch, cleaning the gym and getting involved in practice matches. There were so many practice matches. It was as though Murphy just wasn't prepared to give anyone too much time to think.

It was a time to run and work, to burn our way through the crisis. If we paused, if we thought too much about what had happened to us, maybe we would be ruined. Inevitably, some young players were adversely affected, if not destroyed. John Giles and I have never quite agreed on the extent of the damage caused to those individuals who tried and failed to meet the challenge that came to everyone at the club in the late winter of '58. Maybe because of our different natures and backgrounds, we saw things a little differently. John was passionate in his ambition to play for United – like me, he had worshipped at the altar of Johnny Carey – but he was able to apply a cooling system to his emotions. Those feelings about the game run as deeply in him as in any man I know, but part of his greatness as a player, time would prove, was that he was a man always in control. He didn't dream other men's dreams and that was a claim, certainly at that time, that maybe I couldn't make for myself.

One day the playing staff was assembled for a club photograph, which I supposed was a statement that our football life would go on and that these were the players who would help to heal the wounds. The problem was that when I saw the photograph, I noted that I was the only one in it who didn't get on the bus to Blackpool. I was gutted, probably more than I should have been. I was, after all, still a few months short of my sixteenth birthday.

It would be another eight months before I would feel that I was indeed a serious candidate to fill the boots of the great men who had gone. The breakthrough came on Christmas night 1958, ten months after the crash. I was over at Wocka Collins's house, listening to his record player, when a knock came on the door. It was my mother telling me that the club had called to say I had to report to Old Trafford at noon the following day. I was in the reserve team against Aston Villa.

Johnny Dixon led Villa out. He was the captain who had collected the FA Cup at Wembley eighteen months earlier at the expense of the Babes. Before I went out, Murphy gave me one of his classic pep talks. 'See that bastard, Dixon. He cost us the final – and the double,' he said. My job was to give Dixon not a moment's peace. I had to snap at him all afternoon. Naturally, I followed my orders and Murphy patted me on the shoulder when I came back to the dressing room at the end of the game. Many years later, when I was working with Ron Atkinson at West Bromwich, Big Ron asked, 'Remember when we played against each other in a reserve match at Old Trafford on Boxing Day?' I said I remembered the game well enough but had to apologise for not recalling Ron's burly presence among the opposition. I excused myself on the grounds that, generally, I operated in something of a tunnel and on that day Jimmy Murphy's orders had been quite specific. My one goal was to put the polished old professional Dixon in chains and avenge the defeat of the Babes at Wembley, if that was even a vague possibility in a reserve match before a slim crowd on Boxing Day. Ron said that my duel with Dixon was the point of his question.

'When Johnny came back into the dressing room,' Atkinson said, 'he told us all, "That kid was all over me out there – I feel I've just played against a little bastard who will one day play for England – if he can stay on the field long enough."'

Playing for Manchester United reserves at the end of 1958, I knew well enough, meant rather less than it might have done at the start of the year. But in football, as in most things in life, the obligation is to take your chances whenever they come, and my success against such a knowing and experienced player as Dixon was, I felt sure, a matter of legitimate satisfaction. In the rush for recognition at that desperate time, some of the younger of my club-mates would have been happy enough with something as tangible to measure their progress.

John Giles believed that the crisis at Old Trafford merely accentuated the demands on young players, such as Peter Jones, Reg Holland, Reg Hunter and, ultimately, two direct heirs of the Babes, Alex Dawson and my friend Pancho. John's theory was that, whatever the circumstances, players play the best they can and face judgement on that effort. My view was that these lads were rushed too hard, and that the expectations that came down on them over the months, rather than in just those first emotion-charged weeks following the crash, were in the end simply unsupportable. John was supported in his opinion by our mutual friend Jimmy Sheils, another Irishman, whose hopes at Old Trafford were ended in a collision with reserve goalkeeper Gordon Clayton. For Gordon and Jimmy, the challenge was taken away by their training-field accident. It was a reminder for the rest of us that this life we prized so highly was always just one crushing mishap away. Munich was something off the graph of football's bleaker possibilities, and Gordon had avoided it when a minor injury kept him out of the squad for the Belgrade match. He had made an earlier trip to Europe as understudy to Ray Wood. A picture in the *Evening Chronicle* showed him going up the stairs of the British European Airways plane with the first team, wearing a long mac and a bright and eager face. I was filled with envy when I looked at the picture, but then, so quickly, it was all over for him and Jimmy.

Gordon told me how it was travelling with the first team, how Roger Byrne, as the captain and oldest player, was a little aloof from the rest – and how Busby was a little wary of him because, unlike the others, he didn't lap up everything that was said by the boss and Jimmy Murphy. Roger felt he was the gaffer of the dressing room and had a duty to question Busby and Murphy about arrangements and tactics. In those days, that really wasn't done. Mostly, I quizzed Gordon about Coly. What was he like away from the field?

'Oh, he was a good lad,' said Gordon. 'He didn't have any airs about him. He was a good, Salford lad.' I was pleased to have the picture I had always had in my head confirmed.

Unlike Jimmy, who returned to Ireland and became a successful businessman whose interests included one of the most popular pubs in Londonderry, which he always pointedly refers to as Derry when he is among Englishmen, Gordon lingered at the club for a while. But his injury effectively ended his chances at Old Trafford, and he left after playing just two games for the first team, against West Brom and the giants of his native Black Country, Wolves.

Also unlike Jimmy but in common with so many football men, he found that he was permanently wedded to the game. Nothing, he decided, could really replace it.

Gordon scarcely lasted a season with Tranmere Rovers in the old Third Division north, then slipped into non-league football with Cheadle Town, GKN Sankey and finished as a part-time professional with Radcliffe Borough. But he couldn't be done with football. He kept dreaming dreams, scouting for Manchester United and Derby, moving back to Cheadle Town as manager and then taking the assistant managership at Northwich Victoria. He died in that job in 1991 at the age of fifty-four. For some years we lived near each other in Stretford, a short walk away from Old Trafford. He never wanted to forget those years when he rubbed shoulders with the great team, and when I heard he had died I thought of the pictures of him walking up the stairway of the plane with Byrne, Taylor and Coleman. No one could ever take that away from him.

Gordon, who felt the elation of gaining an FA Youth Cup-winners medal in a team that seemed to offer all its members the fast route to the top of football, was one of the big losers after Munich, along with Jones, Holland and Hunter, who were rushed into the vacuum left by the crash. Soon enough the three of them – all lovely lads – were playing for Wrexham, who were a Third Division team producing very cultured football under the player-managership of Ken Barnes, who had been such a skilled and popular player for our fierce rivals Manchester City.

A few years ago I saw Peter Jones for the first time since those dramatic days at Old Trafford. He came to an old players do and we finished up having a drink in one of the watering holes of former United players, Terry Corless's Circus Tavern in Portland Street. Peter was a Salford lad who imagined that he would walk in the footsteps of Coly, but he got just one shot at the big time

– a First Division appearance against Portsmouth in 1957. He understudied the England captain Roger Byrne – an unpromising task. He told me he had always enjoyed his football, with Wrexham and then Stockport County before playing into his forties with Altrincham. He was a skilful player but when his trial came at Old Trafford, when Jimmy Murphy was driving so hard, his chance came and went, probably, I suspect, before he really grasped how much was at stake. It had all started so promisingly with an amateur season with Wolves, United's one serious rival as the glamour club of England in the fifties, and then he was lured to Old Trafford and ushered into the all-conquering youth team. According to my theory, he was one of those who was caught and broken by the convulsion of Munich.

Alex Dawson and Pancho Pearson had similar pedigrees, and of course they suffered less obvious damage. But I cited Dawson, the son of a Grimsby trawlerman, as my most compelling evidence when I argued with John Giles and Jimmy Sheils that if the aftermath of Munich offered great opportunity to the next wave of United players, it also asked too much of them, too soon. Dawson was strong beyond his years, but soon enough he showed evidence of burn-out. He arrived as a fearless, dark and hugely powerful young man. He was an England schoolboy international who was a big factor in two of United's Youth Cup triumphs. He scored in his first games for the first team in the League, in the FA Cup and the League Cup, and at the age of eighteen years and thirty-three days, just a few months after Munich, he scored a hat-trick in the FA Cup semi-final replay with Fulham at Highbury. Suddenly, he was the great hope of Manchester United. There was the wonderfully smooth skill of Bobby Charlton, and there was the raw power of Alex Dawson.

But such power, in my opinion, needed more careful handling, and maybe this would have happened if Jimmy Murphy hadn't had one thought above all – to keep United alive as a force in football, to win some time. Under this pressure, big Alex had to survive or go down.

He didn't exactly crumble – in 93 appearances for the first team he scored 54 goals – but by 1961 he had given way to David Herd, a £30,000 signing from Arsenal. Dawson, this wrecking ball of a player, had lost some of his force. He moved to Preston North End and was, with another young player who lost his way at Old Trafford, Nobby Lawton, in the losing FA Cup final against Bobby Moore's West Ham. Then he moved on to Bury, Brighton (on loan) and, finally, Corby Town. I will always believe his fire was allowed to burn too quickly, too fiercely.

Pancho, my adviser, tormentor and, in his crazy way, my friend, was also given big billing after Munich. But, like Dawson, his momentum slowed, and in 1963 he was gone – to Sheffield Wednesday for £20,000, and then, two years later, to Fulham. Ten years and two broken legs after Munich, he decided to quit. He was at Halifax Town at the time.

I argued that the reserves had been pushed up too soon. It seemed that everyone at the club was pushed up except me, and I didn't like it at the time. Later, Jimmy Sheils said that the reason I went on to establish myself with United, and John Giles, after troubles with Busby, became a foundation of Leeds United's success under Don Revie, was nothing to do with timing or being shielded from pressure. It was that we had something extra, the means to go the long course. But there could be no easy progress for the first replacements of the lost team because, unlike their predecessors, they couldn't grow under the influence of a Roger Byrne or the amazingly mature Duncan Edwards. They didn't have the confidence that comes when you are playing with great men. When I look back to that time, it just seems like a blur of action, of practice match after practice match, a treadmill of effort.

While everyone agreed that it was the worst thing anyone could ever imagine happening, I know some of the lads said, well, it has happened, and we just have to take our chances. But they didn't realise the effect of playing so far ahead of themselves. They didn't see the danger of burn-out. I said to Jimmy and Johnny, it's all right playing out of your skin, but for how long can you do it? When you have the confidence of everyone around you, when every game isn't the big audition of your career, it made sense in my mind that you could show more of your game, more of your understanding of what was most important. But John and Jimmy said, 'Never mind that – you play or you don't play.'

Whatever John and Jimmy said, I came to look at that picture of all the United players who were taken to Blackpool by Jimmy Murphy, remembered how gutted I felt as their bus rolled away, and thanked God that I was put on hold.

My career ticked along. I went the full course in the youth team, captaining it in my final year of 1961, and while I was doing it, United were fighting to stay in the big time. From 1958 to 1961 we had the desperate years, when it was enough to hang on to First Division life. Tottenham were the great team, bursting with talent and class based on such outstanding characters as Danny Blanchflower, Dave Mackay, Cliff Jones, and the slim ghost of a Scotsman who would soon enough give me the football lesson of my life, John White. We had to live, at least for a while, on the less fashionable side of the street. Matt Busby and Jimmy Murphy, having seen all their brilliant work swept away, had to find the means to consolidate in the First Division, and then launch the real fight-back. They realised Old Trafford needed better organisation, a surer direction, and they appointed a coach, John Aston, and a trainer, Jack Crompton. They were immensely significant signings.

'Crompo' was dour and thorough, far from a typical goalkeeper, although at times he had acquitted himself brilliantly in that role for the club, winning an FA Cup-winner's medal with the great team of 1948 while I was having my head extracted from the sofa in Rochdale Road. He brought organisation to the training at Old Trafford, something that, strangely when you consider how many huge strides the club had made under Busby and Murphy, had been lacking pre-Munich. John and I were delighted by his arrival. It told us that Busby was serious about attempting to make the club great again. Jack gave us weight-training and a proper schedule of running, sprints and distance.

John Aston, whose son John later shared with me one of the two greatest nights in the history of the club, also played a valuable role in moving the players towards a more thoughtful approach to their football. He had great knowledge and, considering he had served as a Royal Marine commando during the war, a surprisingly gentle touch. He had played seventeen times for England and been a key member of United's 1948 Cup-winners and 1952 champions. Mostly he had played full-back, but, when the occasion demanded, he had proved himself more than useful up front. It meant that when he had something to say to you, he could give his advice with great authority.

There were other telling moves. Tony Dunne, who proved to be one of the club's greatest signings, was picked up for £5,000 from the League of Ireland club Shelbourne, and he made a big impression in his first training session. He was as fast as a whippet and he could tackle.

I was mostly playing right-half with switches to inside-forward, and in 1960 the great day came – at Burnden Park, the famous old ground of Bolton Wanderers. I made the first team at right-half, with John in front of me at inside-forward. The feeling was magical even though I felt nervous. I was obliged to feel nervous. Bolton were a good side, and they were also formidably hard.

Their full-backs Roy Hartle and Tommy Banks had a reputation for devouring young players. Their centre-forward was the legendary Nat Lofthouse, the Lion of Vienna, who had destroyed us two years earlier in the Cup final, when all the country looked for a sentimental ending to our season of Munich and instead saw a great footballer simply going about his work.

The nerves, I came to learn quickly enough, were essential. Later, when I had some more experience, and success, there were times when I would get a little cocky, and on those occasions I never played well. At Bolton, I wasn't cocky, just utterly dedicated to making the right start to my career in the big-time. It went far better than I could have hoped. We needed a point and we got one – largely because of the goal John scored from my pass. Somewhere in the jumble of my football keepsakes I have the yellowing headline from the *Daily Express* – 'Stiles to Giles – all Smiles'.

The memories of those early days in league football are so vivid they may have happened yesterday. It was a new, big, glorious world but there was so much to learn, and so many mistakes that you had to learn from quickly or go under. Later, when I was still fighting to nail down a permanent place in the first team, I learned one of the big lessons. You have to be very sure about your preparation for a big game. You can't afford to have doubts about what is best for you. The need for this was underlined in a match at Arsenal. Already I had adopted the ritual of going to bed early, no later than 10.30, but it was a holiday time and I went to a neighbourhood party. I told everybody that I could stay for an hour only because I was travelling to London the following day, but in fact I didn't get home until the early hours of the morning. It played terribly on my mind on the train journey down to London, and my mood didn't improve when John and I told the staff at the President's Hotel that we were hungry. They said there was nothing in the larder except cold milk and Colman's pies. Disgusted, we went to bed and slept, in my case uneasily. But then there was never any question about John sleeping soundly. He could nod off on the coach going to the ground. He snoozed while my nerves twanged.

We started brilliantly at Highbury. For fifteen minutes we ran Arsenal off their feet, but that was it. We couldn't score, we couldn't give ourselves any ballast, and we finished well beaten. Long before the end, I said to myself, 'Nobby, you weren't the only one who stayed late at a party.'

But mostly that first run in league football went well enough. Apart from the good headline in the *Express*, Maurice Setters, the hard wing-half-defender who had joined us from West Bromwich in another Busby move to bring some firmness to our transition period, gave me a flattering reference in his column in the *Chronicle*. He said that I was a kid to keep an eye on.

I scored my first goal, against Newcastle, the one I dedicated to Eddie Colman. There are two things I remember clearly about that game. Naturally, the goal is set in my mind for ever – your first goal in the big league is a 'keeper' memory. It tells you that the world might just be at your feet. The other strong recollection is of one of the great characters of football at that time, Jimmy Scoular. He was a soft-spoken Scot but there was nothing gentle about his tackling. He brought down Bobby Charlton, who, as the old pro Scoular had no doubt noticed, was winding himself up into a brilliant performance, and as the new hero of Old Trafford went down in a heap in the middle of the pitch, the culprit turned to every corner of the ground and waved an imaginary baton. He was conducting the angry crowd and I couldn't help thinking, 'Here's some man – some player.'

Scoular was part of the great wing-half tradition of British football, a man who mixed fine football skill with the sharpest of edges. His countryman Dave Mackay is probably the ultimate example of this combination of velvet skill and cold steel in the tackle, but Scoular was very much of the same breed. I had marvelled at the way he had destroyed our rivals Manchester City in the 1955 Cup final, feeding beautiful passes to Newcastle's talented winger Bobby Mitchell and making tackles that I was sure you could hear in every corner of the ground. Scoular was an important experience for an eighteen year old making his way in the game, and surviving it whole, and with my career still intact, was, when I think about it now, probably as much reason to celebrate as scoring the goal.

Busby had a strict policy about blooding young players, at least when the post-Munich pressure began to lift a little. He put you in for a few games, then ushered you back into the shadows to regather your strength, 'laddie', and to make sure that your feet were still on the ground. I re-emerged at Bloomfield Road, Blackpool, on Good Friday – an outing to the home of the great Sir Stanley Matthews.

It should have been an afternoon of uncomplicated pleasure but it was anything but that. The crisis came at lunchtime at the Norbreck Hydro, which a few years earlier had seemed the most attractive place on earth when the first-team bus rolled away from Old Trafford without me. My problem came when the waitresses started to serve the food. It was toast and steaks. I thought, 'Oh my God, it's Good Friday and we will be kicking off in a few hours' time, when normally I would be an altar boy assisting at the Stations of the Cross – and not only that, I'm about to eat meat, a great bloody chunk of it, on Good Friday.' Instead of acknowledging it was the day Our Lord died for us and went off to heaven, I had a knife and fork poised above a fine example of Angus beef. John was at the table but he was no help. He was eating away. Maybe, I thought, I should ask for fish, but I wanted

My brother Charlie was always my minder. He couldn't go anywhere without me – not even to his first communion.

I put on my best smile for my own first communion at the age of seven. It's not true that I was already practising my approach to referees.

Dad, me, Charlie and Mum head for the beach in Bray, Ireland. It was our only family holiday apart from day-trips to Blackpool. Dad had come up on the horses.

I manage a smile as a I stand next to Miss Morgan for the class picture at St Pat's in 1953. It took some effort. She was a firm believer in corporal punishment.

Johnny Carey – one of my first heroes. Dad said, 'Look at his shorts at the end of the game. They are always clean. He never loses his balance.'

Sugar Poole, third from left front row, was captain of our winning under-14s team. Later, it was Sugar who invited me to the pub from which Charlie banished me. John 'Wocka' Collins, extreme right front row, was my best friend and came to my wedding in Dublin. I'm third from right, back row, and in one of my rare growth spurts.

...hake hands with Field Marshal Montgomery at ...embley in 1957 before my first schoolboy ...ternational. The sun is shining on our team. ...e scored after thirteen seconds. The great Joe ...ercer's widow sent me the picture.

My idol – Eddie 'Snakehips' Colman. I cleaned his boots. I worshipped him. I tried not to believe he had gone.

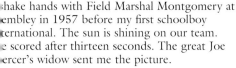

...e front and back pages of the *News Chronicle*, which told the story of Munich. I ...ayed that none of it was true.

I make my debut at Bolton Wanderers aged eighteen, aching to show a little of that Colman style.

Courting Kay on one of her visits to Rochdale Road. Charlie's baby is in the pram.

Manchester United going into the Cup-winning season of 1962–63. *Back row, left to right*: Sir Matt Busby, Maurice Setters, Jimmy Nicholson, David Gaskell, Shay Brennan, Mark Pearson, Noel Cantwell. *Second row*: Bill Foulkes, Sammy McMillan, Tony Dunne, me, Nobby Lawton, Jack Crompton. *Front row*: John Giles, Albert Quixall, David Herd, Denis Law, Bobby Charlton.

The happiest day of my life. Cutting the cake with Kay in Dublin on 18 June 1963.

Kay and the girls at the wedding, including sisters Pauline and Anna, second and fif[th] from the left back row, and sister-in-law, Anne Giles, second from right, back row.

Friends, family and team-mates at my wedding include brother-in-law John Giles and Eamon Dunphy, then a United player, now a controversial author, third and fourth from the right, back row.

A brotherly kiss for Kay from John Giles.
Their father Dickie (*centre*) concentrates
on the camera – unlike, next to him, my
dad Charlie.

Our first-born, John, had all our
attention when he arrived in 1964.
He was another reason for me to
make my mark.

Showing the championship trophy with George Best in 1965. Another reason to
celebrate – I didn't forget my teeth.

My England debut – and the big challenge, marking the Lawman.

The road to the World Cup – arriving in Cardiff for a match against Wales, with Terry Paine and (*left to right*) Ro Springett, George Cohen and Jack Charlton.

An early bite into Germany. I score the only goal at Wembley in a friendly in February 1966.

desperately to reclaim my place in the team. I wanted to build up my strength. So I ate the steak and immediately developed a blinding headache. I put the headache down to a massive onset of guilt. As I ran out on the field I found myself throwing up. Guilt, nausea – it was a twin attack, and the crushing result was that when I scored it was for Blackpool. I headed into my own net. There were two consequences – I was out of the first team, and I would never again eat meat on Good Friday. I switched to poached eggs on toast, which was good for my conscience and my digestive system.

So already I was able to tick off a whole list of lessons learned. Don't preen yourself on the ball. Don't stay out at parties when you should be in bed, trying to get to sleep despite all the thoughts racing through your head about what the future might have in store. Don't eat meat before games, especially if they fall on Good Friday. Above all, don't say one thing to Matt Busby and do another. If he gives you an order, follow it. That, at Old Trafford, was the rule of survival, and on the club's most important day since Munich, I broke it. I thought for myself and deep down I still shudder at the consequences.

May 1962 was supposed to be the time when Manchester United returned to the big stage. We played Spurs in the semifinal of the FA Cup at Hillsborough. It's true that the club had played two semi-finals within a few months of the crash, winning one, in the FA Cup against Second Division Fulham, and losing the other to AC Milan in the European Cup. But that was when United were buoyed by sentiment and an extraordinary flood of adrenaline, which had run its course by the time Bolton beat us in the 1958 FA Cup final. This, in 1962, was a new United, fashioned around the great talent that was miraculously salvaged from the crash, Bobby Charlton.

Before the game, I took a walk with Bobby and Shay Brennan.

From that day, taking walks before big games would become another don't. It wasn't a great ramble on to the moors, but I was troubled as Bobby and Shay ambled along, filling in the dead time before we had to go down to the ground. I thought of John Giles, back in the team hotel, snoozing and storing his strength.

Every ounce of strength you had, both physical and mental, was needed against Bill Nicholson's Spurs. Busby's team-talk followed its usual pattern. We should go out to play and express ourselves. Show that we didn't fear the team of Blanchflower and Mackay, White and Jones. But he did make a few specific points, and they included my assignment for the game. I had to cover John White like a blanket. Wherever he went, I had to go. The other man-marking job went to Nobby Lawton. He had to shut down Danny Blanchflower. Nobby was a nice player, he passed the ball well, but he didn't have a lot of pace, which was a particular problem that day because Blanchflower was at his best, stretching us repeatedly with some beautiful passing. Spurs took a two-goal lead and were well worth it.

At half-time Busby, as always, remained unflustered. Just keep playing the way you have been, said the boss, we could turn it around. I raised an objection. I said that I was wasting my time. White, who could run for fun, had been dragging me out of position, but he had not been doing us any serious damage. It was Blanchflower's day. But Busby said, 'No, son, keep on White. That's your job.'

After just a few minutes of the second half, Bobby Charlton conjured a moment of brilliance and the score was 2–1. After being completely outplayed by the puppet-master Blanchflower, we were back in the game. Maybe the old fox was right. It was time for United to make a big push and also, I decided, for me to throw aside my orders. When White made still another run, I said to myself, 'I know where you're going but this time I'm not coming with you.' Instead, I literally got hold of Blanchflower. Unfortunately, as I was attending to the Spurs captain, there was a great roar. I turned to look down the field and saw Tottenham players celebrating. White, uncovered and with plenty of time to pick his spot, had played a pin-point pass to Cliff Jones, who promptly ended the contest with another Spurs goal. As the Spurs players broke off from their hugs, White called to me, 'Where were you, Nobby?' I was heading back for another stint with the reserves. Later, in the dressing room, Busby could probably see my pain, and he contented himself with one of those looks that said, 'That wasn't Manchester United.'

It was quite soon after that he went up to Glasgow and bought himself another right-half. Paddy Crerand, of Celtic and Scotland, a fine creative player, arrived at Old Trafford as one of the foundation stones of a new United. Where did that leave me? Looking for alternative employment.

I would find it soon enough and, remarkably, it would return me again to Manchester United's first team. The odds against that, I would have said as I marched off the Hillsborough pitch with my head down, were huge. John White left the field a hero in pursuit of another FA Cup-winner's medal. But then football, like life, teaches you that the line between success and failure can be very fine indeed. It means that you have to celebrate your victories when you can. That was John White's lesson to me at Hillsborough. The one he gave to all of football came a few months later, when he was struck dead by a bolt of lightning.

6

MY CUP OF TEA

THEY say one good turn deserves another and if it is true, as I believe it is, it means that, every day of the last forty-odd years of my life I have had reason to celebrate the first time I invited John Giles to sample some of my mother's Sunday cooking. The digs the club had put him in were not very much to his liking. The food was meagre and not very well cooked and his eyes, and Jimmy Sheils', lit up when I said I thought my mother could probably do quite a bit better.

John had taken a different route from me to the Old Trafford dressing room. He had signed for United as an amateur and the club found him a job as an apprentice electrician when he arrived from Dublin as a fifteen year old. He loathed the distraction from football and worked hard, hungry for recognition, in the twice-weekly training sessions he attended at the Cliff.

Soon after his first visit, John moved into our little house. It was the start of a friendship that has shaped my life. What goes into a great friendship? I suppose there are many elements – an easy liking, of course, an admiration for certain qualities, respect. John inspired all of those reactions in me, and down the years those traits of character that I first detected in a young kid from Dublin who, like me, operated in the shadows and the footsteps of men we had come to revere, have become more pronounced in my mind.

Reading his columns, first in the *Daily Express* and now the *Daily Mail*, I have always found a point of identity for an old pro. They have also helped me understand why, after some great early success with West Bromwich, and profitable stints with Shamrock Rovers in Dublin and Vancouver Whitecaps, he decided that the life of a football manager was not for him. It involved too many frustrations, too many compromises. In this, our lives would stay on parallel lines. I too had a little bit of success when I took over at Preston North End after working there with Bobby Charlton, but there were aspects of the job that I always felt, deep down, worked against my own nature.

When John tried to remove some of the injustices that had so angered him through his career as a player, he was told by one director or another that it could not be done. He wearied of a job in which he could not put all his knowledge to full use without requiring approval by men who lacked a fraction of his experience and understanding of the game. The *Express* billed him as the 'Man the Players Read', and though I cannot speak for a younger generation, I know that many of the players of my time do indeed pick up on John's comments, and see in them the old threads of their thinking. The game has changed so much but in its fundamentals, it still makes the same demands on character and commitment in exchange for true success.

Going into his sixties, John has developed to a fine, mature point those first insights that were so easy to detect in the teenager. He sees the whole picture, and he is particularly hard on those who insult the intelligence of people in and out of the game. He has always had a built-in detector for false claims of greatness, and what I particularly like is that he is, unlike a lot of our generation of professionals, open-minded. He doesn't automatically assume that everything is wrong in the modern game just because it is modern.

Sometimes I speculate on what might have happened if he had been more prepared to live with some of the inevitable frustrations of the manager's life, if he could have suffered football fools a little more comfortably. In his time, he had opportunities to run Leeds United, Tottenham and Arsenal, but on each occasion the circumstances were not quite right for him. He wouldn't take anyone's first offer – as a player under the great Sir Matt Busby or as candidate for some of the game's top jobs.

I always thought he should have been the cornerstone of Manchester United. He should have done for the club he adored from a distance when he played street football as a boy on the quayside of the Liffey in Dublin, while I was marching across the Red Rec and Newton Loco, what he did so brilliantly for Leeds. But, ultimately, there was something in the air at Old Trafford that didn't agree with John, and something in his attitude, his refusal to accept things as they had always been, that created a negative reaction in Matt Busby and Jimmy Murphy.

But all that would come to a head a little further down the road. His rebellion was just stirring when he moved into Rochdale Road.

We did play together in the red shirts of United, and he achieved something that would always elude me in my fourteen years at Old Trafford. He won a Cup-winner's medal. He snatched it against a tide of what I can now see only as prejudice, a sense that his face didn't quite fit.

The reason I was able to invite John to stay at our house was that my brother Charlie got married and moved out, leaving a free bed. John and I shared the second bedroom and talked long into the night, mostly about football. John seemed a lot older than his years when he spoke about the game. Right from the start he had impressed me as someone who knew what he was about, and his knowledge of football ran very deep. I provided a lot of passion in those conversations in the back bedroom. John's contribution was more calculated. He had the knack of thinking things through.

But there was something else about John. It wasn't the strength of his convictions or his sharply individual view of the game we were both committed to playing and making the core of our lives. It wasn't that he seemed so clearly to me to be a footballer touched by the hand of destiny. It was that he had a sister who knocked my head off the first time I saw her. They say that young Italians know the Sicilian thunderbolt – perhaps I was experiencing something that might be described as the Collyhurst Comet. Certainly nothing else would ever shine so bright in my sky.

In fact, John had three lovely sisters, Anna, Kay and Pauline. It was Kay who did the damage to my equilibrium. It was Kay who made the Giles family home off the Navan Road the place that held my most stubborn dream. I felt like the love-imprisoned character in 'My Fair Lady', the one who sang 'On the Street Where You Live'. If I could sing, I would have given it full throttle.

John and his father Dickie, a well-known figure in Dublin football, met me off an early boat at the docks on Dublin Wall and took me home for breakfast at their house near Phoenix Park, a place that celebrates the struggles of Irish heroes. John's mother Kate made us a magnificent breakfast of eggs, bacon, sausages and white pudding. I had never been a fan of the northern delicacy black pudding, but this pale Irish version was delicious. Then Kay came down the stairs and my legs turned to jelly.

I was sixteen at the time and, apart from my earlier admiration for Doreen Bracegirdle, and the fact that I had been to the pictures a few times with a girl called Alma from Stretford, who was a friend of my cousin's, I was not exactly a ladies man. Kay, I learned gloomily, was 'walking out' with a certain singer, and when I stuttered my 'good morning' she said, 'Oh, hello,' and, without waiting for an introduction, sailed on out of the house. She was going to church. It was, I realised straightaway, going to be a long campaign.

Apart from the singer, I had other rivals, and one was another singer. Later, I confided my fears to Jimmy Sheils that I couldn't compete with the glamour of these crooners but Jimmy tried to reassure me on that point, at least. 'Don't worry about those guys,' he declared. It was one small crumb of comfort.

I conducted the campaign with the patience and relentlessness that befitted a midfielder. However, after being invited into the heart of a warm family, and at the end of my first visit, it was Kay's elder sister Anna who said, 'Nobby, it's been great having you, come and visit us again soon.' I said to myself, 'I'll be back, no danger.'

My first visit was for a week, then I returned for a fortnight and within a couple of years I was spending all my free summer time in Dublin. Kay was the magnet, but I loved the family and the city, and my friendship with John, as we fought for recognition at Old Trafford, deepened quickly to the point where I knew it would always be a cornerstone of my life. My relationship with Kay took a much longer, and agonising, time to catch fire.

My cause wasn't helped by my lack of musical ability and a disastrous record at the Plaza dancehall in Manchester. I despaired of ever getting a dance at that place although I was never sure of the steps I would make if a girl ever allowed me to sweep her on to the dance floor. It didn't help that I was shy, but then it was also true that I was game enough. I had, after all, auditioned for a part in the Minstrel Show, and once at school I had dressed in a kilt and attempted to perform a Scottish reel. I can't imagine Kay would have been too impressed.

Her singer would pick her up and I would wait up for her return, watching the clock until I heard the sound of the bastard's car drawing up outside the house. I couldn't sing the words of any Everly Brothers or Elvis song, or any of the old standards that the family performed with enthusiasm at regular sing-songs – ironically, for me, John's party piece later became 'Don't Cry for Me, Argentina' – and so there were inevitably times when I felt like a sore thumb. But there was one hand I could play better than any of the singers or, I decided, any young man alive. I could woo Kay with devotion, pure, blinding devotion, and patiently waiting for the sound of the car, rushing to make a cup of tea, engaging her in all those late-night conversations, finally worked. The fact that she continued to take my breath away every time I saw her, which presumably I eventually managed to convey with more force than some stuttering, lovesick kid, got me to where I wanted most to be – occupying the high ground of the man in the life of Kay Giles. It had taken about two years, but I had my first official date with Kay and I was so happy I wouldn't have called the King my cousin.

While I had been trying to court his sister, John was engaged in something that seemed equally challenging. He was attempting to teach me to play golf, something he has been doing on and off for the last forty years. We had some wonderful days out on the course. For a Collyhurst boy, the smell of the grass was intoxicating enough. At the ninth hole the pleasure increased when we stopped with two of John's friends, who were tick-tack men at the racetracks and also worked some time at the docks, for drinks and prawn sandwiches. The prawns came, how legally I was never quite sure, from the docks and, though it feels a bit traitorous to say it, the sandwiches were far superior to those soggy tomato specials Charlie and I used to wolf down at Old Trafford cricket ground.

Dickie Giles was the head of the family. He was a character celebrated not only in football circles but also in many of the pubs and bars of Dublin. He was a man of great enterprise and had he been born into different circumstances, if he had inherited or won some capital, he could well have been Ireland's answer to Richard Branson. He never had a factory job, and the only way he could be described from a professional perspective is as an entrepreneur. He wasn't the most organised man in the world. John would often have to tramp up to the Navan Road for a gallon of petrol in a tin can after Dickie's car had run dry at some late hour of the night.

Apart from running football teams, renting pitches and leasing them on to clubs, and buying shirts and footballs in bulk and selling them for some profit, he had two main business initiatives. One was the production of a home-made version of Pine disinfectant. He would make it in a shed in the big back garden and sell it round the pubs. The sales part of the job he obviously found by far the most agreeable aspect of the operation, and John told of days as a kid when he sat outside a bar with a lemonade and a bag of crisps while Dickie went about business, which John noticed ruefully seemed to require his father to buy a drink for everyone in the pub.

His other line of business was running his own lottery. He bought books of tickets and sold them, also around the pubs. Kay's mother Kate used to remark how amazing it was that so much of her husband's work made visits to the pub not a pleasure but a simple business requirement. He would laugh and say it was a terrible hard life being a business entrepreneur.

He was a real Dublin character and you had a strong sense of that at his funeral. The church was filled with friends and admirers. He may not have been the most disciplined man the world had ever known but he touched so many people with his love of life – and not least with his passion for football. He was a great judge of the game, and a huge influence on John, although he could often be maddening. He used to drive John crazy at times, especially when he ran out of petrol, but there was always respect for his knowledge of football and his instinct for what made a genuine player.

Dickie had a hard sense of what was important in the game, but he was quite the opposite of my father. While my dad was a pessimist, always worrying whether my team would win a game, Dickie was filled with optimism. When I was carried off injured while playing for a United team as an eighteen year old in a friendly game at Tolka Park in Dublin, Dickie offered me instant encouragement. He said I might consider it a bad night, but in his opinion I was a certainty to play for England.

One of my great memories of those days, as I think about it, is the relationships of fathers and sons and their friends. It was as though the generations touched quite seamlessly, and one of the worries I have when I think of my own sons and their families is that the days are so different now. I have a lovely pack of grandchildren, and they are among the great pleasures of my life, but sometimes you want to hold them tight against the perils of a world that can be a little hard to understand. I suspect it was so much easier for the generations to merge back then when I fell under the thrall of Dickie Giles; and John and Jimmy Sheils got on so well with my own father. There was a linkage, a strength of understanding of what was important in life and, of course, for both families football occupied that extremely high place.

It didn't impress Kay, though, unfortunately. The singer's ability to carry a tune was for a long time more attractive to her than my own capacity to kick the shit out of a football and, sometimes, anybody who happened to be trying to keep it out of my possession.

I don't really remember the details of our first date, which you may think a little surprising, but I suppose it's because the whole affair from my perspective was one long effort to win her approval. We did the usual things. I met her when she came off her shift as a hairdresser. We went to the pictures. We walked in the park. We listened to music. Necessarily, long periods of courtship were conducted entirely by letter. She would visit Rochdale Road at Easter-time, and I would spend the whole summer in Dublin and, when I was injured, I would sneak a trip across the Irish Sea.

I was nineteen when I asked Dickie for his daughter's hand. I had asked Kay the big question while we listened to music in the family parlour, and then I went to Dickie and said, 'Mr Giles [I never called him Dickie] can I have a word? I would like to marry your daughter.' Apparently, he had been expecting this development for some time. He said he was chuffed. 'It's a pleasure, son,' he said, and poured us both a drink.

We were engaged for a year before getting married in Dublin. By this time, John was courting his wife Anne, who lived just around the corner from the Giles house. She, too, was brought up with strong sporting connections. Her brother, Paul Dolan, ran for Ireland in the Olympics. Kay and I used to babysit for her other brother, Joe.

My brother Charlie came over for the wedding as best man along with Wocka Collins. Jimmy Sheils was there and he tells some haunting stories about the state I got into before the priest finally announced that Kay was officially my wife, declared under the rites of the Catholic Church and the force of my passion, if not punctuality. Shamefully, but perhaps inevitably, I was late for my own wedding. Kay and Dickie had to make two circuits of the neighbouring streets before getting the signal from Charlie that I had finally arrived, trussed up in a morning suit and with my heart in my throat. Kay was apparently as cool as ice. She was repeatedly told that I would show up, and she said, 'He can please his bloody self.' When I walked down the aisle I caught Jimmy Shiels out of the corner of my eye. He was killing himself laughing.

It had been the ordeal of my life. I'd stayed in town with John and Charlie and our first problem came with the car John had parked on the quays. I was horrified to see that it had a flat tyre. John had just learned to drive but his newly acquired knowledge did not include a clue about changing a tyre. Between the three of us, there were just enough ideas to get the job done, but as soon as it was completed we found that a woman had blocked us in. Sweating in my morning suit, I knocked on her window and said, 'Could you move your car, love, we're late for a very important date.' When she um-ed and ah-ed, my patience snapped. 'Move the fucking car. I'm supposed to be getting married,' I yelled.

The day had started much more smoothly. I got into the morning suit Kay had insisted I should wear despite long and desperate protests by me, and, at John's suggestion, we walked down to a barber's shop and were shaved. It was a brilliant idea. It meant that even if I arrived late, I would not have my face decorated with bits of newspaper mopping up the blood from razor slashes.

I got to the altar twenty minutes late but as soon as Kay said 'I do' all my tension and fears drained away and it was the loveliest of days. The reception was out at the Grand Hotel in Malahide, and at 4 p.m. we were driven to the airport. We were heading for Paris, Rome and, I knew, the stars. I'd booked the trip with Thomas Cook's in Manchester and I don't really know why we chose those particular locations. They just seemed liked the most exciting places in the world when we looked at the map. In fact, the honeymoon was brilliant, and not least because we had a guardian angel – a man of great kindness and, very helpful to me at the time, great sophistication. It was the famous Italian football agent Gigi Peronace.

Gigi had brought Denis Law to United after his brief stint with Torino, and I had met him just once before, a month or so earlier after the FA Cup semi-final against Southampton at Villa Park. The club always threw a dinner at the Midland Hotel in Manchester at that time of year and Gigi, who had become a friend of Busby during the Law negotiation with Torino, was invited. Kay was over from Dublin and when we were introduced to Gigi we told him that we were planning to spend our honeymoon in Rome. He said he would see us there, which at the time I thought was merely a matter of politeness. It was surprising, then, that when we arrived our room was filled with a great array of gladioli and there was a bottle of champagne sitting in an ice bucket on the table. They had been sent by Gigi.

We didn't really drink then, so didn't finish the bottle of Frascati we had when we went out to dinner that first day. The waiter said he would put a cork back in the bottle and keep it for our return. Gigi had other plans for our honeymoon, however. He appeared at our little hotel and said that he was going to spend the day showing us around the Eternal City. It was a brilliant tour. He took us to St Peter's and pointed out all the sights, including the statue of Moses in the great church and the Sistine chapel, and we also went to the Trevi fountain and the glittering Via Veneto. Then, over a superb dinner, which he insisted on paying for, he said that it was too hot to be in Rome at that time of the year. All the Romans who could fled to the sea or the mountains, and he was going to take us down to the coast.

He took us to a fabulous hotel at the beach of Latina – an exclusive little place that had been plagued by mosquitoes and malaria before Mussolini cleaned it up as another gesture towards making Italy a place of high efficiency. We know how all that ended, with Mussolini hanging upside down from a lamp-post in Milan, but Kay and I were certainly grateful for his efforts in Latina. We had long lunches and dinners at the verandah restaurant overlooking the beach. It was a fabulous time. I still had some battles to win at Old Trafford – the arrival of Paddy Crerand had reminded me that nothing could be taken for granted in football – but I felt that a young man could not have been provided with a greater incentive do well. I had married the woman I loved and now it was my job to make a good life for her in the game that I also loved.

I could only count my blessings, and they included the great kindness of Gigi Peronace. He had returned to Rome to see some friends, but he said he would be back, and when he came he brought great men – John Charles and the Tottenham manager Bill Nicholson.

Big John, the hero of Juventus, who was still idolised in Turin, had moved to Roma as he approached the end of his career and it was thrilling to eat and talk with this man whom I had admired from a distance. He was a big, lovely quiet man and he ate very carefully and neatly with his napkin tucked into his shirt. After having a dance with him, Kay said that she was not surprised he was such a great footballer. She said he was the best dancer she had ever known, his steps were easy and feathery. Years earlier I had seen him play for Leeds United, and he had given the same impression of wonderful timing and neatness of movement out on the field as he did on that little dance floor beside the Mediterranean.

Nicholson had been touring South Africa with Spurs and was persuaded by Gigi to stop off in Rome on his way home. It would be a nice little break for Bill – and for Gigi if he managed to persuade the Tottenham manager that it would be a good idea to sell Cliff Jones to a top Italian club. Nicholson, a dour Yorkshireman in some ways but also a man with a twinkle of humour, seemed happy enough to be Italy – at least until he roasted himself out on the beach – but he made it clear that he would not part with his brilliant Welsh winger. The offers could be as generous as the gush of wine in the fountains of Frascati, but Nicholson was not about to dismantle the team that had already won the double and, with the addition of Jimmy Greaves, seemed certain to dominate English football for some time.

But if Gigi didn't get his man he did get his woman – a beautiful young Italian girl who took walks on the beach only when she was chaperoned by her grandmother. One day I saw Gigi looking at her with some intensity and I said to Kay, 'Watch out, I think Gigi is going to make a move for that young lady.' Kay said I was imagining things, but, sure enough, he launched a campaign that brought rather quicker results than my Dublin effort. Originally, he had brought a girlfriend down from Rome, but she was missing when he returned. Another thing I imagined about Gigi was that he would from time to time sip a glass of cold tea. I asked if he ever took his tea hot, and he shook his head and said, 'Nobby, the tea is for you English – this is whisky.'

Soon enough, Gigi married his Dream Girl of Latina and a few years later Mr and Mrs Peronace and their children arrived at our house in Stretford for a visit. We were thrilled to see him and his family and touched that he had taken the trouble to track us down.

Back on the honeymoon, I was less than thrilled when another Italian attached himself to our party. He was an extremely handsome young man who told us that he had played for the Italian Under-23 team. In my insecurity, which I suppose is not that uncommon in a new, twenty-one-year-old husband, I was more concerned about his undoubted sex appeal than his football skills. I thought to myself, 'Oh dear, Kay is going to fancy this handsome bastard.' It didn't help that he was bronzed and immaculately dressed while I had been broiled to a pale shade of lobster.

I must have done a few things right, however. Our eldest son,

John Charles – the Charles was for my father, not big John – was born the following spring, and when we returned to England we had the sense that no two young people could have had a better start to their married life. We had had a time that we could always look back on with great happiness and the richest memories. A couple of kids had been taken in hand by a man of great sophistication. As a young footballer, I had been allowed to rub shoulders and while away some memorable hours with one of the greatest players of all time, and with a manager who had set new standards of excellence for the English game. Kay had been regaled with attention and discovered that if I played a game for a living, it was one that crossed boundaries and touched all kinds of people all over the world.

So we travelled home with a new idea of what the world offered – and a box containing an exquisite piece of Capodimonte china. It was Gigi's parting gift. He presented it to us at the hotel in Latina just before we left. It was the gift of a man of the world to a young couple who were in the process of discovering it. I would like to say that this fine gift is now accorded a place of honour in the Stiles house, that occasionally I look at it and that it conjures up memories of lazy days in the Italian sun when it seemed that my life had moved on to a new and wonderful plane.

Unfortunately, I broke it, jabbing my finger through the box as I collected our luggage. It was around about this time that I acquired another nickname. It was, if you haven't already guessed, Inspector Clouseau.

7

ON THE EDGE

THE Capodimonte was shattered in the little box in which it had
been carefully wrapped – and it was also true that a few weeks
before I was married to Kay, my career at Old Trafford was, it had
seemed to me as I stormed out of the treatment room with tears
of anger and frustration prickling my eyes, in pieces.

As a man, I had won the greatest prize of my life in Dublin, but
as a young footballer in the spring of that year I had been denied
a trophy that would always elude me. I share with Bobby Charlton
the distinction of being the only Englishmen, for at least forty
years and possibly for ever, to hold winner's medals for both the
World Cup and the European Cup, and this was on top of two
First Division title medals. But a few weeks before my marriage in
Dublin, Bobby also won an FA Cup-winner's medal, and I sat on
the bench at sunlit Wembley seething with bitterness and already
forming in my mind the outline of a transfer request I would make
to the club I had adored every waking moment of my life. For that
to have been even a possibility reminds me now of the strength of
the resentment that flowed through my body that morning in the
treatment room.

In a difficult season, I had survived the arrival of Paddy
Crerand, as I had another glamorous signing much earlier, the

blond-haired Albert Quixall from Sheffield Wednesday. I had also weathered Matt Busby's conclusion after the semi-final defeat by Spurs the previous year, the game in which John White had delivered to me that devastating sucker punch, that he needed sharply to upgrade his playing resources if he was indeed to return United to the élite of the English, let alone the European, game.

I was making my way as an inside-right, not without intense competition, it is true, but my play had been effective enough to earn me selection for two of the most important games of the season – the FA Cup semi-final victory over Southampton and, ten days before the final, a vital relegation game against our closest rivals, Manchester City, at Maine Road. We needed a point out of City and we got it. Harry Dowd, their goalkeeper, made a mistake and conceded a penalty, which we scored. We had saved our lives in the First Division but for me the cost was a hamstring injury that put me out of the Saturday game against Leyton Orient, which was suddenly a match that didn't matter. It was won comfortably and quite a number of our players showed up very well. Nevertheless, I reckoned I was good for my place in the final. I had plenty of recovery time and what happened on the field against Orient, and would happen in our final league match at Nottingham Forest on the Monday night, was irrelevant. In the games on which the success or desperate failure of our season had depended, I had done my stuff.

The treatment room on the Sunday morning after the Orient game looked like a platform at Euston Station in the rush hour. Everyone seemed to have some kind of niggle or knock, and names were being ticked off the list of candidates for the trip to Nottingham Forest – and the risk of fresh injury that would keep them out of the final – like a classroom rollcall conducted by Sister Veronica. I wouldn't get my free ride to Wembley. I was on the team for the Forest game. The physiotherapist Ted Dalton said I would be fine and would benefit from the outing, but it seemed to me on that Sunday morning that of all the contenders for a place in the final, I was the only one carrying a real injury.

Back at Rochdale Road I confided my fears to John, who would also be playing at Nottingham and had apprehensions of his own. We just had to put our fears on hold and do what we could. Unfortunately, my leg went again in the first minutes of the match. It was useless. I couldn't really play but in those days of no substitutes, I was obliged to play out the game, as I had at Maine Road, carrying the injury. At Maine Road, of course, no one had to explain the need for a little self-sacrifice. The club was playing for its life. Here at Nottingham, all I seemed to be doing was hobbling my way out of a Cup final.

When I reported for treatment at Old Trafford on Tuesday morning, I did so with the heaviest of hearts. All around me was a buzz of expectation. John had travelled in to the ground with me and he tried to comfort me as best he could, but what can you say to a friend in those circumstances, especially when you have to subdue your own excitement about the prospect of being involved in the great day so soon? John was very sensitive to my situation but it didn't help much when I went into the treatment room and got on the table for the physiotherapist to do his work. I was stripped down to my shorts and being worked upon when Matt Busby came into the room and asked to speak to me in the little referees' room next door.

'Why did you play injured last night?' he asked. I told him what Ted Dalton had said, that I would be fine and needed the work-out. Busby shook his head. 'No, if you hadn't played last night, you would be in the final,' he said. I felt the tears coming to my eyes, and a terrible anger. Why hadn't I been looked after? Why, when all those others were pleading injury, when they plainly were not, hadn't some hard decisions been made? Why had I been sent

into the action when I was most vulnerable to losing my chance
of playing for something I had slaved for?

But if I thought those things, I didn't say them. You didn't
speak to Matt Busby in that way. You didn't challenge the Father
of Old Trafford. I walked back into the treatment room to collect
my trousers, which were hanging on a big hatstand.

'Where are you going?' asked Dalton. I said I was leaving. 'You
can't leave,' he said. 'You need treatment.'

'Oh, I need treatment do I?' I replied. 'I need treatment even
though I've got no chance of playing in the final – the one I would
have been in if you hadn't said I was fine to play at Forest, that I
needed the run-out.' As I spoke I could sense the other players in
the room, including the captain Noel Cantwell, snapping to attention. Young kids didn't speak to senior United staff in that way.
But they hadn't heard anything yet. 'You know what you can do
with your treatment?' I asked Dalton as I pulled on my trousers.
'You can stick it up your fucking arse.' I heard a few gasps in the
room as I stormed out, slamming the door behind me.

I went up into the stand, sat down and stared at the great field,
my brain buzzing and the tears rolling down my cheeks. I sobbed
my heart out. Then I recalled someone saying that Wolves had
expressed some interest in me. I would put in a transfer request.
I would say, 'Sod Manchester United – I deserve better than this.'
For me, that was the ultimate blasphemy. It would have been like
raising my fist at the high altar back at the Convent Chapel, like
telling Canon Early what he could do with his ideas of punctuality and respect.

But then it was also true I was due to be married in a few weeks'
time. I had to take a little time over this and, in the next few days,
I was grateful for the fact that I wasn't hauled into the presence
of Busby again and asked to explain my tirade against one of his
trusted aides. I didn't get the 'that wasn't United' speech and so

I owed some kind of debt to Dalton. He hadn't run into the boss's office with a report of my rebellion. The transfer request didn't go in even though I was so hurt by the episode. It still hurts when I think about it, because what is more romantic for an English footballer than going out on to the field on a spring day at Wembley with all the nation watching as you play in the game that Sir Stanley Matthews made his own, for all time, and that as a boy you always greeted as the great moment of the season, whatever the fate of your team's championship campaign?

But if I can still conjure up that long-ago pain so easily, it is softened by a little knowledge of the responsibility of the football manager, more so when I look back and try to reconstruct the way Busby's mind must have been working when he made the decision that effectively ruled me out of my one and only chance of playing in an FA Cup final. The way I told the story, it might appear that it was Dalton who played the principal role in denying me my chance, but it didn't work like that at Old Trafford. It was the big man who called all the shots. It was he who settled the contracts and decided when it was time to pull a player out of the side.

Always the breaking of the grim news followed the same pattern. Busby would call you to his office and ask the question that had become a dark legend, the doomsday question. 'How do you think you're playing, laddie?' he would ask and the chances were, at least the first time you were asked, that you would play the modesty card. Well, maybe you could be playing better, you would allow, and when you said that Busby would strike like a cobra. 'Aye, that's what I think – and that's why I'm going to give you a wee rest.'

John, who was naturally bolder than me when confronted by the great man, tried another tactic. 'You're the manager, Boss, you tell me,' said John. So, of course, Busby told him. He could do better, and he would be given a rest.

The second time I was asked the question, I said, 'Well, Boss, I think I'm playing well.' But Busby was more than equal to that. 'Aye, Norrie,' he said – he never called me Nobbie, only Norrie – 'but do you think you could be playing a little better?' You had to agree that was always possible, and he would leap on that, too. 'Yes, Norrie, that's why I think you would benefit from a little rest.' You would go out of his room shaking your head thinking, 'He's done me again – like a kipper.'

I suppose I'll always carry a little bitterness about missing that final, but each time I think about it I can understand a little better the Busby rationale. He knew how vital it was for United to win the Cup. The years were rolling on since Munich and it was essential for United to put something back into the trophy cupboard. A link with the great days of pre-Munich just had to be forged. Without the use of substitutes, he had to be very sure about the fitness of every player who started the final against Leicester. When he weighed up the wider situation, and balanced my yearnings against his and the club's need for a win, I suppose the result was inevitable. But that conclusion could never take away the pain of reading United's line-up for the Cup final match I had done quite a bit to make possible.

Shay Brennan and goalkeeper Harry Gregg were also aggrieved when the team was announced. It read: Dave Gaskell in goal, Tony Dunne and Noel Cantwell full-backs, Bill Foulkes and Maurice Setters in the centre of defence, Paddy Crerand attacking wing-half, Albert Quixall and Denis Law at inside-forward, David Herd striker, and John Giles and Bobby Charlton on the wings. Harry was inflamed that Gaskell had got the nod between the posts and Shay was angry that Dunne, who could play on either flank, had been moved to right-back to make room for the club captain Cantwell at left-back.

The three of us formed a small circle of resentment as we travelled to the team hotel in Weybridge. At such a time, when the wounds are so open, you don't spend much time reflecting on the nature of the game, the fine lines between joy and pain. I had particular reason to understand this because had I passed my fitness tests, there is no doubt about the identity of the player who would have lost out. It would have been John Giles, despite the fact that he had played in all the Cup games and that he was in good form. He already had a sense that he was on the margins of the team after the semi-final victory over Southampton. His reward for playing well in the semi was to be dropped for the next game, a league match against Wolves. John, being John and sensing the way the wind was blowing, immediately challenged Busby over his decision. He said that he disputed the basis of the selection, both in fairness and in the reality of his form against that of his chief rival, Quixall, a player of some skill but one who really had never begun to justify the big reputation that accompanied his expensive move from Sheffield. John's protest, the unfolding events would make clear enough, was another serious black mark against him in the minds of both Busby and Jimmy Murphy.

I have never been able to analyse the failure of John and Busby to forge a real relationship. It has to be one of the great mysteries of football in the fifties and sixties, this breakdown of understanding and trust between the great manager and one of the most influential players of his generation. Later, Busby would say that John Giles represented his greatest mistake. In the spring of 1963, though, it didn't seem so complicated. It seemed to me a simple matter of a kid suffering from a touch of too much independence of mind and spirit.

All through that season of the big freeze-up, when the winter stretched so deep into the spring, it was a battle for survival, individually and collectively. We were winning in the Cup, and John was playing a significant part, but in the League any kind of team rhythm was elusive and, whatever he did, John couldn't seem to please the management. There was a classic example of this in one team-talk. Busby said to John, who was playing on the right wing at the time, 'When you come to the full-back, you take him on the outside, get to the by-line and cross the ball,' and John said, 'Yes, Boss, isn't that what I'm supposed to do?'

'Why don't you mix it up?' said Busby. 'Why don't you sometimes go inside the full-back?' John nodded, and said, 'Fine.' But of course the end result was the same.

John saw the winger's role as one of the classic attacking functions. Give the team width, stretch the opposing defence, get to the line, and load up the ammunition for the inside men. In a subsequent match he simply took the inside option but with the same result – progress to the by-line and give a good supply of centres. Again there was the old question from Busby – 'John, why don't you mix it up?' John said, 'Well, I go on the outside, and you say why not go inside? Then when I go inside, you still say mix it up. What do I do now?' Busby said, 'Well, can't you just hit it across from where you receive the ball?'

I sometimes think of that old issue now when I see David Beckham play. Of course, Beckham doesn't generally go by people. He often hits it from where he receives it, which often works fine because of his great ball-striking skill. But if you keep doing that, John knew well enough, it makes it easier for a defence to pick you up. John, as he would prove all through his playing years, had a brilliant understanding of the need for variety, making feints, always keeping a defence in two minds. All this was bubbling inside him at Old Trafford and so much of it was contained and frustrated. When we came out of the meeting, John said to me, 'Nobby, what do you think of that?' He was shaking his head.

However, John was in for the Cup final, he had a big stage on which to prove his ability – and Shay, Harry and I went down to

London with our spirits growling. Shay and I broke ranks on the Friday night before the game. We were living in a void and we had to fill it somehow. We had a few pints and came back to the hotel after 10.30 p.m. When Jack Crompton, who was on curfew patrol, saw us, he demanded to know, 'What the hell have you two been up to?' We said we had had a few pints. We hadn't seen any reason not to. Jack was a disciplinarian, all right, but he was also a man of the world and he knew the depth of our disappointment. We were good pros and in the last few days we had had to absorb a lot of disappointment. He didn't report us to Busby. He let it ride.

Our rebellion didn't end with the little bout of drinking. Maybe rebellion isn't quite the right word. It was more a sullen statement of disagreement with the way the final selection had worked, and our resentment expressed itself on the bench during the match. John Giles became the central point of our protest. He had a brilliant game. Paddy Crerand got most of the headlines, and it is true he put in a fine passing performance. Crerand sent Denis Law in for an early goal, and although Leicester City were the favourites, they couldn't shut down the invention of a United team that was having its finest hour since the horror of Munich.

John was terrific, confident on the ball and setting up a stream of chances. Shay and I were appalled at the lack of appreciation of John's play demonstrated by our bench. Neither Busby nor Murphy, two men whose basic judgement on the game we admired so much, had a good word for John that afternoon. His excellent work went unremarked and any slight lapse was singled out. Shay and I appointed ourselves the Giles cheerleaders. 'Brilliant, John,' we shouted against the silence of Busby and Murphy, and, I noted, Jack Crompton. The fact that John's face suddenly didn't fit seemed like company policy.

Our victory was given aid from the most unexpected quarter –

the goalkeeping talent of Gordon Banks, who was already on his way to becoming the world's best. Banks failed to get hold of a drive by Bobby Charlton, and David Herd was there to tuck away the loose ball. After Ken Keyworth had given Leicester a late charge of hope with a headed goal, John worked himself free again before putting in another dangerous cross. Banks, maybe unsettled by his earlier error, again could do no better than push the ball into the path of the predatory Herd – 3–1 and United were winners again, but of the heroes John Giles would remain unheralded.

His relationship with Busby continued to slide. While I retreated from that first instinct to march out of the club, John's departure became more and more inevitable. He had a testy exchange with Busby over his contract, and within a few months of his superb performance at Wembley he was no longer a United player.

His standing with the boss was probably not enhanced by an incident that occurred on the club's tour of Italy soon after the final. John had shown fine feelings over my disappointment. He knew that my injury had given him his place in the final – although no one, I believed, could have questioned the fact that he deserved to play in his own right – and he took care not to flaunt his Cup medal in front of me. But maybe because of the chemistry of their relationship, John was less sensitive to the pain of Harry Gregg. The big Irishman, hero of Munich, had not been quiet about his own omission from the big game, and John, who, when the mood was on him, could be a major wind-up artist, had managed to slip easily under Harry's skin in the bar of the team hotel. He had done so to the point that, a few minutes after John and his room-mate, Shay Brennan, had gone upstairs, Harry came clattering down the corridor crying for John's blood. John and Shay had anticipated such a development and had pushed a sideboard across their door. Harry was undaunted. 'I want that bastard, Giles,' he cried, and smashed through a panel of the door. It was my fate to be sharing with Harry, who returned to our room bellowing his frustration.

When an angry Busby, who had been notified of the incident by hotel staff, arrived at the Giles-Brennan room, he was greeted by the mystified victims of a bizarre incident. Their door had been smashed but beyond that they knew nothing. When the manager appeared at our door, Harry and I of course also pleaded ignorance. Busby knew all about the turbulence of Harry Gregg's spirit and he knew that it was common practice for team-mates to close ranks when one of them had strayed over the disciplinary line. But no doubt the thing about the incident that registered most with him was the involvement of John Giles, the young Irishman who refused to toe the line.

It meant the breaking of what I had imagined would be a charmed circle of life in the shadow of Old Trafford. John and his new wife Anne had moved into a club house just around the corner from us in Stretford soon after Kay and I had come back from our honeymoon. It had seemed such a perfect arrangement. Kay and Anne, two Dublin girls, could help each other fight any onset of homesickness, and the friendship of John and I could develop along with our progress in the United side. But suddenly that pretty idea was shattered. John was sold to Leeds United for £37,000. I was both outraged and heartbroken. For one thing, I was amazed that Leeds United, then in the Second Division, were apparently John's only pursuers. I was sorry for John, sorry for myself, and, quite as much, sorry for United. I thought they were letting slip, for a pittance, a major talent.

John was emphatic about the wisdom of the move, however. He told both Wilf McGuinness and me that we had our dreams and they were closely tied to Manchester United. He cared for

United, too, but it was a thing of boyhood which he knew he would outgrow. Old Trafford simply wasn't right for him. He could feel it in his bones. He realised Matt Busby was a great manager, but if a situation wasn't right for you, no amount of wishful thinking would change the reality. He would make something of himself at Leeds. He would make a new start.

Of course, it turned out to be the perfect move. The manager, Don Revie, who had been a player of great skill and understanding, saw the potential of John to grow beyond a merely clever inside-forward or winger. He saw the makings of a field general, and when Bobby Collins, the man who was running Leeds with a hard and brilliant instinct, had his leg broken, John naturally moved into the vacuum of leadership. He was the Pied Piper of a crop of brilliant young players including Eddie Gray, Norman Hunter, Peter Lorimer and Paul Madeley. Revie gave Billy Bremner the captaincy because it was important to that great little player, but I think the manager knew that John's authority was unspoken and came from the sense that this was a man who knew what he was doing and was completely in charge of himself. Billy led with a brilliant passion and John was always at his side, pointing here or there, changing the emphasis of the game, endlessly seeking the ball, and when he had it, discovering a whole array of options for himself and his team-mates.

It is to Busby's great credit that when he came to review his reign at Old Trafford, and itemise his mistakes – which, when you think of all the storms he had to survive and the decisions he had to make, were amazingly few – he unhesitatingly said that John Giles was the diamond he never polished. Nobody knew better than Busby the price he had to pay for that omission. He watched Leeds United grow into one of his greatest rivals, and always he saw John at the helm, probing and nagging and whipping his team-mates along.

John never won a World Cup – the man who shaped England's one triumph in the great competition, Sir Alf Ramsey, said that he 'most regretted' the fact that John Giles wasn't born an Englishman – and he never won a European Cup, although he came heartbreakingly close to it in Paris in 1975, when a Leeds in transition were cruelly hindered by some harsh refereeing decisions in the final against Franz Beckenbauer's Bayern Munich. But he won two FA Cup-winner's medals, the second coming in 1972 when Leeds beat Arsenal. In the end, his haul of medals was impressive enough – those two plus two league championship medals with Leeds plus the Uefa Cup. These were good rewards for the most ambitious and gifted of professionals, but I will always believe they could have been so much greater if he had been persuaded to feel at home at Old Trafford. That it didn't happen was everybody's loss, and it doesn't help that much to know that it was a truth the great Sir Matt Busby took to his grave.

8

SEEING THE FUTURE

HARRY GREGG has a wild, big heart. He proved that between the sticks on so many occasions and nowhere more so than in the pain and chaos of that snow-covered Munich airfield, where he worked so heroically to pull injured team-mates clear of danger. Although you might have doubted it the night he raged through the corridors of the team hotel seeking John Giles' blood, it is also a kind heart, informed by a keen eye. It means that any re-living of my career, and explanation of how it was I finally came through to success beyond even my highest hopes would be incomplete without mention of the crucial role played by Harry.

He saw that I had a huge problem, one that was crippling my chances. More sharply than anyone around me at United, he saw that I was playing my football, and generally living my life, half-blind. After one card session on the way to an away game, Harry went to Matt Busby and said, 'You know, Boss, you just have to do something about Nobby's eyesight. The kid is really struggling. He's putting down the wrong cards. He just can't read them. We just have to imagine how it's affecting his play.'

It was a situation that went right back to the schoolroom where I rubbed my watering eyes and peered at the books so closely. You

119

come to terms with a handicap like that and, certainly back in those days, you just hoped that you could get by. Deep down, though, I knew I had a terrible problem. Between my debut in 1960 and the crisis of my omission from the '63 Cup final and my flirtation with a transfer request, I appeared in the first team sporadically. I would have one good game and then I would slip back into the reserves. The problem came to a head in my own mind during a match against Everton at Goodison Park. I went to receive a throw-in from the wing-half and I suddenly realised I was guessing when it came to timing the ball and to where and to whom I was going to play it. I was given a man to mark, and in the flow of the play I frequently lost sight of him. It was a terrible shock but, perhaps out of fear of what I would be told if I raised the issue with Busby and was sent to see specialists, I kept quiet. I would try to get along in the fog. It was a silence Harry Gregg smashed through in the same forthright style he attacked John and Shay's hotel room door. 'The boy needs help,' Harry insisted.

I was sent to see a top eye specialist in St John's Street, Deansgate, which was Manchester's answer to Harley Street. For me as a kid in Collyhurst, those fancy consulting rooms might have been a thousand miles away, but now I was a potential Manchester United first-teamer with a career to be saved. The first thing I discovered in St John's Street was that there was no easy cure. I had to wear big, hard contact lenses and squirt blue lubricating fluid into my eyes. I also realised, when I walked out on to Deansgate, that I would have to re-learn the most basic steps I had made in the game. They put these big things in my eyes and told me to go out and have a walk. I'll never forget walking down Deansgate that time. Everything was so clear. Suddenly, Manchester was a brilliant place of clean lines. The sky was a vivid blue. The clouds were white and fluffy. The ends of the buildings were clearly defined. Everything was so sharp. I found myself stepping off the kerbside a foot too soon, and when I came to play the game again I was guilty of some horrible miscalculations.

One of the problems with contact lenses in that early stage of their development was that after a while your eyes dried out with the lack of oxygen. I used to get rings around my eyes like a panda and if a match went into extra time I would have problems under the floodlights. For a while I lost my place as a contender for the first team and slipped into the reserves, occasionally even the A team. There were some despairing days, but fortunately I did grasp that sometimes you have to take a step backwards if you truly want to move forward.

Slowly, but with sharply increasing confidence, I began to make progress. I was no longer heading the ball a fraction of a second too early. I was able to let the ball come to me. I wasn't snatching at the ball, lunging into tackles, playing it by ear as much as eye. Those who were supposed to be marked, stayed marked. My passing became much more accurate and towards the end of the 1963–64 season the breakthrough I had waited for so desperately finally arrived.

Now, ironically enough, I could have a simple laser operation that would end the need for contact lenses or glasses. My stigmatism could be burned away, but really I see no need. My big specs became part of my image, such as it was, and in 1966 after the burst of fame which came with the World Cup I was voted Bespectacled Man of the Year, beating Eric Morecambe into second place. As in so many aspects of my life, including crucial decisions at various stages of my football career, I have to thank Kay for getting me through the most difficult days.

At first I was very self-conscious while performing the ritual of fitting the lenses, taking myself off to a toilet, away from everybody. Sometimes I was so frustrated I decided I would try to get by without the contacts but whenever I did that I was reminded that I was suffering not just an inconvenience but a serious handicap.

As is so often the case in football, the good fortune that established me as a fixture in the first team came at somebody else's expense. There is always a victim of circumstances and in my case it was Maurice Setters who was obliged to give way. The sequence of events started in the clutter of action that is the peculiar burden of an English club experiencing some success. We were still in the FA Cup and the European Cup-winners' Cup, which we seemed well on the way to winning with a 4–1 victory in the first leg of our quarter-final tie with Sporting Lisbon at Old Trafford. I was playing well enough at inside-right, but I probably didn't delight the management when I refused to go through with a penalty-kick routine that we had practised on the training field.

The plan was for me to run up to take the penalty, then, instead of firing at the goal, sidefoot it to Denis Law. It was perfectly legal and worked well enough in practice, but when the time came I just couldn't do it. Maybe it just seemed wrong to me, too laden with risk, and perhaps, at a time when I was trying so hard to nail down my first-team place, I lost it for a moment and did something I have always despised in other players. Yes, maybe I bottled it. Anyway, I said, 'No, I'm not doing that.' The Lawman stepped up and banged in the penalty, and he scored another one in the same match.

In our defence of the FA Cup we were involved in a tremendous quarter-final dog-fight with Sunderland. It seemed like a disaster in the first game at Old Trafford, when they leaped into a 2–0 lead, but we clawed our way back into the game and earned a replay at Roker Park, where it was our turn to jump into the lead. I was moved to outside-right, with Phil Chisnall inside, but in the second half they fought back to earn another replay. We won the final game at Huddersfield. On the previous Saturday I had played, along with nine reserves, in a 2–0 win over West Ham, who would be our semi-final opposition if we beat Sunderland. You can imagine the pressure that came with such a string of important games, and after my longest run in the first team it may be that I had become a little stale. So, whether Busby had noted that an edge was leaving my game or was nettled by my refusal to execute the penalty manoeuvre, I was out of the semi-final against West Ham. Under the youthful leadership of Bobby Moore, the Hammers played composed football and won 3–1.

It was an unexpected blow, but there is always instant consolation for the players who have been left out of a big match that goes wrong. As we flew out for the second leg of the Cup-winners' tie in Lisbon, Paddy Crerand assured me, 'You're a certainty to be back in the team, at inside-right.' It was a pretty thought but it didn't happen. It all went wrong for the team – we suffered our biggest defeat in Europe, 5–0, and were swept out of the competition – and for Setters, who alongside big Bill Foulkes had taken a terrible mauling in the middle of our overstretched defence, it carried on going wrong after the game.

We were staying in the big Palace Casino Hotel in Estoril, down the coast from Lisbon, and in the time-honoured way of footballers we went to drown our post-game sorrows in a bar – not heavily, just a few glasses of beer and a few mournful recollections of a game that had been torn from our grasp despite a three-goal lead from the first leg, which had seemed so impregnable at the first whistle. Everyone was steady on their feet as we returned to the Palace in good time to avoid the ire of Jack Crompton, but as we walked through the marble-floored lobby, Maurice Setters slipped and fell awkwardly. He hurt his knee – and changed my football life.

You're supposed to feel compassion for a stricken team-mate, know that he has suffered the fate that could overtake you at any moment. That's a nice theory. The reality is that football has a cruel law that says one man's catastrophe is another's great opportunity.

On the face of it, this shouldn't have been my chance. I had never played in the back four – which was the new shape of defence – at any level. I could tackle, naturally, but my career had been spent shuttling between the old wing-half and inside-forward positions. I was, certainly in my own mind, an heir of Eddie Colman, not some dreadnought defender. But I always had a sense that I could play at the back. I was quick and competitive and I could read the play quite acutely. Tony Dunne would kill me over twenty or thirty yards, but over five to ten yards I was whippet-quick, and with those few yards of genuine pace, I could exploit the good defensive antenna that would ultimately bring me my greatest success in the game.

Setters failed to respond to treatment and when we flew to London for a Saturday game at White Hart Lane with our great nemesis Tottenham Hotspur and their sensational striking acquisition Jimmy Greaves, I agonised over whether I should speak to Busby to ask him to give me a shot at a new position. I said to myself that I needed to make my case. It was something I was very sure about, and I could have put forward a good argument, but the more I thought about it, the more my nerve ebbed away. In the end, I resorted to a simple prayer – 'Put me in, please put me in.'

Meanwhile, Busby and Jimmy Murphy were discussing the problem and, though I've never known for sure, maybe they had some in-put from Foulkes, the former full-back who had built a new empire for himself in central defence. Perhaps they simply reached the same conclusion as I had, noting my speed in the tackle and my ability to read the play. I knew for sure Bill wanted me alongside him. On the practice field, he had registered that I was very quick off the mark. For a big man, Bill was very quick when it mattered, but in that position you need all the speed you can get around you. It does wonders for your sense of security, and at times like the débâcle in Lisbon I suspect that Foulkes thought to himself, 'I could do with that little bastard back here.'

On the Saturday morning, I got the nod. I was back in the team alongside Foulkes. Furthermore, I would be marking Greaves, the stiletto man. I couldn't decide whether it was a daunting challenge or a wonderful opportunity. Fortunately, I came to the conclusion that it was the latter.

I had the strictest game plan, and it was based entirely on the principle that there was only one way to mark Greaves effectively. He was the quickest and arguably most natural striker to emerge in the English game, so I knew that I had to get tight, without selling myself, and that if I could do it he would be unable to perform his potentially deadly turns. I would not let him turn and come at me, and if that meant going with him ten or fifteen yards back, I would do it. As soon as the ball was knocked off, I could haul him back. There would be no diving at him from the back. You couldn't take liberties with Jimmy Greaves. You had to respect him every inch of the way. I held Jimmy Greaves throughout the game. We won 3–2, which, after Lisbon, was psychologically a huge result. The Sunday papers made very good reading. According to them, I had 'curtailed' and 'curbed' Jimmy Greaves. I felt like a kid gunfighter who had survived a brush with Doc Holliday or Johnny Ringo.

Soon enough it was clear that the game at White Hart Lane was the clinching moment in my great battle to become a fully accepted member of the United élite, a name that would appear automatically on the teamsheet. It was the key to everything good that came to me in the game, it persuaded the press that I was a significant player and, most vitally of all, it drew me to the attention of Sir Alf Ramsey.

The confidence that came to me with the performance against Greaves and that quite literally improved vision meant that I had moved on to another and much higher plane. A place in the first team alongside Foulkes was no longer a gift – it was something I owned. I had a strong sense that this might be so straight after the Spurs game when Matt Busby came into the dressing room and put his hand on my shoulder. He was quite emphatic when he said, 'Well, played Norrie, well played son.'

Many years later, Malcolm Allison told me that I made Bill Foulkes look a much better player with my quickness in the tackle and reading of the game, but it was an argument I rejected with some force – and not just out of loyalty to a senior team-mate who had provided vital support at a crucial stage of my career. Foulkes was a tremendous, instinctive defender, very strong and very sure about what he was doing. What was important, though, was not to give him too much time on the ball. Defending with power, getting rid of the ball in the simplest way, these were the foundations of Bill's game, and they served United – and me – brilliantly as we finally turned our backs on the bleak post-Munich years.

There was a growing confidence in the team, and when I look back I see that it was the time when the natural self-belief I had in my own ability was at last fully expressed. I had the arrogance to believe that I could play against anybody if I attended to detail, if I did my work and cared about the game in the way displayed by one of the greatest players I had ever seen, Alfredo Di Stefano.

Looking back over my playing days, it is easy to see many moments of revelation. There was the hard word from Pancho Pearson when I got a little carried away with myself in that youth game. There was the time I was skinned by John White. There was the sight of Jimmy Scoular defying the great, hostile crowd at Old Trafford and getting on with his work. But probably nothing concentrated my mind so much on the proper priorities of a professional footballer than the time I saw the great Di Stefano ripping into a team-mate, angry and indignant at the performance of his colleague. There were two stunning aspects to his rage. One was that it came in a friendly match. The other was that the cause of his anger was not some fringe player but a star who shone quite as brightly as the maestro himself. It was Ferenc Puskas, the roly-poly magician who had bewitched Wembley with his skill and shooting power in the shafting victory of Hungary over England in 1953.

The match was at Old Trafford in 1961, one of a series that Matt Busby had arranged in the wake of our first European Cup defeat by Real Madrid in 1957. Busby used the games to familiarise United players with the level of performance that was required if we were ever to get back to, and then beyond, the standard that was being achieved before Munich. We had taken some heavy beatings and in the last match we had played against Real, at the great Bernabeu stadium, had conceded six goals. The fans knew that these were friendly games in their billing only. They had a hard purpose and much pride was at stake. Unfortunately for a young side like us, trying to find our feet at the highest level, nowhere did that pride burn more fiercely than in the heart of Di Stefano.

At half-time we were winning 2–0. I was nineteen and had run myself silly against the great men in white. As I came off the field I noticed that Di Stefano was giving Puskas one of the biggest public bollockings I'd ever seen. He pointed his finger at the Hungarian. He gesticulated. He raged. That went on all the time they walked off the field and into the tunnel. I was fascinated. Di Stefano was so intense and Puskas was shrugging his shoulders as if to say, 'Hold on, Alfredo, this isn't the European Cup final, this is a bloody friendly match.' But what I could see so clearly was that Di Stefano was saying that in his book there was no such thing as a friendly. There was only a football match in which you always carried your pride.

I had already established the difference between a real game and a friendly but Di Stefano was challenging that. He was saying, it seemed to me, that you could never really let down your standards. Within reason, you had to play your game. When it was time for the second half I was first out of our dressing room, and I hid behind the half-opened door of a storeroom in the corridor leading down to the tunnel. I wanted to watch Real Madrid come out for the second half. I wanted to see if anything had been resolved between Di Stefano and Puskas, two of the greatest players the world would ever see.

Nothing had been settled, at least not to the satisfaction of Di Stefano. He and Puskas came out of the dressing room together and the bollocking was still going on. I didn't need to know Spanish to understand what Di Stefano was telling Puskas. He said he wasn't putting it all in. He was letting his side down.

Madrid were a lot different in the second half. Di Stefano, the man with the big chest, was hungry for the ball and so, now, was Puskas. Final score – 2–2. Real Madrid had pulled themselves up and it was a lesson I would never forget. A great player had shown me something I needed to know at that stage of my career. It was that you never just turn up for a game; you come to play the best you can. It doesn't matter what you have done in the past; what matters is how you perform now, what integrity you bring to every game. The significant fact that at an early stage of my playing days I had got to share the same field with Di Stefano twice – the following season we went to the Bernabeu and won – was a bonus I would never discount.

Off the field, there was also a lot of inspiration. The blow of seeing John and Anne Giles pack their bags and move across the

Pennines was a heavy one, but there were huge compensations, which survived some youthful stupidity by me.

Our first son John was a beautiful baby, and I was thrilled by his arrival, and to set up house with Kay. However, I did not distinguish myself as a thoughtful young husband and father. Kay must have missed her family and friends in Dublin as I tore about the country playing football and, on Saturday nights, chose to go to the dogs with my father and brother Charlie. Fortunately, Kay was patient and I came to my senses soon enough. In 1965 we bought the house from the club and were very proud householders. After arranging a mortgage, we paid £3,500 for the house, where we lived until I was transferred to Middlesbrough six years later. It wasn't Beckham Towers but we couldn't have been happier. We had an arch in the lounge and a shed in the garden, where I put up nets in preparation for children playing. Peter arrived in 1966, as I was competing for a World Cup place, and Robert in 1969, in the wake of the European Cup.

Of course, so much separates the life of a young footballer and his family then from the fantasy future of the Beckhams. I couldn't help thinking of this recently when David, wearing his red bandanna, announced the birth of his second son, Romeo, outside a private hospital in London. You could see by what extent the life of a footballer had changed. When Peter was born, I snatched one weekend visit home in the first six weeks of his life. Kay asked if I could break from the Lilleshall training centre where I was preparing for the World Cup so that I could be with her for the birth, but the truth – and it will probably shock today's generation of young marrieds – is that I didn't have the nerve to ask Sir Alf Ramsey for the time. You see, I was on England duty, and according to Alf, England always came first – and second and third.

Back then you snatched what you could and in 1964, when I stopped to think about it, it seemed to me that I had everything a young man could want. When John was born I got the call to go to the hospital in the middle of the night, and when you see your first child for the first time, you know you will never have a feeling quite like it ever again.

It meant that I charged through '64 and into '65 with the sense that everything was before me. I had my family and my football future. I was now a key part of a team that was coming into its own. It was a settled team moving confidently into a new age of the game. Bobby Charlton was laying down his claims as a great midfielder, the orchestrator of both his club and his country. Denis Law had the supporters in the palm of his hand. He was electric. By now, we had a trinity of great players because Georgie Best had arrived on a bright sunlit autumn day in 1963 and was doing staggering things with the ball. Busby and Murphy had done it. They had conjured greatness again. Busby had worked his genius for spotting players of dimensions that soared beyond the norm. Murphy had done what had always been at the core of his work, the organising of proper defence, the provision of that foundation without which even the most talented team will always struggle to find lasting success.

Although the goalkeeper's spot would not be cemented until the arrival of Alex Stepney from Chelsea in 1966, a new signing, Irishman Pat Dunne, was competing with Gregg and Gaskell and the rest of the defence had become impressively grooved. The full-backs Tony Dunne and Shay Brennan brought pace and assurance and as the months flicked by, my relationship with Bill Foulkes developed very quickly. Foulkes was strong and resilient, powerful in the air and extremely solid in the tackle. My role beside him was one of watchfulness and quick intervention. It meant that while the fans increasingly celebrated the virtuoso play of Charlton, Law and Best, within the game there was a growing sense that United's annexation of the 1965 championship race was as much to do with defensive security as attacking brilliance. Murphy knew better than anyone that in a winning team such balance was not so much an asset as a fundamental requirement. The reshaping of the club had been achieved cleverly. I had to concede that, even though I had been made so restive by some of the decisions along the way. I was bitter about the treatment of my brother-in-law and far from convinced that I had always been treated fairly, but when you stepped back you could see clearly enough that Busby and Murphy just could not have afforded to be too sentimental. Nobby Stiles's personal ambitions were one thing; the development of the club, its resurrection after Munich, was quite another.

The signing of Crerand was plainly a success. The work of Jack Crompton and John Aston, despite some opposition from Noel Cantwell, who wanted less running and more ball practice in our training sessions, had brought greater discipline and better fitness; and the presence of old pros Cantwell and Maurice Setters, who had experienced football life beyond Old Trafford, had proved hugely valuable.

Not so long ago I got the impression while talking to Noel that he and Maurice had felt great resentment from some of the young United players including John Giles and me. They had the sense that we believed their arrival could only retard our progress towards the first team. I was happy to tell Noel, whose brightness I had always admired, that he was quite wrong. It was good to listen to them and gain some new perspectives.

I remember Noel with particular fondness for his efforts to improve the financial prospects of young players. When we qualified for the 1963 Cup final, it was Noel who organised the players pool and took the first steps towards setting up the United souvenir shop, which now makes millions for the club. We built a little hut outside the ground to use as the base of our commercial operation. Noel had a brochure printed and sent John and me, among others, out into the town to sell adverts. We didn't have a bloody clue. After being turned away from the Dolcis shoe shop, one of our many failures, we agreed that if the football failed, we could forget any idea that we might become super salesmen.

Thoughts of alternative careers were fast fading, however. I was just flying in '64. Maurice's slip on the marble floor in Lisbon had finally opened the door for me and this time, I knew it for sure. My vision was sharp and my confidence was soaring. I swore to Kay, 'No one is going to take the United shirt off me now.'

I played in the last twelve games of the 1963–64 season, my longest unbroken run in the team, and with each match my sense of belonging increased. I was putting in extra training so that when it came to the regular sessions I had the edge on everyone. When we went on runs, I was killing them.

At the end of the season I took Kay and John to Dublin and that time will always live vividly in my mind. I woke up first every morning, just as the sun was coming up, made the bottle for John and went out into Phoenix Park to do my training. I said to Kay, 'I have to do this because this is a chance I'm not going to let go.' It was wonderful running through the park in the early morning sunshine. I'd never experienced such a smell of grass, such exhilaration at being alive. I thought of Kay and John and the life that was spreading before us. I breathed the air in great gulps and wanted to yell 'Top of the fucking morning' to everyone I passed.

9

TAKE THAT, LAWMAN

SUDDENLY, my horizons were deeper and broader than I could have dreamed in those days when I scuffled and squinted on the edge of the first team, but they were not entirely uncomplicated. Indeed, in February 1965, I had to make one of the toughest decisions of my life in football. I had to choose between Matt Busby and Alf Ramsey, and if that wasn't tricky enough, Kay told me that if I made the wrong move, if I took what she might consider a cowardly course of action, it would colour all the feelings she had for me. In fact, it might mean she would not be sure she wanted anything more to do with me. She might even walk out.

Ramsey picked me for the England Under-23 team to play Scotland in Aberdeen just a few months before I would cease to qualify for this important level of international football. It was a chance to make a real impression on the England manager on the run-in to the 1966 World Cup. The *Evening Chronicle*, which had so often been the source of joy and pain in my United career, announced that I was in the Under-23 squad and that I would be released by the club for the game on a Tuesday night after playing for United on the Saturday. This news wasn't as straightforward as you might imagine. In those days, the club and country issue was an unending source of controversy. The big club managers, preoccupied with their own fight for honours, often advised their players of the need to sustain a diplomatic injury which would prevent them risking a mishap on behalf of their country rather than their club. But the impression on this occasion was that United, despite their first serious involvement in a championship race since before Munich, were rubber-stamping my call-up by Ramsey.

My selection wasn't altogether a surprise because my form in a winning United team had been very good. I was growing in assurance beside Bill Foulkes, and in exhilaration at being picked for the squad, I asked my friend Wilf McGuinness, who now assisted Ramsey with the Under-23s as well as being a trainer at Old Trafford, if he would have a word in Ramsey's ear about where he might play me. I told Wilf that despite all my experience at wing-half and inside-forward, I saw myself as exclusively a back-four operator, and perhaps the England manager might bear this in mind. Wilf looked at me a little sceptically, but said he would do as I asked.

Kay was thrilled by my selection. Rightly, she saw it as my big chance to break back on to the international stage I had experienced at schoolboy and youth level. With the schoolboys I had met the great Monty and hobnobbed with big-name Scottish players Bobby Collins and Tommy Docherty, and with the youth team I had had a particularly lively time in Sofia, Bulgaria, in a tournament in which I had quite a lot to say for myself, on and off the field. I had been appalled when the bus we had been given, a battered old bone-shaker, groaned and wheezed its way to the stadium while our opponents, Greece, showed up in a sleek, air-conditioned coach. I told the England coach, the former Bolton Wanderers player Harold Hassall, it was a disgrace that a team representing England should be treated like that. Hassall, a gentle man, also had to put up with another tirade from me when one of our players was fouled badly by a Yugoslav and just brushed himself down and got on with the game. Hassall singled out that mild response for special praise. 'That's how players wearing the England shirt should behave,' the schoolmaster Hassall said. I said, 'Bollocks to that. If you let somebody get away with a foul like that, they're going to be all over you.' I don't think I received a glowing commendation from the coach when he submitted his report to the Football Association, but I was happy enough with my contribution to the team. At the very least, I had got stuck in.

Now I was about to pull on an England shirt again, and by way of celebration Kay, just as my mother had done before my trip to Plymouth for my schoolboy international, went out to buy me what seemed like a whole new wardrobe of clothes. She bought me a lovely sports jacket, smart slacks and a short, white mac. I felt good and Kay assured me that I also looked good in my new outfit, but unfortunately it turned out that it wasn't simply a case of getting on the train and riding to glory.

That's how I was imagining it would be as I got out of the bath after the Saturday league game, but Busby shattered that happy idea. He came into the dressing room and said, 'Norrie, could I see you in my office? I want a word.'

He told me that we had a tough game on Tuesday night at Sunderland, and we desperately needed the points to maintain our championship race. Sunderland, who had been promoted with John Giles's, Leeds, were a difficult side and Busby wanted every available key player. At last the championship was within our grasp again but obviously the talented Leeds team assembled by Don Revie and Bill Shankly's Liverpool were going to chase us all the way. 'I need you on Tuesday night, Norrie,' said Busby. 'Don't make a decision now. Think about it and give me a call tomorrow.'

I was gutted, of course. The World Cup was coming into focus and the chance of impressing Alf Ramsey had filled most of my thoughts for days. The complication was that, just as I had reflected after the club had put me through the fitness test at Nottingham Forest, which had ruined my chances of appearing in an FA Cup final, I could see the situation from Busby's angle. The club paid my wages, they had nurtured my football ability since I was a kid and they had given me far better eyesight than I had been born with. Now they wanted a little payback. In a way, it was reassuring that Busby considered me so indispensable to the team that he was prepared to put my chances of an international career at risk.

All these thoughts were banging around in my head as I made the short journey home to Stretford, and as soon I got through the front door I blurted out the problem to Kay. She listened patiently as I went through all my thoughts, swinging first one way and then the other. When I had finished, she said, 'Nobby, what are you going to do?' That started a fresh bout of agonising. I told Kay that Manchester United was in my blood, that deep down I would always be a supporter and so it was still the most important thing in the world for them to win, whether I was playing or not. If the great Busby felt I was crucial to United's chances, what could I do but tell Ramsey that I couldn't take the place he had offered on his World Cup caravan.

Kay was not sympathetic. 'Look, Nobby,' she said, 'sometimes you have to put yourself first. It's a big tough world out there, and in football, like anywhere else, it's so easy to get pushed on one side. Will United care so much for you if you get injured and are no longer any good to them?' It was a hard speech and, of course, I knew she was right, but that wasn't all she said. She said I might be turning down the chance to play for my country, might be closing the door on a great future in the game. She would think a lot less of me if I did that. In fact, we might just be finished.

It wasn't supposed to be like this. Football, or life, wasn't supposed to be so complicated. I thrashed about in bed that night, woke up several times and felt the weight of the world on me. All that certainty of recent months, all that smell of success, seemed to have disappeared and I was quite drained when on the Sunday afternoon I picked up the phone to call Sir Matt Busby at his home down the road in Chorlton-cum-Hardy. I'll never forget the brief conversation.

'Hi, Boss, it's Nobby.'

'Hello Norrie. Well, what are you doing?'

'Boss, I've decided I would like to play for England,' I gulped. There was a brief pause.

'OK,' and the phone went down. There were no words of comfort or understanding, no wishing me good luck. Matt Busby, the father of Manchester United and, some said, the father of football, could be a tough, cold taskmaster, and if I hadn't known that before, I knew it now, and I would be reminded of it later when Kay's words would come swirling back into my head. But for the moment, and with the stiffening help of my wife, I was still on course to be a young master of the football universe. I was taking the high road to Scotland for an audition before the man who had promised to return England to the top of the football world.

When I arrived in Aberdeen, Wilf McGuinness reported Alf's cool reaction to my plea to be a contender for a place in central defence alongside big Jack Charlton.

'Alf listened to what I had to say,' said Wilf, 'and I did point out to him how well you had adapted to your new position, and what an important part you had played in United's success. But he wants you to think about a few things. The first thing you should consider, Alf said, was that to win through to the England team you have to get in front of not just Bobby Moore but also Norman Hunter.'

I told Wilf that the point was taken. When I got to know Alf better, I realised the folly of trying to tell him where I should play. His great talent was to identify a player's strengths in club football and then move him into the international game without asking of him anything that he had not been able to accomplish for his own team. I would learn soon enough that he had already earmarked me as a possibility for a key role in his emerging England team. I would, if I showed the right instincts at this level, operate in front of Moore and Jack Charlton, winning the ball, covering when George Cohen and Ray Wilson went on forays down the flanks, read the flow of the game and, from time to time, take on specific marking roles.

At half-time in Aberdeen, Alf got very specific. He said, 'Nobby, Charlie Cooke is giving us a lot of problems. Sort him out.' I asked him what he meant. He said, 'Well, put him out of the game.'

In the case of Cooke this was rather easier said than done. A wonderfully tricky dribbler, Charlie had extremely quick feet and he was not the kind of player who was easily nailed. You had to line him up and wait for the right situation, so that when the ball came between you, you could take the ball and the player all in one emphatic and crunching movement. Soon enough, I got my chance and the tackle went in perfectly. My victim shot into the air and finished up in a crumpled heap. Naturally, I trotted back to my position with an air of some satisfaction. The job had been assigned, and now it had been accomplished with some thoroughness. I was thus a little surprised when Norman Hunter came up beside me and said, 'What the fuck do you think you're doing?' I said I was doing what Alf had asked me to do, taking Charlie Cooke out of the game. Hunter said, 'I think you'd better look again, you stupid bastard.' At this point I should probably report that in all the excitement of leaving for Aberdeen I had forgotten the fluid for my contact lenses. I asked Norman what he was talking about. He said, 'You didn't do Charlie, you did Billy Bremner.'

I had taken on one of the meanest, toughest little Jocks ever to put on a pair of football boots and for a moment my blood ran cold. As it turned out, though, it was really the start of a beautiful friendship. After the game we had the first of many drinks we would share down the years until his untimely death in the nineties. Billy, like me, would know his disappointments when his playing days were over – he had an unsuccessful stint as manager of Leeds United – but he had a wonderful playing career. He was one of the ultimate competitors, hard and bright and with a brilliant instinct for attacking the jugular of an opponent. The combination of his drive, hardness and brilliant attacking instinct and John Giles's generalship made competing with Leeds in midfield a nightmare for so many years.

He exacted a long, sustained revenge for that clattering tackle in Aberdeen, and the first instalment came a couple of months later when Billy scored the winner in the FA Cup semi-final second replay that denied me another trip to Wembley for the final. He was an irrepressible character and he kept scoring goals against United. He did it with a special delight, but invariably we would retrace the battle over a few drinks.

Shortly before he died we were involved in a marathon celebration of the good days and great battles we had shared on the pitch. The occasion was the Irish version of 'This is Your Life' dedicated to the career of John Giles. In Ireland, the show runs for a couple of hours, and by the time we retired for drinks at the Burlington Hotel we were ready for a little celebration. With John and Kay around, there was inevitably a sing-song, and when I threw in the towel around 3 a.m. and finally persuaded Kay to return with me to Jimmy Sheils's house, where we were staying for the weekend,

Billy could be heard performing his party piece, 'I Left my Heart in San Francisco'. A few hours later, I was woken up by Bremner in full flow. He came crashing into the house, up the stairs and into our bedroom, shook me awake and said, 'Stiles, get your arse out of bed and have a drink – you're the only Englishman I've ever liked.'

It was something I remembered when Billy was buried in a little church in Doncaster. Some of the great names of the game came to recognise a football career that had blazed with passion. Dave Mackay, who was so memorably pictured holding Billy up in the air with one hand, was there to record his belief that the kid whom he had once treated as an impertinent challenger to his own high status in the game had grown into a great competitor. Sir Alex Ferguson, who had been involved in a Champions League game in Europe the night before and had not had much sleep, said that Bremner occupied a special place in the hearts of football men. This was especially so for a Scottish football man who, no doubt like so many others, mourned the decline of that nation's once generous stocks of native talent. My own pride and sadness was that I had forged a great understanding with a rival whom, in many ways, I saw as a reflection of myself – a physically small, driven man who was most at home in the heat of a major football battle.

The sadness was that I would no longer be able to linger over a drink and a reflection or two with the man I fought with so hard over so many years, and to whom I introduced myself with a tackle that shook all the bones of his body. They were bones I came to love.

My experience with Bremner, I think now, highlighted one of the great rewards of playing the game at the highest level – to compete at your limits, to give it everything, and then when the final whistle sounded, to embrace your opponent with both affection and respect. It happens in the boxing ring all the time; in football it was perhaps most famously expressed when Bobby Moore and Pele embraced after the great World Cup match in Guadalajara in 1970. I was on the England bench that day, my career was running down, but I ached to be part of the action. Bremner's gift to me was reinforced by so many of my opponents – Tommy Smith and Norman Hunter, for instance – for whom no battle was too fierce, or hindered by the bonds of friendship.

Maybe my strongest sense of the companionship that grows naturally between the hardest competitors came in Italy in 1968 when Uefa threw a buffet for the four semi-final teams at the end of the European Championship. We were beaten by Yugoslavia in one of the semis in Florence, and then played the Russians in the third-place match. It was, given the fact that neither team could win the championship, a tremendously hard game and I had several collisions with a big, tough Russian. Later, at the open-air buffet, I noticed that the Russians were hanging back while the Italians and the Yugoslavs crowded around the bar. At that time there was an idea that the Russians were monsters lurking behind the Iron Curtain but my suspicion was that behind their masks they were good lads. I certainly liked the honest way in which they played the game. I went to the big lad I had been battling with and said, 'Come on, get your arse to the bar, we deserve a drink.' I got hold of him, we pushed our way to the bar and I ordered up the drinks. He was a big lovely lad and we had a smashing time.

My mood was certainly a lot better in Italy than it had been in the wake of my first performance for Sir Alf Ramsey. Apart from nailing the wrong man, I played terribly. If I completed two consecutive accurate passes it was a small miracle. I was angry with myself for so stupidly forgetting the lens fluid and I felt that I had plunged back into the fog. I was also troubled by Busby's possible reaction to my decision to leave United's championship challenge at a vital point. My mood was further darkened when I saw one of my Under-23 team-mates, fellow midfielder John Hollins, reading a good-luck telegram from his Chelsea manager, Tommy Docherty. When I saw that little piece of manager-player bonding, the crash of Busby's phone dropping back on its cradle sounded even louder in my mind. I was shattered when I got home to Stretford. Kay asked me how I'd done and I owned up to scarcely putting two passes together. I said that the best I could say was that I'd won an Under-23 cap. My passing had been so poor, on that form, I wouldn't have been able to pass water.

Kay, as always, had sound advice. 'Don't worry,' she said. 'You're always your worst critic and I don't think Alf is going to judge you on just one game. You still have everything to play for.'

She was right. Maybe Alf had not been captivated by my passing skills, but he must have liked the passion I had brought to the job, and if I hadn't been a creative master, that was, anyway, something he had probably never seen in me in the first place. The bottom line, as it turned out, was that Alf had noted my ability to stop the most gifted of opponents, in this case Charlie Cooke and Billy Bremner, operating at the top of their powers. Alf had, after all, told Jack Charlton that he didn't always pick the best players but those whom he knew could do a job for him within a perfectly balanced team. My job, clearly, was to read the opponents' game plan and break it down at the most dangerous points. In that respect, I had plainly passed my first test with Ramsey and when he picked his next team for a Football League–Scottish League game at Newcastle, I was in again.

In the relief that came with that selection, I felt a wave of well being, and new confidence. With Kay's help, maybe I had grown up a little during the Aberdeen episode. I had, for one thing, successfully stood up to Busby. There was no mention of the Aberdeen game when I returned to Old Trafford. Busby behaved normally, and I felt that maybe a little of the awe I had brought to United as a schoolboy had slipped away. I was no longer a boy; I was a husband and a father, and a footballer in the running for a World Cup.

I much enjoyed the autobiography of the former England cricketer Mike Atherton, and it was easy to identify with some of the points he made about the growth of a player's competitive nature. He said that if he didn't have the greatest natural talent in the world – in this area he compared himself unfavourably with his Test team-mate Mark Ramprakash – he had the instinct not to take a step back but always to meet a challenge. I think that was also a significant factor in my own career. Of course, Atherton had great talent. You do not score runs and produce the great innings he did under difficult circumstances without enormous talent, and if I am mostly remembered for my willingness to get stuck in, I never had reason to doubt my ability to play the game. The key, as it was for Atherton, was the level of determination I applied. Also, you have to recognise there are times when it is essential to take your foot off the pedal. I know that Athers had that last ability because I once saw him in the bar at Old Trafford as drunk as a skunk. I thought to myself, 'Good luck to you, kid, you have put the work in.'

At one cricket do at Old Trafford, I sat at the table of two of my boyhood heroes, the great pace bowler Brian Statham and the spinner Roy Tattersall, and I spent quite some time asking them questions about their careers. The thing that struck me so strongly was that you can admire sportsmen in other fields at a distance, and then, suddenly, you meet them and you feel perfectly at home in their company. I suppose this shouldn't be any great mystery. There is much shared experience of the challenge that goes into separating yourself from the rest of the crowd at the top end of the competition.

It was in the dressing room before the Football League game that I first met Jack Charlton. We eyed each other across the room and I was not thrilled when he recalled to the world his first impression of me. He said he saw this 'little Japanese-looking bastard' fitting these bloody great things into his eyes. He said to me, 'Hey, look over there – that's the referee. He's dressed in black.' It was the start of an excellent, though sometimes tumultuous, relationship. I loved Jack for his commitment and spirit and his big long legs and tough nature, but there is no doubt he could be a difficult man and there would be times when we looked at each other and saw red mist.

The most notable occasion was in the run-in to the World Cup, when England played in Poland. It was my job to organise the wall defending against a free kick and as I was doing it Jack was mouthing off, and he continued after I told him to shut it. Unfortunately, the Poles sent the free kick past the wall against a post with Gordon Banks beaten, and so of course Jack had another go at me. I just snapped and marched towards Jack. I told him it was my job to organise the wall and he should get on with his own business. It was a slightly ridiculous confrontation, big Jack and little Nobby, eyes flashing and jaws working, but it was Jack who gave ground. In fact, he bolted.

You go through incidents like that with a team-mate when you are operating under pressure, but if there is a degree of respect you put it away easily enough. In the case of Jack, I had enormous respect for him. He is a completely different character from his brother Bobby, but I love them both. The greatness of the team of which I was just becoming part was founded on that willingness to work together and bury differences of nature and style. Jack was the classic example of this. One second he was urging the ultimate stylist Bobby Moore to boot the ball into the stand, the next he was slack-jawed with admiration for a piece of beautiful skill and timing from the same player. Jack could generate white-heat anger one second, gales of laughter the next. His comic mas-terpiece is to describe a goose race in Ireland.

The Football League game went well for me, which no doubt had a lot to do with the fact that on this occasion I had a clear view of what was happening around me. I realised straightaway I could work easily with big Jack. He had so many of the virtues of Bill Foulkes – big strides, a real presence in the air, a big heart.

It was no surprise that a few weeks later I was picked for my first full cap against Scotland at Wembley. I was, it was clear enough, a player Ramsey was prepared to investigate thoroughly on the road to the World Cup, and apart from the progress I might make under his direction, he could see my increasing confidence in a United back four that was acquiring an enviable reputation for flint-hearted meanness.

Ramsey saw my performance against Scotland in a full inter-national at Wembley as a crucial test. I was grateful to Wilf McGuinness for letting me know that this was a match on which my whole future as an international player could well hinge. According to Wilf, Alf had given him quite a quizzing on my playing character. 'Will he be as hard and determined,' asked Alf, 'as he was in the Under-23 game when he comes up against his team-mate Denis Law at Wembley?' I was pleased to hear that Wilf's response could not have come more quickly, or more emphatically. 'No fucking danger,' said Wilf.

In fact, any chance that I might show any deference to the Lawman disappeared in two incidents, one at Old Trafford a few days before the game, and another at Wembley just before the kick-off.

Naturally, I was a little bit tense going into a game that would have brought quite enough pressure without the knowledge that Ramsey had made it clear that he was seeing it as, among other things, an acid test of my ability to produce the best of my game at the highest competitive level. On the Wednesday, the five United players involved in the international – Bobby Charlton, John Connelly and me for England, Denis and Paddy Crerand for Scotland – trained together at Old Trafford. After the session, we all travelled down to London, the English and the Scots on different trains. While walking down the tunnel after the training, Paddy came over to Bobby, John and me and wished us all the best. I shook hands with Paddy and Denis didn't have any alternative but to shake hands with me. The thing was, though, he looked straight through me. I thought that was rather odd, but then, I speculated, maybe he was just putting his game face on, stripping off the sentiment and getting down to concentrating on what he would do at Wembley – a place that always dragged out the deepest ambition of any Scot wearing the blue shirt.

I also thought that maybe the Lawman was pulling rank and trying to burn off the confidence of a younger player, letting me know that this was no ordinary game, no Under-23 picnic, but a full international against England's oldest enemy. But then I already knew that, and I wondered if Denis knew that I didn't really give a damn about how polite and generous he was to a young team-mate before the most important game of his life. I was going to kick lumps out of him whatever he said or did before the game. As Wilf had said, there was no danger about that.

I was determined to prepare properly for the game because I knew that England–Scotland games, whatever the quality of the play, had always been a severe test of a young player, and, having learned my lesson after going for a hike with Bobby Charlton and Shay Brennan before that disastrous semi-final with Spurs, I took care to rest before the match. I followed the advice of John Giles, who always said that it was important to get your feet up before a big match. Whether or not you managed to sleep was not so important, the key was to take the weight off your legs.

So as much as I could be, I was ready for the big test. I stood to attention for the national anthem, I watched the pigeons fly by, I thought about the challenge of playing Denis out of the game, and I tried to control the wave of doubts that always invade you before a game – doubts that you learn to trust because the moment you don't have them, you are at risk of having a nightmare. Inevitably, I was a little nervous when I went up to Denis, wished him luck and offered my hand, this time expecting a little more response in the last seconds before the sound of the whistle. 'Fuck off, you little English bastard,' said Denis, and trotted away. Denis has reported that I kicked the hell out of him that afternoon, and it's true enough that I played ruthlessly, at my limits. It was always going to be so. Alf Ramsey expected nothing less, and for a few years his was the dominant voice in my football life. He was the man who was going to take me to the stars in an England shirt.

It was a hard game, a typically tough battle between England and Scotland, and we got into a 2–0 lead before injuries reduced us to nine men, with Bobby Charlton having to move to left-back. We still would have won, though, if Gordon Banks had not made a rare error. I found myself covering Paddy Crerand and pushing him on to his left side where he wasn't so strong. He managed to get off a twenty-five-yard pass to Law, whose shot on goal took a weird bounce that beat Banks. He was forced to take a kick at the ball and missed. That was the equaliser and a matter of some pain for me, but with our team reduced to nine men, Alf was happy with our performance and the mood was good when we went to the post-game banquet.

Unfortunately, I got lost in the corridors and banqueting rooms of the Café Royal and finished up dining with some complete strangers. I was looking in vain for the rest of the lads when one of my fellow diners asked me if I was a friend of the bride or the groom. I had attached myself to a wedding party, and when I finally joined the rest of the team I realised that my Inspector Clouseau nickname would now be written in stone.

It was something I was sure I could live with, however. At Old Trafford I was known as Happy because of my tendency to moan. Nicknames couldn't break my bones, I thought, ignoring the frown from Alf Ramsey at my late arrival at the dinner table. I was confident that he had noted I hadn't gone missing against the Scots – and especially against my celebrated team-mate Denis Law.

10

THE MERCY OF ALF

FROM the spring of 1965 to the spring of 1968, the smell of the grass and the glory had never been so strong. I was swept along with both United and England. It was, quite literally, the time of my football life and, I came to reflect when the good days ebbed away, of any English footballer's existence.

That statement is embedded in the records of the national game. As I have already mentioned with great pride, Bobby Charlton and I alone among Englishmen share the knowledge of what it's like to win both a World Cup and a European Cup. Both triumphs came at Wembley Stadium; when they knocked down the twin towers, they were demolishing part of my life. But then, I don't need any memorial of bricks and mortar, any more than the medals and the MBE, which came so long after the event, to enhance the sensation of achievement. I always have those days on call.

Of course, disappointment and defeat did not become total strangers. Their tentacles reached out again just a few months before the World Cup when Matt Busby's dream of winning the European Cup, so excited by the astonishing performance of young George Best when he led us to a 5–1 victory over Benfica in Lisbon's Estado da Luz, foundered in the Partizan stadium in

Belgrade at the semi-final stage. The defeat came in the absence of the dawning brilliance of Best, who was injured, and brought some terrible angst for Busby because, of course, it had been from Belgrade that his Babes had flown to their destruction just seven years earlier.

But that was victory and justice delayed rather than denied, and it did little to dampen my belief that a winning destiny had got hold of me and tucked me into its back pocket. I told myself just to look at the tide of my life and my career. I was happily married, my second son had arrived and I had won the respect of two of the greatest football managers the game had ever known. So, given all these happy circumstances, you may be a little surprised to learn how I managed, on a summer's night in England's Shropshire headquarters at Lilleshall in the spring of 1966, to put it all at risk. For so many years it has been my guilty secret, and it still makes my blood run cold when I think of it.

Analysing the incident now, I can only put it down to the misguided belief that I had reached the point where I had become untouchable. It was no excuse, I know now, that there was quite a bit of circumstantial evidence to point me in that direction. I had become a fixture in the teams of Busby and Ramsey. Since he had blooded me against the Scots three times in the first half of 1965, Ramsey had come, it seemed, to scrawl my name on his team-sheet automatically. I was in there not as a triallist but as an integral part of the team of great players – Bobby Moore, Bobby Charlton, Gordon Banks, Ray Wilson and Jimmy Greaves. The caps were spreading over my sideboard in Stretford. I had played in Gothenburg against the Swedes, in Belgrade against the Yugoslavs, at Hampden Park against the Scots, and in Nuremburg against the Germans. But for a home defeat by Austria, which we dismissed as something of a freak, and a 0–0 draw with Wales, nothing had happened to detach Ramsey from his belief that we had an excellent chance of winning England's first World Cup. Indeed, it was a conviction that was thrillingly strengthened in early December when we played brilliantly in Madrid to beat Spain 2–0 and inspire from the Spanish coach Jose Villalonga the opinion that Ramsey was an extraordinary innovator and that our performance would have beaten any team in the world.

Since that cold night in Madrid, when Ramsey unveiled his 'wingless wonders' blueprint and then carefully returned it to its wraps, our confidence had grown still further. We played well in a tumultuous game against an impressive Poland at Goodison Park, a belief not dented too much by a 1–1 scoreline; we beat West Germany in Nuremburg, and went to Hampden Park and, to the great delight of Ramsey, beat the Scots 4–3. We gathered at Lilleshall beneath a clear blue sky for a little fine tuning before a tour of Scandinavia and a return game with Poland in Katowice. This was the last run to the World Cup, a time to gather in all the fruits of the hard work and the growing sense of team and genuine progress. It was again time to smell the grass and celebrate the privilege of operating at the top of the game.

That's precisely what Alan Ball, John Connelly and I were doing until the night we had an overwhelming desire to break out for an hour and have a pint. From time to time, Alf permitted this. He allowed the team to walk down to the clubhouse of the nearby golf course and take a relaxing drink, but he made it very clear that this was not a privilege to be taken up at any time. It needed the manager's explicit approval. On the occasion in question, the night stretched before us according to the unchanging preference of Alf Ramsey. We would see some video film of rival World Cup teams and, inevitably, watch westerns. After tea at six o'clock, Bally and I agreed that we could kill a pint, and John Connelly said that he was prepared to take a chance. Like schoolboys playing hookey, we sneaked off to the bar but, of course, we had no sooner got there than we started feeling guilty. We swallowed our pints, turned on our heels and headed back to the training complex and the authority of Ramsey. It was an old echo of the time my brother Charlie had driven me out of that pub in Oldham Road, and when we got back to the building I had reason to remember all of his words about the difference between taking your chances in life and throwing them away. Wilf McGuinness was standing at the front door and he had a very anxious look on his face.

'Where the hell have you been?' he asked. Bally and I owned up to having a pint, Bally adding, 'We just drank it down and came straight back.'

'You ought to know you're in deep shit,' Wilf said. 'Alf knows you went down to the bar, and he said the place was off limits tonight.'

We protested our ignorance, said that Alf had allowed the team to go to the bar before and we were unaware of his latest order, but Wilf shook his head.

'Everybody knew the bar was out tonight,' he said.

John Connelly had a look of defiance on his face, but Bally and I couldn't conceal our feelings of panic. No one could have valued their places in the England team more than us. Even in a team already notable for its commitment, and its faith in and respect for its manager, we were known as a couple of young players desperate to achieve, and now we were both shocked that we had endangered all our hopes in a few minutes of stupidity.

Wilf reminded us that there had been a similar incident right at the start of the Ramsey regime, when both Bally and me were fighting to get in to the first teams of our clubs, Blackpool and United. On the eve of a foreign tour a group of players, including Bobby Charlton, had failed to beat curfew at White's Hotel in London, where the team were staying. On that occasion,

Ramsey had ordered that the passports of the offending players be placed on their pillows. After anxious nights, they were told that Ramsey had considered calling for replacements, and that they had to understand they had two options. They could be treated like men or erring schoolboys, and if they elected to join the latter category they could have no part in his plans.

'Alf knows about this,' said Wilf. 'He wants you to go to his room.'

I had a terrible vision of being sent away in disgrace. I didn't want to imagine Kay's reaction; she had been so strong in her support when Busby had stood in the way of my first call-up by Ramsey. I could imagine her saying, 'What the hell were you thinking about, sliding away for a pint and putting everything at risk while I'm back at home, pregnant and looking after our son?'

Alf came out of his room with a very solemn expression. Bally and I looked at our feet as Ramsey, after the usual pause, said, 'I didn't say you couldn't go to the bar, I didn't say you shouldn't go. I just expected you wouldn't go. We are here on serious business and I thought you all understood that. We are going to win the World Cup.'

Bally and I practically threw ourselves at his feet. We said we were so sorry, we didn't know what we were thinking about, it would never happen again. Then, to our horror, John Connelly stepped forward with an entirely different approach.

'What the fuck are you two talking about?' he said. 'We only had a pint, which isn't going to do us any harm at all after all the training we've been doing.' Our eyes shot from John's to Alf's face with some certainty about what we were going to see, and we were not surprised. Alf's face was like thunder.

'Get out of here, all of you. Get out of my sight,' he snapped.

Like those earlier curfew-breakers, we suffered sleepless nights wondering whether we had wrecked our chances of making it to the World Cup. Bally and I took a vow of silence; we wouldn't tell anybody, and me least of all Kay. Just last year the secret finally came out, Bally letting it slip when we were having dinner with our wives. Kay's reaction was as I had anticipated it would be all those years before.

'That was great,' she said. 'Me back home looking after John and waiting to have another baby – you supposed to be preparing for a World Cup while nipping off to the boozer.'

John Connelly just sailed on. He was an easygoing lad with a broad Lancashire accent and, who knows, his reaction may have helped our case as much as our hand-wringing. Whatever the reason, we got away with it. We had assured Ramsey that nothing of this sort would ever happen again and, at least in this, we were as good as our word. We had let down the great disciplinarian once and nobody needed to tell us that you didn't do it twice and survive.

The memory of those days underlines how much the life of a professional footballer has changed down the years. When England flew off to the World Cup in the Far East in 2002, I couldn't help noting the fact that they were given a week in a five-star hotel in Dubai with their wives and girlfriends, after negoti-ating a commercial deal with the Football Association worth millions. Very sheepishly, I recalled my own failure of nerve when Kay asked if I could get some time away from training camp to be with her for the birth of our second son. I had just two fleeting visits home in more than two months as Kay had Peter and then took John and the baby to Dublin for the summer. Obviously, a player of my generation may envy a David Beckham the scale of his income, his ability to give his family such a luxurious life, but I cannot say I would exchange my existence back then for the life he leads today. I know David well enough, I worked with him when he was a kid at Old Trafford, and in many respects I found him to be a very good lad indeed. But the lifestyle into which he has grown would have appalled me. I couldn't have stood the distractions and the media attention. No, if I played today, I would be the Paul Scholes type, playing football and otherwise keeping my head down. I always thought there was enough to do keeping fit, fighting for my place in the big-time and listening to the people who had been a bit further down the road than me.

It happened that my run in the England team ended with the first match we played after Bally and I were marched to Ramsey's room by Wilf McGuinness, but it was not the misadventure in Shropshire that kept me out of the opening game of the tour of Scandinavia, a comfortable 3–0 win over Finland in Helsinki. It was a mishap in the sky over the Baltic. I managed to injure myself on the plane. It was, the team doctor said, caused by the way I had been sitting. The doc said I would be fine for the rest of the tour and I duly returned for the next game, a 6–1 thrashing of Norway in Oslo. I now had two strict rules in the build-up to the World Cup. One was to avoid scrupulously the intake of any alcohol without the permission of Alf Ramsey. The other was avoid any further Inspector Clouseau-style disasters while sitting in my seat in an airliner.

We finished off the Scandinavian swing with a 2–0 cruising win over Denmark. In those days, the Scandinavians were a long way from the serious end of international competition, and we knew that the Poles, in their gritty bastion of the coal-mining town Katowice, would give us a much better guide to the state of our form and understanding as a team. At this point we had reverted to a 4-4-2 formation with wingers Connelly, Terry Paine of Southampton and Ian Callaghan of Liverpool vying for the wide positions, and Alf carefully weighing the claims of Ball and Martin Peters. Later, some of Alf's critics claimed that he dallied over installing the system that worked so brilliantly against Spain on that cold night in Madrid, and that it was only injury to another Liverpool winger, Peter Thompson, and failure by the other orthodox wingers to convince him of their value, that had turned the old full-back away from the gamble of jettisoning conventional wing play. I have another theory and it is one I have held to from the day that Ramsey's masterplan carried us through maybe our greatest test of the tournament, the quarter-final against Argentina.

My belief is that Alf had seen how perfectly the wingless approach had worked in Madrid and, having established that it could work so well, simply put it away from the gaze of the rest of the football world. He wanted to go into the finals with something different, something hard and fresh and guaranteed to disrupt the thinking of the opposition.

In Madrid, Bally had put in a phenomenal performance, running magnificently into the open spaces left by full-backs who, lacking any obvious marking assignments, were repeatedly dragged out of position. Joe Baker, a mobile striker who lost his chance of making an impact in the finals because of injury, also had a fine game and afterwards the Spanish coach was plainly stunned by the depth and strength of our running. He said, 'England were phenomenal – far superior in their experiment and their players.'

An English-born Scotsman, Baker was quick and intelligent and perfectly suited to Ramsey's concept of a well-organised but also extremely fluid team. Many years later we met at a dinner in Edinburgh and I said how sorry I was that all the promise he had displayed against Spain, when as a team we had so dramatically shown our potential to go all the way, had come to nothing. Joe shrugged philosophically, but he did say how much he had valued playing, however briefly, under Ramsey. I asked him about the difference between Alf and the previous England manager, the well-respected but FA committee-dominated Walter Winterbottom.

Joe said the key was that Alf was a players' man. He was tough on discipline, but he always had the well-being of the players in mind. Quickly, Ramsey got over the message that whatever he did, it was provoked by one basic objective – the improved performance of the team, something that every serious professional wanted. One of Baker's examples was the difference between press days under Walter and Alf. Alf would say before our training sessions at the Bank of England ground in Roehampton, 'Gentlemen, we have to make ourselves available to the press today. How long should we give them?' Ray Wilson always proposed that we gave them nothing, although he generally put it rather more forcefully. Alf said that of course we had to provide some facilities for the media. We were representing our country, and the press, however much we might disagree with some of the headlines and their angles, were serving the public. But if we agreed a time for the interview session, Alf was emphatic that a strict time limit would be enforced. Under Walter, the journalists' inevitable pleas for another interview, another half hour, were invariably granted. Walter was too gentlemanly to draw down the curtain. Alf had no compunction in saying it was time for the players to get back to their hotel.

This might sound a little petty, even precious, but Alf knew the way it was in the rhythm of a footballer's week. The press days were usually on Friday after morning training. Work on the field was generally very sharp with quite a bit of sprinting. After that you didn't want to be on your feet for an indefinite period. You got mentally tired and irritable very quickly, and often you could give a bad account of yourself. Alf understood this, and acted upon it. When the time was up he would have his assistants Harold Shepherdson and Les Cocker blowing whistles and announce it was time to go. Walter Winterbottom was, apparently, nothing like so commanding. You might think this was something in the margins of our week, but in the psychology of a footballer operating in a tunnel, trying to keep focused, little things can loom large. Alf had been a professional and he never forgot any of the hard lessons he had learned.

There was no doubt about the most important lesson he had absorbed when he played for England under Winterbottom and suffered terrible humiliations in the losses to the United States in the 1950 World Cup in the Brazilian mining town of Belo Horizonte and then, three years later, to the great Hungarian team of Puskas at Wembley and the Nep Stadium in Budapest. Alf learned that a successful team had two basic needs. It had to have organisation and it had to have pride. These were his two great gifts to the men he assembled for the tournament that would wipe away the memories of defeat by a team of American amateurs, and a complete ransacking by Hungarians who appeared to be playing a different and much superior game.

When Alf gathered us together he never said that we *could* do something; he said we *would* do it. He said this before the make-up of the team was finalised or the tactics were completely evolved. He gave us belief before we really did anything. 'Gentlemen, most certainly we will win the World Cup,' announced Alf, and we went away believing it.

After the alarm in Shropshire and injury in the sky, I settled back behind the barricades of Alf's conviction and the sense that despite my brief fall from grace I remained a firm part of his battle-plan. It was wonderful to see fine cities such as Helsinki, Oslo and Copenhagen in the early summer. Following the lead of Bobby Charlton, the boldest eater in the team, I had herrings and a shot of schnapps and saw the midnight sun streaming through the hotel windows. For a kid from Collyhurst, it was thrilling to see a big and ever-widening world.

It was also good to sense the growth of England's football

team. After surviving the free-kick mishap and any disruption of concentration caused by my heated debate with big Jack, we played with great confidence against an impressive Polish team. Roger Hunt scored an excellent goal and we were able to return to England with the feeling that we could go into the backyard of tough opponents and take control.

Of course, Alf still had a few tricky decisions to make and probably the most demanding concerned Jimmy Greaves. He was, no question, one of our truly world-class players but the manager had already made it clear that the making of a team involved something more than assembling the most gifted players. Jimmy was very quiet on the bus after the game in Katowice and maybe he had an inkling that the pattern of Ramsey's approach, with its heavy emphasis on running and high work-rate, put his own position in the team under more pressure than some might have imagined.

It was around this time that I took exception to some remarks made by Malcolm Allison, who had emerged as a big television pundit as well as a coach who was doing a brilliant job down the road at Manchester City. You couldn't help but be impressed by Allison's work at Maine Road and he was obviously a man who thought deeply about the game, but in his opinions on Ramsey's work I thought he had reached one or two false conclusions. The most upsetting to me was his view that Alf had saddled his players with a strict 4-3-3 formation and that if the trend continued it could ruin the game. The fact was that there was nothing restrictive about the way we were being asked to play. Really it was the most fluid approach and gave full scope to the individual abilities of all the players. I saw Sven Goran Eriksson's England making very heavy weather of a similar formation. They called it the diamond system, but unfortunately it didn't shine very brightly on a rainy night against Slovakia in Bratislava. Certainly it didn't touch the fluency or the simplicity achieved when it was in the hands of Alf Ramsey.

Bobby Charlton was in the centre, Alan Ball on the right, Martin Peters on the left with two strikers at the front, but there was nothing static about the way the system operated. The obligation was great movement and biting runs. Bally operated like a runaway train, Martin made ghostly runs that persuaded Alf he was ten years ahead of his time, and Bobby was the creative heartbeat. I won the ball and gave it to Bobby or, on the odd occasion when he hadn't been able to make the right ground and carve himself a little space, someone else who was available. Ball was a huge factor in making things work; his running put defenders, and especially the full-back who was supposed to be marking him, into fevers of doubt. He went all over the field looking for the ball, making an extra man in midfield, and with the strikers running on, the opposing defence was always at full stretch. They also had to pick up the tremendous surging overlaps of George Cohen, who was happy to run all day just for the fun of it.

When I think of all that dovetailing, the way we quickly came to know the instincts of each other, the way Mooro and big Jack worked together, how George and Ray Wilson could go forward, knowing that it was my job to cover any ground they had to leave uncovered, the lack of real preparation that today's England have to overcome when they go into competitive matches fills me with dismay. Friendly matches don't seem to serve any purpose as substitutes stream on to the field. That would have been a horror for Ramsey. His whole campaign was based on the need for players to develop deep familiarity with their own roles and the way they related to team-mates. Apart from handing out a specific assignment, Alf never told me what to do. He put me into the team with basic expectations — I had to make my tackles, read the game, supply Bobby Charlton with a good, quick service of the ball —

and as for the rest, well, I was a professional and he knew what I could do for United, so he expected the same for England. Like all his players, I was required to adapt to the rhythm of every game, impose myself on it. He once said to me that we were not playing 4-3-3, we were not spelling out what we were doing, we weren't running along tram-lines. We were playing football, strong simple football that allowed all his players, including a wonderfully gifted individual such as Bobby Charlton, to express all of his talent.

We came back from Poland, had a brief visit with our families, and then headed to London for the World Cup finals, which would shape our lives. That should have been the entrance to a tunnel from which all distraction was excluded for five weeks, but even for the pick of the nation's football talent there were inevitably other concerns. Alf Ramsey could organise the fine details of our football lives, but he couldn't smooth away our day-by-day cares.

A year earlier, on the strength of my progress in the United first team, I had been persuaded to set up a business partnership with somebody who said it would a nice little licence to print money. I went into the underfloor heating business and we bought a van. The trouble was that whenever a bill came in, it was me who had to pay it. And there didn't seem to be much of a profit. When I should have been exclusively smelling the grass, and scenting victory over the best teams in the world, I found myself worrying about the bank account. From the exotic places we'd been, I was making calls to the bank manager back in a Manchester suburb. He said I shouldn't worry, all business projects had teething problems, it would all work out fine. I wasn't sure.

I had thrown everything into the game, but after a while you do worry about the future. You see players going down with injury and suddenly having to remake their lives. You remember the old warnings – get yourself a trade, think of the future, you have to put food on the table. The hazards of business nagged at me from time to time in those weeks when we faced the challenge of winning the World Cup, and I always considered it good fortune that when we checked into the Hendon Hall Hotel I was assigned a room with Alan Ball. It was up in the loft of the hotel and for five weeks Bally and I helped each other through one crisis or another.

One of them we made for ourselves. We were given the job of picking the five-a-side teams at the end of our training sessions and as a matter of strict policy we decided that we would always keep Jack Charlton waiting until last. It meant that more than once we had to flee through the bushes in the grounds of Hendon Hall with big Jack at our heels. 'I'll kill one of you little bastards,' he roared. Everyone agreed it was very good for team spirit.

11

LIGHT THAT WILL NEVER DIE

So many of those days of the summer of '66 remain alive that I know, thirty-seven years on, they will never fray or shred on the edges of my memory. Of course, you cannot carry such a time around with you like baggage; you have to put it into storage and get on with the rest of your life. But how could it not always be with you, just below the surface to be summoned up whenever you need to bring a little lift to your stride? It is the ballast of your life.

For example, last summer when I watched another World Cup from a hospital bed, recovering from my heart-attack, inevitably my thoughts strayed back to that time when I felt as though I occupied a place near the centre of the world. As I followed the course of another great tournament, I marvelled all over again at the scale of my good fortune in being at a certain place at a certain time and in such good company. I thought of all the tension and the worry before that final explosion of joy and relief which sent me jigging across Wembley. I saw the banners again and I heard the cheers. I remembered how calm Bobby Moore had always been, and the time when Bally was left out of the games against Mexico and France and came up to the loft after collecting some winnings from the bookmaker's, throwing the fivers on the floor and dancing on them, saying, 'Fuck Alf Ramsey,' but I knew that really he was breaking up inside because you had only to look at his face to know that. I couldn't forget the haunted look on the face of Jimmy Greaves, one of the greatest players English football had ever seen, when he began to realise that the tide of good fortune was, for him, maybe ebbing away. I thought of the surge of electricity that shot through the team and Wembley and, I'm told, the whole nation when Bobby Charlton scored his stupendous goal against Mexico – the one that told us we really were in with a chance of winning the greatest prize in all of football.

Most of all, I recalled the brilliant leadership of Alf Ramsey and the loyalty he showed to me when I was being hung, drawn and quartered by the press, the World Cup television panellists and the high-ups in the Football Association, and the world ruling body FIFA wanted me thrown out of the tournament. That was when Alf stood up for me against a world that suddenly seemed very hostile indeed, and when I became indebted to him for the rest of my life. It was, I vowed, a debt I would repay even if it meant running to the ends of the earth, and in that hospital bed, when my strength was so depleted by the heart-attack, I thought of that other time when I took myself to the very edge of my physical limits.

But before that there were other, smaller trials as we made a tentative start to Ramsey's crusade to win the World Cup. We were confident enough before the opening game against Uruguay. The mood in Hendon Hall, given all the expectations that were building around us, couldn't have been more relaxed. Up in the loft, Bally's and my next-door neighbours, the reserve goalkeepers Ron Springett and Peter Bonetti, were good companions, and Springett, a chirpy Londoner with the kind of wacky humour you associate naturally with the men who stand between the posts, could be particularly amusing. His flair for mimicry reached its high-point with an impersonation of the peacocks that preened in the gardens of the Lilleshall complex.

The problem was that the Uruguayans, as Alf had warned us repeatedly, were no mugs. They tackled hard and ruthlessly and got players behind the ball, including their most gifted performers Pedro Rocha and Julio Cesar Cortes, whenever they could. It can be tough breaking down any team that doesn't have a scrap of ambition to score a goal unless it's offered up to them on a silver plate, but the high technical level of the South Americans made the job all the more difficult. Their objective, they made it quite clear, was simply to survive against the tournament hosts with a point to show for their ceaseless running. They put in some tackles, including one on me, that made you automatically feel all your vital parts for the reassurance that they were still connected to the rest of your body. They covered Greaves like a blanket, John Connelly scarcely got a kick and even Bally was forced to shake his head in frustration.

We were booed off the field at the end of the goalless draw, which was a bit disappointing but quite understandable because there had been such a ballyhoo going into that first game. The nation was looking for lift-off but what it got was two teams operating with one clear imperative – they just couldn't afford to lose. That was our particular difficulty because even while they were building their barricades, the Uruguayans still retained the capacity to hit us hard on the counter-attack if we were careless enough to invite them in. We couldn't afford to leave any gaps in our defence even as we mounted attack after attack on the goal of Ladislao Mazurkiewicz, and so at the end, as the South Americans jumped around congratulating themselves on the draw, we at least consoled ourselves that we hadn't been suckered into conceding a goal that could have thrown the entire campaign into immediate chaos. We had, it was important to remind ourselves, confirmed the defensive security that had brought us clean sheets against such impressive trial horses as Spain and Poland in their fortresses of Madrid and Katowice.

Still, the papers made grim reading – Ramsey had to reorganise us, give us more bite; we had to go back to the training field and come up with something new and brighter in the way of tactics. Sometimes you hear it said that managers and players do not read the papers. Never believe that. Everybody reads the papers. Players do it out of insecurity and managers for varying degrees of that, but also to note the difference between what influential reporters say over a drink and a confidential briefing and what they finally come to write.

But if Ramsey was no exception to this rule, he didn't have to act upon what he read, which meant that when he should, according to the press, have been overhauling every aspect of his team, he was in fact leading us down to Pinewood Studios. There, we hobnobbed with Yul Brynner, Sean Connery, Cliff Richard and the Shadows. Kay was a great fan of Yul Brynner's and he gave me his autograph and a message for her as we all let the pressures of the Uruguayan game drain away.

By the time we left a reception at Hendon Town Hall, the wine and beer supplied with the buffet had taken away all of the tension, perhaps a little too completely in some cases. That, certainly, was the feeling of several councillors when they discovered that prawn cocktail and potato salad had found its way into their suit pockets. For Ramsey, the benefit was that when we went back to work the following morning, our appetite for the game, and the challenge, was restored.

Alan Ball, at least on the surface, was a victim of the Uruguayan impasse. For the next game, against Mexico, he lost his place to Martin Peters, with Connelly dropping out in favour of Terry Paine. We knew precisely the challenge we faced against Mexico, who were as determined to frustrate us as Uruguay had been but had nothing like the technical skill with which to do it. Not only did we have to beat the Mexicans, we had to inject some new life and confidence into the team. We had gone flat against Uruguay – along with the whole nation – so we needed a jolt, a spark, something that would get the blood running again. Who better to provide it than Bobby Charlton?

Bobby's goal in the thirty-sixth minute displayed everything about his talent – it had grace, energy and wonderfully controlled power. He collected the ball from Roger Hunt in the centre circle and as the Mexicans retreated, he flowed on their goal. Then he moved to the right, made that famous hitch in his stride, and sent a long shot past the goalkeeper Ignacio Calderon. It was more than a goal. It was a statement that we had someone among us who could do anything on a football field. I had, of course, long known the quality of Charlton; I had seen all the early signs of his genius and the natural physical gifts that supported it. At Old Trafford, his brilliance, and that of Denis Law and young George Best, had persuaded us that we could achieve all our goals. Now that same sense poured into every corner of the England team.

Hunt, who would always be regarded as a workhorse at the expense of any deeper analysis of his tremendous footballing ability, scored the other goal, one of three from him that would carry us through the first phase of the tournament and remind everyone that Ramsey hadn't placed his faith in mere industry. Hunt was right on the spot when Calderon fumbled a shot from Jimmy Greaves, who had been released by Charlton after he had orchestrated a bout of passing down the left.

Greaves got one last chance to make a mark on this World Cup, against the French in the final group game, but again he failed to hit the mark while Hunt scored two more goals during another ninety minutes of running that stretched an opposing defence to

its seams. The French game was also a last chance for an orthodox winger to be kept in at the expense of the restless energy of
Ball, or the subtle running of Martin Peters, but Ian Callaghan,
such a vital factor in the rise of Liverpool under Bill Shankly, could
make no more impression than Connelly or Paine before him.
Hunt shot us through to the quarter-finals and the test Alf feared
most, against the cynical but often brilliant Argentina. Hunt had
done that for most of the team, at least. My own future in the
tournament was nothing like so clear.

The details of the play leading up to my tackle on the French
midfielder Jacky Simon have always been foggy in my memory,
but I remember the tackle well enough. It was the one from hell,
which is exactly where it threatened to put me. As I first recalled
the build-up, we were attacking along the right with George
Cohen on the ball and Simon, a very good player, tracking him.
When the French goalkeeper, Marcel Aubour, gathered up the
ball and threw it out to his team-mate, I was already on the move,
watching the ball looping down and lining up my tackle. George
remembers it differently. He said the ball reached Simon via a
throw-in and that when I came in so late and the Frenchman fell
in a heap in front of the royal box, he said to himself, 'Oh Christ,
that looks bad.'

Maybe I should say what was in my mind as I went in to the
tackle that would create such a storm of headlines and criticism.
It was to hit the ball – and him – just as he turned. It is not a foul
if you go through the ball, hitting it with all the force you have,
and that takes you through the player. That is a hard but legal
tackle, and that was my ambition. The objective is not to hurt the
player but to remind him of the force of body contact in the game,
to announce your presence so that the next time you are in his
vicinity, he will think twice about doing something fancy, and possibly dangerous, with the ball. In my position, you always wanted

the opposing player to believe that he had a good chance of getting the ball; you wanted to encourage the possibility of some serious contact, which is not quite the same thing as Roy Keane's freely admitted, and much publicised, attempt to do damage to his old rival Alf-Inge Haarland.

What went wrong was that while I was following an old instruction of Matt Busby's, who always used to say, 'Norrie, let him know you're there in the first five minutes,' the ball had gone. Simon, the playmaker who liked to stroke it around, had on this occasion whipped the ball away at first contact. That compounded my mistiming, making the tackle look even more horribly late. The crowd shrieked, and although the referee Arturo Yamaski, a Peruvian, took no action, a Fifa observer in the stand did. He booked me and took me within an inch of being banished from the World Cup.

I didn't apologise to Simon as he was getting treatment down on the field. I didn't feel the need to do that. I hadn't tried to annihilate him with a cheap shot. That's how it may have looked, but that hadn't been in my mind or my heart, so I just shrugged and shut my ears to the buzz of the crowd, and regretted that my timing had been off. These things did, after all, happen from time to time in the football trenches, though I have to say I was relieved to see him get to his feet and rejoin the match.

About five years later we met at an indoor tournament at Wembley and I asked him if there had been any long-lasting effects of our collision. He told me he had played on in the French team for another two years and said, yes, it was a thing that could happen in football. We shook hands and embraced, but for a while most of the rest of the world was rather less forgiving.

The headlines screamed at my 'atrocity', the television panellists, with the exception of Jimmy Hill, launched into me. Joe Mercer, whose widow would later send me the old photograph of my meeting with Monty, said I had committed a terrible foul, one to shame English football. Danny Blanchflower and Billy Wright took up pretty much the same theme.

Jimmy Hill, and of course Kay and my team-mates, provided just about the only kind words in the storm. Hill said that this was a kid who was striving to do his best for England, and that while maybe he had got this tackle wrong, he shouldn't be crucified for one mistake. Every day in the build-up to the game with Argentina, it did feel like a form of crucifixion. I was being slaughtered in the press and on the television and I got so down that Kay had to give me a rallying speech during one of our evening phone calls. 'Why are you so down?' she asked. 'Remember, it's your job to win for England, tackle for England, so instead of moping around, just bloody well get on with it.' She also sent her love, which had never been more important.

The question was whether I would be allowed to persevere in the challenge Kay had defined so precisely, and it stabbed into me at the Friday training session before Saturday's game with the Argentines. I was working on corners when Alf walked across the field and called me over to him. At that time I didn't know that Alf had been called down to FA headquarters and told that he had to get rid of me, that I was an embarrassment to England and that the best thing he could do for the image of the tournament was to give me the boot. I didn't know how Alf had replied.

'Well, gentlemen,' he had said, 'most certainly Nobby Stiles can be thrown off the team, but I must tell you that I see him as a very important player for England, one who has done very well for the team since he was first selected, and that if he goes, so do I. You will be looking for a new manager.'

Alf did not ask me for any detailed explanation of what happened when I tackled Jacky Simon. He just gave me a hard look and said, 'Did you mean it?'

'No, Alf,' I said, 'I didn't. I mistimed the tackle.'

He looked me straight in the eye and said, 'You are playing tomorrow.'

I will never forget the wave of relief that swept over me at that moment. Suddenly I was training again rather than going through the motions. Later, I called Kay in Dublin and she wished me all the best for the Argentina game. John and Dickie Giles also came on the phone and told me that I should just put all the other stuff out of my mind, it was over now, and concentrate on playing to my limits. Kay reinforced her phone message with a telegram and many years later I found it, faded and crumpled, at the bottom of a drawer. It sent her love and said, 'You can do it.'

But the Simon affair wasn't quite over. Alf had another card to play. He made a statement to the football world and the nation. He said that Nobby Stiles was a great young Englishman who was proud to play for his country, and had done it very well. He said that I was not just a good player but a great player. I saw him on the television and heard him saying it. I felt tears coming to my eyes and my skin went prickly, and I thought, 'Alf, thank you very much.'

I received another charge to my spirit going up Wembley Way in the team bus. Bally nudged me and said, 'Nob, look at that banner.' It was huge and it declared, 'Nobby for Prime Minister'. Another, smaller one said, 'Nobby, go and get the bastards'. I was so moved because all the criticism had really got into my head; I had developed a belief that whatever I did in the rest of the World Cup, a shadow would be over me, and any achievement would always be set against the effects of the Simon controversy. The banners, the cheers and the thumbs-up gestures as we went along Wembley Way banished that feeling. I felt I had returned to good standing in the eyes of the nation.

Alf, having resolved my problem, had settled on his final,

winning solution. The wingers had been tried and found wanting; Greaves had, partly through injury sustained in the French game, lost his battle to keep out the sharpness, hard running and power of Geoff Hurst; and Ball and Peters were back in the team. The Madrid masterplan had been reinstated and I was particularly delighted for my friend Bally. He had become almost the legs of the team, running fiercely and with unbreakable wit and optimism, and it had been terrible to see his despair when he was left out of the group games against Mexico and France. One night I talked to Alan Ball Senior, a fierce, professional football man who had moulded his son's playing personality since he was a toddler. Alan's father was in constant touch with his son, buoying him up, telling him to work hard because there was no doubt his chance would come again. I told Ball Senior that I agreed with him, and I thought the chance would come against Argentina. I just couldn't see Alf going into a match like this without Alan's energy and bite.

The manager's team-talk was low key, practical. Don't get involved in anything off the ball, he said. Walk away from everything, just get on with the game; remember at all times what you have to do – win the World Cup for England.

There was quite a lot to walk away from. Argentina had wonderful skill, and a technically brilliant captain in Antonio Rattin, but they were spoiling from the first seconds. We had to deal with a tide of petty needling – and spittle. The spitting never stopped. Time after time they gobbed in your face, and when you went down in a tackle they were grabbing your boots, yanking your legs. You just had to keep telling yourself not to take the bait. I remember how, after I went down on the ground and was getting up, the Argentine who had gone down with me got hold of my foot, lifted it up and then fell back as though I had hit him. You knew it was going to be a hard day and that was confirmed when

Bobby Charlton was booked. For me, of course, this was the day of all days when I couldn't lose my head. The need for self-control had been reinforced by Ramsey's assistants Harold Shepherdson and Les Cocker. Separately, they got hold of me before the game – Cocker even pushed me up against the dressing-room wall – and told me that I just couldn't let Alf down. 'You'll never know,' said Shepherdson, 'what Alf has gone through for you.' I said he shouldn't worry, I knew what Alf had done, and there was no way I would disappoint him now. Cocker, it should be said, was not above the passions of the game, or the need for a team to exert itself physically. He was, after all, Don Revie's trainer at Leeds and they were not exactly a team for stepping back politely. In fact, when Cocker was giving me his fierce talk about the need to behave myself more scrupulously than ever before, I couldn't help remembering an incident from the previous year, when we played an Under-23 international against Germany.

A German opponent left me in a heap after I'd nicked the ball off one of his team-mates. I'd carried the ball away and when another German stepped into my path as I came to him, I planned to knock the ball off. The guy chasing me pushed me and I fell over the ball; as I did so, the new man turned his shoulder and hit me in the solar plexus. As I struggled for breath, Cocker treated me. When my breath came back, I said, 'That little bastard did me in a big way. If I find out who it was, I'll sort him out.' As Cocker picked up his bag and trotted away, he said, 'It was number four.' Ten minutes later it was the German trainer who had to come on to the field.

But there was none of that 'live by the sword, die by it' philosophy from Cocker as we prepared to go out against Argentina, and he reinforced Shepherdson's message. Cocker gave me a dig and said, 'Just don't let him down – he went in and batted for you.' I said the same as I'd said to Shepherdson – 'Don't worry, Les, nobody needs to tell me what Alf has done for me.'

In the games against Uruguay and Mexico, Alf hadn't given me a specific assignment. I had my usual brief of reading the game, looking for interceptions, covering George Cohen and Ray Wilson on the flanks and, as an absolute priority, winning my tackles. Whenever possible, I was to supply Bobby Charlton with the ball. Against France, however, I had been given the fateful job of marking Simon, and Alf gave me another shadowing role in the Argentina game. As usual, Alf's decision appeared to be the result of consensus. In the team-talk, Alf pointed out that the Argies had a clever playmaker in Ermindo Onega. Should we man-mark him? There was a chorus of yes, and Alf asked who should get the job. Led by Wilson, everyone said I should do it, which was quite touching after the tumult that had come with my tackle on Simon.

The fact that Wilson led the vote was very encouraging for me. He was the quiet man of the team, very much the brooding Yorkshire introvert off the field, but he carried a lot of influence with the players, and although Alf always basically knew what he wanted to do, I did notice that he tended to prick up his ears when Ray had something to say.

So I tracked the tricky Onega, but very carefully. I'd probably never played a more conservative game, but I did make my tackles and I did read the game. It was like walking through a minefield, and later Geoff Hurst said that it seemed to him he had taken more stick and received more goading and taunts in those ninety minutes than in all the rest of his career to that point. Rattin was the goader-in-chief. I'd never seen anyone 'rabbit' so relentlessly on the field, and as he protested and yelled, the German referee Rudolf Kreitlein was increasingly the object of his scorn.

It seemed to us that we just had to play our game because this tremendously gifted Argentina seemed to have programmed themselves for self-destruction. In the thirty-sixth minute the referee snapped and Rattin, who looked so assured and talented on the ball, paid the inevitable price of his madness. He was sent off, and as he eventually walked away from the field after giving his famously sad tug at a corner flag, and his team-mates bitterly protested and threatened to abandon the game, we looked at each other and agreed that if we kept our heads our route to the semi-finals was probably guaranteed.

It seemed like an absurd waste of talent. We knew that if the Argentines had concentrated on football, if they had relied on their skill rather than every devious little trick they could come up with, we would have been involved in a hell of a game. Instead, they made a mockery of the idea that we were all meeting the challenge of trying to prove ourselves the best football team in the world.

The Argentines were so skilled and sound in their technical approach to the game that they were hardly any easier to beat down when they were reduced to ten men. It meant that Hurst and Hunt just had to keep running in that snakepit defensive zone, Cohen and Wilson had to overlap and stretch them whenever they could, and when I wasn't supplying Charlton I had to watch for a moment of defensive breakdown that would have shattered all our efforts. But the defence, with Moore and Jackie Charlton perfectly grooved, held again – we had yet to concede a goal in the tournament – and the moment of our breakthrough was perfectly conceived and executed.

The goal was designed and made in West Ham, but Alf and the rest of us had put plenty of work into making sure it was incorporated as a prime weapon in our campaign. As a Manchester United player, I knew well enough the threat posed by the Hammers. Their front players would at some point split and make a big move on the near post. At Old Trafford, we always insisted on the need to guard the post. The Argentines were not so aware of the threat and the Peters–Hurst combo delivered the sweetest of knock-out

175

blows. Peters floated a superb ball to the near post and Hurst timed his run and header as if by clockwork. There were thirteen minutes left.

Alf had always said that he felt Argentina were much more of a threat than Pele's ageing and battle-worn Brazil, and when we got into that lead we had the powerful sense that the most difficult obstacle had been cleared from our path, and we could indeed go all the way. For Alf, particularly, there was much satisfaction but little joy in the vital victory. For him, the pleasure of it had been torn away by the behaviour of our opponents, and for once the restraint he prided himself upon broke down. He angrily intervened when George Cohen was about to exchange his shirt with Alberto Gonzalez, and when he came to talk to the press he didn't even try to hold back. He said the Argentines had behaved like animals. The quote caused outrage in Argentina, dismayed the Foreign Office, but what could have been worse than that spitting, gouging, needling travesty of a performance by a team that had the wit and the talent to play their way to the peak of the game?

Despite the reputation I'd gained through the Simon episode, I was as angry as anyone in our dressing room about the way the game had been conducted. Yes, right from schooldays I had played hard. I had always sensed it was the only way I would make it to the top of the game, but I had respected both my opponents and the game. There were rules and I played to the limits of them, but I always recognised their existence. It was as if the Argentines had made their own rules, and their own morality, and they didn't give a damn about whatever anyone thought of them. When they came to our dressing-room door at the end of the game, shouting 'We're gonna kill you,' and the security guards worked to clear the area, I had to agree when big Jack said, 'Let the bastards in, and we'll have a real fight.'

Back in Collyhurst, I had come to recognise that fighting with my fists would never be my forte, but I did fight. I responded when someone said, 'Come on, how would you like some, Nibs or Nebs or Smebs or whatever you're called,' but in my heart I knew I would never be a real fighter. I put everything I had into being a footballer. But on this occasion my blood was up and I was ready to fight, really fight, and the same was plainly true of all our players.

Before the game Bobby Moore had said, 'We accept in our guts it's going to be hard, maybe brutal.' Later he confirmed it, saying, 'They did tug your hair, spit at you, poke you in the eyes, and kick you when the ball was miles away and no one was looking.' Hurst also gave a graphic account of his difficulties as he and Hunt ran at the front through a gauntlet of jabs and kicks and gobs of spit. He said he felt as though he was walking down a dark alley in a strange town. 'At any moment you thought that, for no reason, you would be attacked from behind. Twice, when I was nowhere near the ball, I was kicked on the ankles and each time I swung round there was a sea of blank faces.'

I suppose more than anything it was a collision of cultures; what we held important, they didn't, and vice versa. I have to admit that in those days when referees were so much more lenient, when you could make a tackle from behind, there was always a temptation to bend and to push the rules as far as you could, but some things were beneath contempt – diving, spitting and shirt-tugging, for instance. I played football as hard as I could, and when I found my vocation in the centre of Manchester United's defence, my goal was always to make it as difficult as possible for an attacker. I would tackle him anywhere from the eighteen-yard box to the halfway line, and if it happened that the other team kept the ball, I beavered away to make sure my ground was recovered and that the line held. I always thought, and never more so than on the day Argentina never began to produce the best of themselves, that if you dived, pulled shirts or spat at people, you were accepting the principle of cheating; you were letting the idea take its first bite into you and from there it was just a few strides to becoming rotten.

What I had, I always knew, was a rage to get things right on the field – right for myself and for the team. It led to some ferocious arguments with my own team-mates from time to time, and these included my two greatest friends at Old Trafford, Bobby Charlton and Shay Brennan. When John Giles left the club, they looked after me and guided me through those early days when I felt a bit lost, but when the whistle blew for the start of the action, and the blood rose, no one was spared in the matter of lashings of the tongue. In a league match against Villa, I gave Shay a ferociously worded order as I supervised the defensive wall for a free kick, and he came up to me with a very hard look in his eyes. 'What?' he said. It brought a little chill to my blood and I made a mental note to go a little easier with my friend in the future.

Bobby tended to sulk after I'd spoken to him sharply. On a Monday morning after a weekend league game, when maybe a few words had been exchanged, he would just grunt when I said good morning. But they both knew I adored them, and nobody needed to tell me how much they had done to give me the confidence in myself that helped me fit so quickly into the England dressing room. In just over a year, I had come to enjoy with the England players the same levels of friendship and understanding that were such crucial factors in Manchester United's return to the front rank of the English and European games. The reality of that was confirmed to me as I stood in the Wembley dressing room, just one match away from a World Cup final, and said, 'Hear, hear,' when big Jack bellowed, 'Open the door and bring on the bastards.'

12

KEEPING THE FAITH

THE flame of Catholicism that burned so strongly in my youth and drew me from my bed into the cold Collyhurst dawn, across Rochdale Road and up the stairs to the Convent Chapel and the withering gaze of the high priest of punctuality, Canon Early, slackened considerably over time.

It was something I did as instinctively as pulling on my socks. I didn't question the need to do it, or reflect that a few streets away 'Prod' kids were burrowing deeper in their beds as I watched my cold breath steaming on to my toothbrush. I suppose it is a common experience among cradle Catholics, reaching the point of asking yourself why, and do I need to do this? When something is so strongly enforced, when religion is such a powerful influence on your life, the freedom that comes with being an adult works against the discipline of an old church. But in 1966, as we moved towards our World Cup destiny, there was no question that I was still firmly in its grip. The Latin phrases rolled around in my head, along with the obligations they brought. Emotionally, I was pretty much the same person who rocked back and forth in his grief in St Patrick's church on that cold afternoon when it was confirmed that the Busby Babes had been wiped out, and prayed so hard that there had been

179

some terrible mistake, that somehow God could review the events of the day and with one stroke make them right.

I went to mass every morning of the World Cup. I walked from Hendon Hall through the nearly empty streets to Golders Green, which was a surprise to the few players who got to know about my routine, and not least George Cohen, who has recalled many times his amazement that there was such a thing as a Catholic church in a place that he said probably had more synagogues than Israel.

There was one huge difference, however, between the altar boy and the World Cup player. I no longer walked in terror of what might lurk in the sidestreets and alleyways of the early morning dark. It was as though I was playing out the last acts of boyhood, and what was happening was the conclusion of the rite of passage that started all those years ago when Jimmy Delaney's niece draped me in the shirt of her famous uncle, and a lot of the old fears about the big world and my place in it were falling away. I had a status – and a confidence – that I couldn't have dreamed of when I scurried from the convent chapel with my face burning after Canon Early had snapped his fingers and waved me away. I had a wife and two sons and a place in a potentially unique piece of English football history, and that was more than enough to put a zip into my stride as I marched along the North London pavement.

I also had tremendous companionship. If there was an edge of tension in the loft at Hendon Hall, there were also frequent bursts of laughter. On one memorable occasion I was on the phone to Kay when Ron Springett appeared dressed only in a piece of lingerie. He had got hold of a present I had bought for Kay and chose a deadly moment to do some modelling. My response came a little later when Bally and I arranged for a bucket of water to fall on his head as he left his room.

Not so long ago I was telling Jimmy Ball, Alan's son, about the way I had concealed my church-going from his father each morning as I tiptoed around our room at the hotel, shaving and dressing as quietly as I could, which was not the easiest challenge for someone who had been christened Inspector Clouseau. From across the table, Bally, who is the kind of person who can carry on several conversations simultaneously while also listening in on several others, shouted, 'Jimmy, that is a complete load of bollocks. He woke me up every morning, clattering around, knocking into furniture, screaming out when he cut himself with a razor. It was like trying to sleep through the Calgary Stampede. I just pulled the sheets over my head and said to myself thanks a lot, God. Please tell me this, too, will pass.'

Of course, it did – but not until after considerable torment, for both Bally and me. Five years after my moment of spiritual truth at the Norbreck Hydro in Blackpool, when the choice I had to make was between a piece of steak and a slice of haddock, I was back on the anvil of the conscience that comes to a young Catholic along with the incense, the pomp and the splendour of the brightly coloured vestments. It is something that goes into you very deeply and each night before I went to sleep in the loft room at Hendon Hall I battled with my problem of whether or not to go to mass.

The conflict this time was between my desire to be as well rested as possible for the training and the matches, and the fear that if I changed anything to do with the rhythm of my daily life, if I went missing from the back pew of the church in Golders Green, I might break the spell of winning England, and bring all kinds of disaster on my own head. The dilemma was real enough. The Wembley pitch was extremely draining; when you left it, you had the feeling that you had to get as much rest as you could before your next visit. This had to be balanced against the still vivid memory of what had happened in Blackpool when I ate the meat on the Good Friday – the headache, the vomiting on the field, the own goal and the certainty that when Matt Busby picked his next team my name would be missing. In the World Cup I just couldn't afford to risk such dire repercussions. A formula had been created and in the end it overrode Bally's need for peaceful dawns. I went to mass and England won – I went, we won. It was quite fixed in my mind.

Other benefits accrued from my early morning walks to church. Nobody bothered me as I knelt in my regular pew or walked in the streets. I could think about where I was in my career and my life and what I had to do and, as I have said before, I'd always loved the rituals of the church. It was a different time, of course. People said hello, but they gave you some room of your own, a little space. It is something the World Cup veterans frequently recall when we consider the life, and the pressures, facing today's young footballers. When we went shopping around Hendon, we did so without the fear that sooner or later we would be trapped in a crowd and treated as pieces of public property. We didn't have autograph books stuck in our faces. We could go about the business of taking a breather without the fear of having to snap to attention the moment a bunch of strangers walked, unannounced, into our lives.

As in Lilleshall and Phoenix Park, I loved the morning, inhaling the smell of the grass in the grounds of the hotel and hearing the birdsong. After the crisis brought on by the Simon affair, I felt secure, back in the heart of something very strong, and apart from attending mass, I wanted to build up a routine that would carry me unscathed through the days of mounting pressure. Whenever I went to the stadium for a match, I had to make sure I was wearing all the same clothes, everything, right down to my underpants. If I played at the weekend, I had to remember there was no laundry on Sunday. You could easily be caught out by something like that, letting your matchday socks and underclothes be taken away with the rest of your washing. They had to be kept separate. Blue was the lucky colour. Above all, I always had to wear my blue shirt.

Before the semi-final against Portugal, Alf handed me my most specific instructions since I played for him the first time and Charlie Cooke gave us a bit of trouble in that Under-23 game in Aberdeen. 'Eusebio is capable of giving us a lot of problems, Nobby,' he said, 'so I want you to take him out of the game.' According to George Cohen, I'm supposed to have replied, 'How do you mean, Alf, just for this game, or for life?' I don't recall saying that, but it is possible – but only as a joke. There is no doubt that I was extremely aware of my debt to the boss, But I'm pretty sure it would not have run all the way to the professional assassination of one of the world's greatest players.

Not in question was the fact that Portugal were rated by Alf as a threat to our chances close to the level of Argentina despite their scare against North Korea in the quarter-final game at Goodison Park. When the Koreans raced into a 3–0 lead, it was Eusebio who brilliantly led the counter-attack, scoring four of Portugal's five. After his second, he famously rushed to retrieve the ball from the net of the shock-troops who came from nowhere.

Apart from Eusebio, Portugal had formidable strength distributed through their team. They had a tremendous midfielder in their captain Mario Coluna, great touch and speed on the flanks with José Augusto and Antonio Simoes, and the big striker José Torres had skill on the ground as well as menace in the air. Alf told us we couldn't let up for a second. The Portuguese had the capacity to strike at any hint of weakness, and we had come too far, worked too hard, to throw it all away now. Alf had the ability to underline the realities of any football situation without hammering home his points and creating undue pressure. He just had this knack of guiding us to where we should be, mentally and physically; and fused into everything was the sense that we were indeed on a very important mission, one that could shape the rest of our careers and our lives. Looking around the room during that team-talk, I had the most powerful feeling about the extent of Alf's greatest achievement.

The most significant monument to Alf's work will always be that he built a team in the purest sense. Like putting building blocks in place, he was meticulous about its weight and balance. He had started with five world-class players, Bobby Charlton, Bobby Moore, Jimmy Greaves, Gordon Banks and Ray Wilson, and now, sadly, Greavsie, for one reason or another, had fallen away. But more important than any individual component was the fact that the manager had achieved his most important goal – he had settled on a way of playing that was most effective for eleven players he had come to trust, and who trusted each other. He had cleared away the doubts and the confusion, and he had brought the psychology of the team to a perfect level. We knew what to expect of ourselves and our team-mates.

From time to time, I made fresh evaluations of my team-mates, and whenever I did this, it seemed that they would go up a notch or two in my mind. No goalkeeper ever did more than Gordon Banks to fulfil the greatest demand of his position, which is to generate certainty among his colleagues, to give them the freedom to play their game with the confidence that at any moment, and out of a clear blue sky, disaster is not going to arrive behind their backs. Banksy created a circle of confidence in the defence. You knew that if the ball came in from the right, he would move it out to the left. He would do it unerringly, and if our security system broke down, you always knew that the odds were that the goalkeeper would have the nerve, the reflexes and the sheer talent to prevent us paying too punishing a price. As a bonus, Banksy was one of those rare goalies who gave you the reassuring impression that he wasn't living on the brink of madness and would suddenly, and with killing results, completely mislay the plot. He had a dry, Midlander's humour and I never saw him behave as anything less than a fully fledged gentleman. When the pressure was cranked up against you, it was always possible to say, 'Well, we've got Banksy, we can get through this.'

George Cohen made some terrible accusations against me in his autobiography. He said that when he joined Bally, Roger Hunt, Ray Wilson and me at Buckingham Palace in 2000 when we received our MBEs, the consensus view was that that lounge suits should be worn because the idea of me marching down the Mall in top hat and tails was just too preposterous. He also said that at a moment of glory and joy when I planted a full, smacking kiss on his lips, it was a bit like being snogged by a piece of cold liver. But I forgive him all of that, plus the fact that he sat next to me stony-faced for a full performance of Ken Dodd, one of my favourite comedians, because as a Catholic I still remember that we are all born in a condition of original sin – and also because I love him. If there was ever a better-hearted, fitter, harder-running, more professional footballer than George Cohen, well, I never got to play with him. I have never met a more honest, more decent man, and the fact that he so quickly became an integral part of Alf's grand plan can be easily explained. Alf knew that if he asked him to, George would run through a brick wall, partly for fun. He gave us so much strength and energy along the right side, and in the final stages of the World Cup that flank of Cohen and Ball took on a life and a force all of its own. Dealing with the pair of them brought glazed eyes to world-class defenders, who must have felt like Butch Cassidy and the Sundance Kid when they looked back and saw the posse that just wouldn't stop coming. 'Who are those guys?' In the World Cup, when the crunch came, they were the firm of Cohen and Ball.

Off the field, Ray Wilson, the undertaker, was all dried-out Yorkshire, tough and gritty and speaking only when he felt he had something to say. On the field, you heard his voice constantly. Here, there, he was always offering a team-mate an option, and on the rare occasion he made a mistake, the slip was accompanied by one certainty – he would not be lost from sight. He wouldn't seek the shadows, quite the opposite, in fact. Wilson had moral courage to burn. I never saw him do once what most of the greatest players I have played with or against have done from time to time – he never blinked or flinched at a moment of heavy pressure, and if he did make a mistake, it was as if he was saying, 'Right, here I am, just see if that could possibly happen again.'

At the centre of our defence, Bobby Moore and Jackie Charlton grew in understanding to a point where the results were often nothing less than amazing. Jack's huge legs carried him to the retrieval of balls that seemed certain to put us in desperate trouble, and Mooro was always around, watchful and reading the play as though he was equipped with radar. Jack and I developed a rough working relationship that seemed to succeed in all things except provoking applause from lovers of fine language. A typical exchange was, 'Come on, you little bastard,' Jack; 'Fuck off, you big twat,' me.

Watching Mooro operate in the Cup was stunning, and it brought back a harsh memory of the first time I played against him. It was a league match at Old Trafford and for some time before the game I had made at bit of a study of him. Of course, anyone could see his skill, his polish, but I thought he was a little static, that if you ran at him, really got into him, you would probably ruffle all those sleek feathers. So I put the hustle on him when he was bringing the ball into our half. The next thing I knew was that our goalkeeper, David Gaskell, was picking the ball out of the back of the net. Mooro had sent it in from thirty yards, the ball flicking off my body in its flight. He'd caught me agonising over the need to get at him and to cover my own ground, and he had struck with great bite from behind a front so nonchalant he might have been turning a page of a book.

Mooro didn't shout; he left that to big Jack, Ray and me. He led, minute by minute, second by second, by sheer example. He was so immaculate, on and off the field, that someone once speculated on whether he ever took the fivers out of his wallet to iron them. But behind all the elegance and poise, there was iron, and incredible, instinctive judgement. A supreme example of that came in the game against Portugal at a time when, very unusually for us – a set of defenders who had not conceded a goal in more than 360 minutes of World Cup football – we left ourselves open to the charge that we had sold ourselves.

I had been playing Eusebio quite conservatively but on this occasion we had seriously extended ourselves. Both George and Ray had gone upfield at the same time, and I had decided to push up from a holding role in midfield and go for the ball, but the Portuguese got there first. When I'd made my move, Mooro was out on the left and not covering me. When they knocked the ball off into space, I thought, 'God, this is it. They've caught us out, we could be dead.' At such times your blood runs cold because it is the breakdown of everything you work for, on the training field and in your mind. You strive for control – vital space always occupied, every potential opponent covered until the danger recedes – so that all life and optimism is squeezed out of the other team. One slip and you could be finished, but, as I feared the worst, Bobby came strolling from nowhere on to the ball. When I looked back over my shoulder, I could hardly believe what I was seeing. One moment he was out of it on the left, the next he was closing the door in the middle of our defence. I had always been proud of my ability to read the flow of a game, but this, I thought, was something that had gone off the graph. This wasn't shrewd defence; it was mind-reading.

Another graduate of the West Ham academy, Martin Peters, also had brilliant timing. He was a cool character, and far tougher than his boyish appearance suggested. You might have seen him ghosting into a dangerous position, or passing the ball with all that West Ham style, and imagined that he wouldn't be around when the harder aspects of the game were more apparent. But you would have been wrong, and painfully so if you happened to be marking him. Off the field, Martin was a quiet, lovely lad, and his wife Cath has always had a great sense of humour. In those weeks of the World Cup, however, no one could have shown a sharper edge of ambition than Martin. He could be quite ruthless on the field. He stored up in the back of his mind the cheap shots scored against him, and you could always be sure that, sooner or later, there would be some retribution. It was the tough streak that runs through all good players, but in Martin it was all the more strik-ing, and in a way surprising, because he looked like a kid who didn't need to shave – he still does.

As I've said, Bally was the team-mate with whom I could most easily identify. We were both driven, determined to put everything we had into the game, and when he danced so defiantly on the fivers he had thrown on to our bedroom floor, I felt his pain almost as much as if it was my own. We came from the same part the world, and the same part of life.

Roger Hunt had tremendous moral fibre, and if it bothered him that he never received the credit he deserved, he didn't show it. He never stopped running, never ignored the tough option of that extra stride or two when his body was crying out for rest. He formed a tremendous natural partnership with Geoff Hurst, partly because they shared the hard work, run for run. They trusted each other's instincts, and worked slavishly to give each other vital time and space. They shared another great quality – it was impossible to discourage them. They could miss a chance without it beginning to touch their workrate or their belief that if you did the right things, if you didn't try to find a corner in which to hide, you would get the team where it needed to be sooner or later.

So there they were, a team of formidable ability, but more than anything a group of characters who knew what they wanted and were very confident that they could achieve it. At the heart of this conviction was Bobby Charlton, the best player I ever lined up with, which is something I am able to say because of two facts of my career – I was too young to play alongside Duncan Edwards and I never shared a dressing room with Alfredo Di Stefano.

This remains a massive statement when you think of the blinding talent of Georgie Best, who went out and destroyed Benfica after the boss had told us to take it steady for twenty minutes. When Benfica were a heap of smouldering ruins, Bill Foulkes said to me, 'Didn't anyone mention the plan to George?' And when you think of the thunder and lightning of Denis Law, the man I kicked so relentlessly in that first international game I played at Wembley, partly because he dismissed me as a little English bastard but also because I knew well enough that he could do anything at any time.

No, there is no doubt that Bestie and the Lawman were magnificent players who lit up the sky above Old Trafford, but Bobby, I will always insist, had something that separated him from every other one of my team-mates for both United and England. He had this tremendous energy and grace. When you saw him for the first time up close in the dressing room, you were struck first of all by his size and his strength. While Jack was long and stringy, Bobby was compact and, it seemed, filled with natural power. He had wonderful balance, exploding off either foot, and the first time you saw him play, you knew you would never forget that initial impact on your imagination. It was like seeing for the first time a great waterfall or a range of mountains. When you watched him play, you saw the beauty and the power of the game. It was a true revelation, and once you had it, you would always be a believer.

That's probably the reason why, at an age when both of us should have known better, my old team-mate Paddy Crerand and I had to be stopped from exchanging blows. The dispute followed Paddy's assertion that for Manchester United Eric Cantona was a more important player than Bobby Charlton. For a while we merely debated the issue. Then we roared into a fully fledged argument. Paddy said that Cantona had been a catalyst of Sir Alex Ferguson's Manchester United, and my response was that of course that was true, but when you came to consider the full sweep of the careers of the two players, there was really no comparison. Cantona never helped carry his country to a World Cup, he never shone in the European Cup, and as I pointed out, Bobby reached both of those peaks. The breaking point in the argument, which took us so close to a fight, was when doubt was cast on Bobby's ability to score goals in the important matches.

'Doesn't his World Cup goal against Mexico count – the one that made us believe we could win the greatest trophy in football?' I spluttered. 'Or the one in the European Cup final against Benfica? Or the two that beat Portugal in the semi-final of the World Cup? Or all the forty-nine he scored for England, which twenty years after he stopped playing remains the all-time record? Or the two hundred and fifty-three he scored for United?'

It is never sound policy to argue passionately with Paddy, as the late sportswriter Frank McGhee was no doubt told the morning after he had narrowly escaped a formidable right-hander. Frank, a great but also highly opinionated character, had infuriated Paddy in a bar in Poland, when the press and the players mingled, as was the custom in those days, for an after-match drink. At the precise moment Paddy drew back his right fist, which had earned him respect in the Glasgow of his youth; McGhee's head slumped down into what proved to be a very deep sleep. There was little chance of such salvation for me. Defending the playing reputation of Bobby Charlton was a task that could be accommodated until the first streaks of any dawn. Fortunately, Paddy, whom I have always admired for his skill and liked for his passionate character despite the fact that he was brought in to Old Trafford to take my place, and I were able to disengage from the argument without any blood on the floor.

Later I reflected that in football it can be hard to take an objective view on another player's talent if you don't exactly see eye to eye with him. There was no doubt that Charlton and Crerand experienced a little friction in their relationship from time to time. The fact was that Paddy was a passionate Scotsman and Bobby was an equally fervent Englishman. There was always going to be a point when this didn't make for a blissful working partnership.

It was a combination of Bobby's passion and skill that carried us to the World Cup final. He scored the first goal in the 2–1 win when he sidefooted the ball into the Portuguese net after Hunt had caused havoc; his second, with eleven minutes to go and us leading 1–0, ripped into the net from the edge of the box. It was another Charlton classic, this time set up by Cohen with a ball down the line, and some fine work by Hurst. That should have signalled a cruise to the final through the last ten minutes. Portugal seemed resigned to the fact that their World Cup was over although they had played some good football and big Torres had given big Jack all the work he could handle. Augusto might have been conceding the day when he ran over to Bobby Charlton and shook his hand in the wake of the second goal, but suddenly our assumption of victory was made to seem premature. With just nine minutes to go, Simoes, who had moved over to the right wing, hit a high ball to the far post, Banksy came out and, for once, missed it. As Torres headed for goal, Jack was obliged to handle the ball. Eusebio stepped up to convert the penalty, and it was 2–1. We had conceded our first goal in seven matches, which is still a record for England, and now the high road to the final had filled with unexpected danger.

My contribution in that game, and especially my handling of Eusebio, has been widely praised, and I would have to say that in some ways it was my best, and most controlled, performance, but my most valuable moment went virtually unnoticed. It came in those last, draining minutes after the seemingly beaten Portuguese perked up with the hope brought by Eusebio's penalty. I made the move, the interception of my life.

I was shadowing Eusebio when I saw José Augusto beat Ray Wilson out on our left, and cross the ball. Torres got above big Jack, but he didn't get much power into it. As the ball dropped down a few yards from goal I saw Antonio Simoes coming into the picture. Instinctively I left Eusebio to cover the new threat. Simoes was on the point of shooting when I jabbed out my foot and turned the ball out for a corner. I scoured the newspapers the next day but saw no reference to the incident. It didn't matter because I knew, and my team-mates knew, that in a moment that could have ended all our hopes, I did exactly what I was on the field to do – I read the danger and I cleared it away.

It was something to soften the pain when, in that final desperate phase of the game, Banksy punched my ear. The Portuguese had slung in another high ball, which Banks had come for without shouting his intention. Almost invariably he called out, but not on this occasion. As I went up he punched for the ball, missed it and

192

landed on me. As I lay on the ground gasping for breath, Banks kept saying, 'Nobby, I'm sorry.' When I could, I said, 'Banksy, don't worry – you were doing your job. Never stop coming for the ball.'

The important thing was that we survived, we made it to the final, and although my ear throbbed, I consoled myself with the prospect of a celebratory drink back at Hendon Hall. However, the doctor said that I would need an injection if I didn't want to spend the rest of my life with a cauliflower ear, and I couldn't have a drink because if I did, the injection wouldn't work. I went downstairs with the glum idea that I would be obliged to sip orange juice while my team-mates relaxed in the way that we had after beating Argentina.

However, Alf had once again changed the plot. He made a speech that took away my envy.

'Gentlemen,' he said, 'congratulations on a fine performance and on making the final. You have done well for yourselves, for me and, most important of all, for your country. But tonight I want you to have just two pints. After the Argentina game you were, well, how I can put it, rat-arsed. But not tonight, gentlemen, just two pints because we have a World Cup to win on Saturday. When you do it, I will make sure that you are then, and for quite some time, permanently pissed.'

13

DANCING IN THE SUN

WHEN Saturday, 30 July 1966 finally came, I felt great. I walked briskly to Golders Green for mass. There was rain in the air, and, I decided, a winning destiny. A man in the street said, softly, 'Good luck, Nobby. You're going to do it, mate,' and I said, 'Thanks, I think you're right.'

At dawn I'd seen George Cohen in the lobby of the hotel, and he told me he hadn't slept so well. We seemed to be the first up, though of course I did have that apparently false impression that up in the room we shared, Bally had been left blissfully undisturbed. I told George he would sleep like a baby when the battle was over. He would have the dreams of a winner. I said I could feel it in my bones.

My legs felt light, and I was able to compare the sensation with that feeling I had taken into the FA Cup semi-final with Spurs a few years earlier, when I thought John White had possibly assassinated my career. Then, my legs felt so heavy it was as though I'd been running on sand all day. Today felt so different. It was a day when anything was possible, and there was nothing desperate about my prayers when I knelt in my usual pew at the back of the church.

I thought of all the days that had carried me to this point. I remembered Charlie's speech in the pub on Oldham Road, when he said he would fight for my chances. I thought of the line in John Mulligan's first report – Nobby Stiles will play better than this. I recalled how first my mother, then Kay, had gone out to buy new clothes to make me feel good when I went off on important engagements in international football. So many images came into my mind. I saw my dad watching me from a distance on the train down to Plymouth and the boat to Ireland, and the awe I felt when I met the war hero Monty on a sunny day at Wembley. Inevitably, Coly and big Dunc came into my mind, and Di Stefano bollocking Puskas, who held out his hands and shrugged his shoulders when the big man said that in football you had to fight for everything. Already I had a storehouse of memories and now, at the age of twenty-four, I was hitting a peak that might never be surpassed. I had to play better and fight harder than ever before. It was as simple as that.

Alf reinforced my mood of confidence in the morning teamtalk. He said we had to do it for England and for ourselves; we had done our work well and now we would collect our rewards. Yes, the Germans were a good side, they had discipline and talent, and Franz Beckenbauer, most certainly, was an excellent player. But then we had Bobby Charlton, and in Alf's opinion that was strength beyond anything the Germans possessed. The value of Bobby was particularly relevant to Bally and me, the manager suggested. He knew that in my case he didn't have to stress the point. He had seen me play enough times for United and England to know that I understood my role well enough – win the ball, hard and quick, and give it to Bobby, or for United, Paddy Crerand. I might moan about it sometimes, I might say, 'For fuck's sake, stop giving the ball away, stop taking chances,' and then, *boom*, Crerand had cut a defence clean in two with a forty-yard pass, or Bobby had sent the ball billowing into the back of the net and was skipping away, his arms stretched skywards along with a wisp of hair that sometimes looked like the feather of an Indian brave.

Alf must have felt that Bally needed a little more priming on the importance of delivering to Charlton because he said to him, out of the blue, 'Do you have a dog at home?' When Bally said he did, Alf asked another question. 'Do you take it for a walk, and if you do, do you have a bone with you – or a ball?' The rest of the conversation went like this:

'I take a ball.'

'What do you do with the ball?'

'Well, I throw it for the dog, Boss.'

'What does the dog do?'

'He goes and gets the ball and brings it back to me.'

'Exactly. That's what I want you to do for Bobby Charlton.'

So it was official – Bally and me were dogs of football war.

Alf's assessment of Charlton, we saw in the first minutes of the game, was mirrored by that of the German manager, Helmut Schön. He had decided that Bobby was such a threat he had to be marked by Germany's best player, Beckenbauer. Later Schön admitted that he made a mistake, even though it is also true, as Bobby would probably concede, that the final, despite the fact that he was voted man of the match, wasn't one of his all-time best performances.

But if by his standards Bobby didn't have a great game, there was no doubt that the Germans were most hurt by Schön's decision. Germany had a clutch of fine players, all working well together, as we had been doing on the approach to the final. They had Wolfgang Overath, an excellent midfielder with a great left peg, the quick winger Sigi Held and, in Uwe Seeler, one of the game's most effective strikers. Helmut Haller was an aggressive, clever forward who had made a name for himself in the Italian game, but they had no one else in Beckenbauer's class. Even in his early twenties, Beckenbauer had wonderful skill and maturity, and – an ability Germany would most miss as he shadowed Charlton – the capacity to run on goal and threaten the most serious business.

So Bobby ran, as fluently as ever, and Beckenbauer countered. That was the central battle of the game, and the more intensely it was fought, the more the threat of Beckenbauer as an attacking force faded from our radar screen. Before that game, no one could have realised what a great natural athlete the German was. He had to be to have a chance of matching Charlton's phenomenal energy. The great thing about Bobby was that, like John Giles, he wasn't concerned about how well or badly he was playing. He was always showing for the ball, always accepting responsibility and always covering great stretches of ground.

His total occupation of all Beckenbauer's resources meant that there was an opening for another man-of-the-match, one who might not be as purely talented as either of the great figures locked in hand-to-hand combat but who had enough nerve and heart and raw ability to meet the challenge presented by the greatest day of his football life. We had some formidable candidates for the role. We had the immaculate Mooro, who would never drive us so hard in his cool, quite way. We had Geoff Hurst scoring goals, and Roger Hunt again breaking records for stamina and commitment. Most of all, we had my room-mate Bally. Alf had given him a fetch-and-deliver assignment but as the game wore on, after an unpromising start for us, the clearer it became that the red-haired kid from Walkden – pronounced Wogdon in East Lancashire – had found, when he and his country needed it most, an entirely new level of performance. Bally was fantastic, on fire, and the man who was trying to mark him, the distinguished, Italian-based Karl-Heinz Schnellinger, quickly realised that he was involved in not so much a football match as the ordeal of his life. Long before the end the blond full-back looked hollow-eyed with strain and exhaustion. Bally never stopped. His energy was staggering, almost inhuman. All that passion and ambition flooded into an astonishing effort.

But before Bally imposed himself so strongly, and we got the sense that in a close game, against difficult, tough opponents, we were developing an edge, there were worries that I hadn't anticipated as I came on to the field.

Later, George Cohen said that the doubts he had felt in the morning had still to clear when the buzzer went for us to leave the dressing room. Much later, he also said that he had looked at the film of us walking out on to the field and had seen the strain on his own face. I could only say that he had made a tremendous act of will to play so well, with such conviction, after carrying such doubts. For myself, I was lapping up everything – the edge of excitement, the anticipation of the crowd. When I came up the tunnel and hit the light and heard the roar of the fans, I remembered my father's advice from years ago. 'Look around,' he'd said. 'Enjoy all of it because you might not pass that way again.'

What none of us could enjoy, and least of all Ray Wilson, was that the Germans went into the lead in the thirteenth minute. The goal came from a rare mistake by Wilson. Sigi Held hit a big cross to the far post and, apparently, when Banksy shouted for Ray to leave it, his call was misheard. Ray thought that Banks was calling a warning and headed away too early, which resulted in the ball rolling into a tempting position for Haller to shoot, and the shot squeezed past Banksy and big Jack's outstretched leg. It wasn't quite what we had in mind, and it took a massive effort from Mooro to get us back into the game. It took him six minutes. He went powering down the left, won a free kick, didn't wait for the referee's whistle, and sent a perfect ball into the German box. Hurst headed it in. The rest was hard, battling football. We had our chances, and at half-time Alf was critical of the forwards for snatching at their opportunities. We had the beating of them, said Alf, but in the second half we had to be more ruthless.

If goals remained elusive, the conviction of our play grew in the second half. Ball was inexhaustible, wearing the Germans down to breaking point, and in the seventy-eighth minute we had the breakthrough, and believed that the job was just about over. It wasn't a classic. Bally sent a corner to the edge of the box, from where Hurst shot on goal. The ball was blocked by the defender, Horst-Dieter Hottges, and flew into the air. Peters, beating big Jack by half a yard, reached the ball before it hit the ground and shot past goalkeeper Hans Tilkowski from close in. A Charlton special would probably have been more uplifting, but we were still ready to weigh Martin's goal in gold. We had the game, and the World Cup, and now all we had to do was turn a few screws.

As I saw it, we just about deserved the spoils. Both teams had played hard, without managing truly to punish the opposition, but on balance we had posed the more consistent threat, and there was no doubt that, thanks to Bally, we had carried the game to the Germans. But for some time – and to me it seemed endless – that would be old, meaningless opinion. The Germans, so sickeningly I felt as if I'd been disembowelled, brought the game back to life when it should have been dead. The disaster came with just a minute to go.

The referee decided that Jack Charlton had fouled Held, but the big man angrily insisted the German had 'made a back' for him and conned the official. While he was doing that, I was dragging the wall into place and checking with Banksy that he had a clear sight line. He nodded, but suddenly our goalkeeper's vision was far from clear. The powerful Lothar Emmerich, who had a poor game, smashed the free kick into the wall and as the ball bounced around in the box, Wolfgang Weber got a foot to it and put it past Banks.

Alf was still one rallying speech away from fulfilling his mission. Again he did it brilliantly. He said that we had won the World Cup once – now we simply had to do it again. He made it seem entirely possible. He said our duty to England would be completed successfully.

Ten minutes into extra time, I made my last clearly conscious contribution to the game. It was the first phase of the most controversial goal in the entire history of the World Cup. Big Jack later said the ball I sent into the right corner was just me playing for time, and I hadn't had a call from Bally, who scampered on to it. That, I informed Jack, was complete bollocks. The ball was totally intentional. I knew Bally had the beating of Schnellinger – by now it was written in the sky over Wembley – and I played the ball in for him. As in all other things that day, Bally immediately saw his opportunity. He raced on to the ball and put in an early cross. Hurst beat the exhausted Willie Schulz to the ball and sent his shot crashing against the underside of the crossbar and down.

Did it cross the line? Roger Hunt threw his arms in the air and the linesman, Tofik Bakhramov from Azerbaijan, told the Swiss referee Gottfried Dienst that it was a goal, a decision that every member of the German team will die saying was wrong. Me? I accepted the goal with thanks. It came at the end of a long, tough, glorious road and I did feel we were the better team, if only by a fine margin. The old film doesn't prove the case either way, and in the state of physical and mental weariness that was beginning to overtake me I could only thank God that the verdict was in our favour. At that moment, any other thoughts drained away with the last of my strength.

The fact is that the rest of the game, including the final moments of drama when, with just a minute left on the clock, Hursty raced away to score his third goal, has always remained a blur. My memory returns only at the point when I got hold of

George Cohen, kissed him and told him, after he asked me what the hell I was doing, 'George, we won the fucking World Cup.' He seemed a little embarrassed that I was lying on top of him in front of the royal box at the time. I felt as though I had come out of a long black tunnel into the light.

The darkness came when, with the score locked at 3–2 for us in the second half of extra time, I ran ahead of the ball and took a pass from Bally in the outside-right position. The roar of the crowd swelled as I raced on the overlap. I looked up and said to myself, 'Yes, near post, I'll go for that,' but when I came to make contact with the ball something shocking and terrifying happened. I felt everything go. The sensation was of *whoosh*, and everything had left me. The ball trickled off the toe of my boot and over the line. The crowd sighed and fell silent. I just stood there, empty, and one concern was that my bowels had emptied, which would have been a terrible embarrassment because unlike my team-mates I didn't wear a jock strap or a slip beneath my shorts. But if my worst fear proved to be unfounded, I still had a dreadful problem. In the last desperate minutes of a World Cup final, and at a time when the fresh legs of substitutes were not available, it took a tremendous effort just to move. Bally had run to take a return pass and as he came past me, rooted to the spot where the breakdown had come, my socks around my ankle, his eyes were blazing. 'Move you bastard, move,' he screamed. Bally was on fire and prepared to run for ever. Before the mist came I knew the best I could do was drag one foot in front of the other. Later, I asked my team-mates if they had noticed anything happening to me, and they said no. I had played on. I had got through it.

I can't remember going up the steps to collect my medal from the royal box. There is a picture of me looking up into the stands and I know by my expression that I was looking for Kay, but I cannot tell you if I spoke to her before I went down on to the field and danced my jig. Kay reports that she doesn't think we talked before the moment of my almost total national exposure because she has been haunted for thirty-six years by the fact that she wasn't able to say some precious words at the moment of my supreme football achievement. They wouldn't have been, I have to say, tender words along the lines of 'Nobby, you are my great hero and I adore every bone in your body.' What she would have said, it turns out, was, 'For God's sake, put your bloody teeth in.'

From that flood of celebration, a few points of memory do survive the years. One was Alf's reluctance to join us in front of the crowd. 'You won the Cup,' he insisted. 'This is your time.' Alf was emphatic that he wouldn't move from the shadows of our great day. He said he already had all the satisfaction he had ever desired as a football manager. He had won for his country; he had fulfilled what he had always considered the squandered potential of our national game and our football character.

The greatest thing was the companionship we all felt and in the next twenty-four hours or so there were many examples of this, the most basic – and one that didn't seem anything at the time – probably being our spontaneous and unanimous decision to split our £22,000 winning bonus equally among the squad, irrespective of how many games each individual had played. Mooro knew us well enough to take an instant decision. Alf had gathered us together and said, 'Gentlemen, we have something to discuss. You have been awarded a bonus of £22,000 to be shared between you. One way of doing it would be for everyone to have a basic £500, with extra money being paid for appearances.'

Without a moment's hesitation, our captain stood up and said, 'No, Boss, it will be £1,000 each. We were all in this together and that's how we will stay.'

He hadn't previously consulted Banks, Cohen, Wilson, Jack

Charlton, Bobby Charlton, Roger or me – the seven players who, apart from himself, had appeared in every game in the finals. He knew that it was unnecessary. We had come to know each other very well and it seemed that after the battle had been won, this was the final, and perfect, expression of the team. spirit our manager had worked so carefully to build.

Alf nodded, and said, 'That's very good, Bobby. Somehow, I rather thought you would say that. Now we have a little more celebrating to do.'

I have to say we were not overwhelmed by the generosity of the Football Association. We had heard the Germans were being paid quite a bit more, maybe as much as £10,000 a man just for reaching the final, and it didn't help that later we found out that because of incompetence in their office, the FA were paying far more tax than was necessary. A lot of money had been given for ground improvements for the World Cup, and all of it qualified for tax relief, but because they didn't make the proper claims, the FA were paying £250,000 to the government.

When tax was taken away from my share of the team bonus, I had just enough to buy myself out of the business that had caused me so much worry through the summer, and had provoked me to make so many phone calls throughout the tournament. When the Germans were beaten we knew we had many reasons to celebrate, but a burst of wealth certainly wasn't one of them.

Down the years, I have little memory flashes of the twenty-four hours or so that followed the World Cup final, some of them triggered by old newsreel or a fading newspaper. At a sporting night I attended, a prize in the raffle was a copy of the *Sunday Mirror* dated 31 July 1966. Its front page reported that London had not had such a night of wild celebration since Victory in Europe twenty-one years earlier. Looking at that and seeing the youthful, smiling face of Bobby Moore brought back all the excitement, and when I thought about it again, it had so little to do with money and was so much more about a sense of achievement, of fighting our way to something that would always be part of the folklore of the nation.

From Wembley we travelled through crowded streets, with the hoots of car horns and cheers ringing in our ears, to the Royal Garden Hotel in Kensington where we went out on to the balcony and waved to the crowd. The noise was thunderous and I think it put most of us into a kind of trance as we met our wives briefly before being guided into the banquet that had been arranged for the players and officials of the four semi-finalists, and of course great banks of FA and Fifa 'blazers'. It was around this time that a little reaction set in. You live at a terribly intense pitch for all those weeks, you play, literally I had discovered, to the point of complete physical and mental breakdown, and then you are asked to sit around and listen to a lot of speeches. It is not quite what your spirit craves. You want to be around your loved ones and your team-mates, and as the evening wore on we became increasingly restive.

The burst of renewed energy that came to me in those first few minutes after the game, when I did my dance and waved my medal to show to Kay, was draining away again and we were increasingly irritated by the fact that our wives had been ushered away to another room in the hotel before the banquet started. There they were given drinks and snacks and told that they could watch the official proceedings on closed-circuit television. Perhaps we were conditioned by our times, but our protests didn't quite turn into rebellion. There would be no tabloid headlines screaming 'World Cup team storm out of banquet', but perhaps there might have been if Mooro hadn't whispered into Alf's ear. We said to Bobby, 'Look, we haven't seen our wives for three and a half weeks. They've been sitting at home looking after the kids and now they're shoved off in another room like second-class citizens.' Alf reacted quickly enough. He came to us and said, 'Thank you for everything, gentlemen, now off you go and have a good time. Most certainly, you deserve it.'

Mooro said that we would all be welcome at the Playboy Club, which seemed like a suitably glamorous place to reward Kay for all the weeks she had been without my help while attending to the nappies and the bottles of our baby Peter and the demands of our toddler John. Bally and John Connelly and their wives, Lesley and Sandra, joined Kay and me and we all squeezed into the first cab racing up Park Lane to the Playboy. When we arrived there was a great throng around the door and we were greeted with cheers, but our hopes of being taken to a table and perhaps being served a glass of champagne were immediately frustrated. A flunky told us that we should stand behind a rope and wait for a photographer to arrive. A photo session had been arranged. I think I spoke for our party when I said, 'Fuck off.'

Fortunately, we had another option. Before we had left the Royal Garden, Geoff Hurst said that he and his wife Judith were going down to Danny La Rue's club and we were welcome to join them. We called another cab and headed for Danny's place. There we found a real welcome. We were taken to a big table and given jugs of beer and Bacardi, and after a brief introduction, we were allowed to get on with our celebration. What impressed us most was that Danny didn't make some big publicity occasion out of our visit. There were no phone calls to the newspapers or television and when we left in the small hours of the morning, not altogether steadily, the maître d' dismissed our attempts to pay, saying, 'Danny told me that on no account should I take a penny from you. He's just delighted you came to celebrate in his place.'

Some time later I went to a dinner at a hotel in Stockport and was told that Danny was a guest. I got on the house phone and when I announced myself, Danny said, 'Oh, hello love.' I said I just wanted to thank him and added that he had made the night for us after we had won the World Cup. He said, 'You have nothing to thank me for – it was the best night we ever had at the club.'

I remember that night in Danny La Rue's for many things, and not least the fact that from time to time we would turn to each other and say, 'We did it, we won the World Cup,' and then lapse into silence for a little while as we tried to take it in.

I also thought of another place where, many years before, I had celebrated football victories. It was a little room above a coalyard in Chapman Street in Collyhurst, near where the Kidd brothers grew up. We went there to celebrate the victories of St Pat's. We had tea and sandwiches and a few fancy cakes, and we thought it was great. At Danny La Rue's I thought of how far I had come from the room on stilts above the coalyard.

The day after our great night we were taken, with our thick heads, to a small theatre where we were shown the Pathé News film of the game. It was engrossing. It took me back to some of the action that had become fuzzy and blurred by sheer fatigue. I was amazed all over again by the vitality of Bally, his willingness to cover every relevant blade of grass, and the calmness of Moore, and when Hurst ran away to score the clinching goal it was if I was seeing it for the first time. I was also relieved by my own presence on the big screen. I didn't quite look like a man on the verge of collapse.

Later, as we flew to Dublin where our sons had been staying with the Giles family, Kay mentioned something that happened in the theatre which I had completely missed as I peered up at the screen through my spectacles of the year. She noticed that early in the running of the film, Alf got up and went to the elderly lady usherette who had shown us all to our seats. She was standing to one side. All the seats had been taken. Alf took her by the hand and led her to his seat. He watched the rest of the film standing up. Kay said that Alf was a good-looking man who seemed to care a lot about other people, however strong he was in his ambition.

Maybe she had seen what lay at the core of England's World Cup. It was the strength – and the heart – of the man who had always said that we would win the greatest prize in football.

14

VICTORY IN EUROPE

MY fondness and respect for Alf Ramsey, and my gratitude to him, is on the record now, and in many ways all those feelings I have for him are less complicated than the ones that come to me when I think of the other legendary manager who shaped my football life. Sir Matt Busby was a great man and a great character, but as I have already said, his role as the boss of Manchester United meant that from time to time he had to make decisions that caused me pain and, right to the end of my career with United, moments of disillusionment.

Matt did amazing things for a great football club, and if at times people were hurt, if they thought well, here is this great, kindly father figure who is capable of taking decisions that can upset and even shatter a player's hopes, they also had to understand that it was to a large extent the nature of his job. You show me a successful manager and I'll show you someone who is tougher, I know, than I could ever be. I learnt much later that another knight of Old Trafford, Alex Ferguson, could also be hard when it came to doing the necessary business of discarding an individual who for one reason or another no longer fitted the club's needs. You might feel that your guts have been taken away, but if you have been around the game for a while, you know, when you get right down to it, that it is the way the game has always been, and is always likely to be. They never made a silver cup for sentiment in football.

It was a job that Matt did superbly and I'm sure that in their many conversations, when Ferguson tackled the difficult task that faced him when he arrived from Scotland and Busby was the wise old owl up in the little office he was given by the club in his last years, the new man was given the soundest advice. Although their styles are quite different, it is easy enough to pick out the common characteristics that shaped the huge success of both of them. Matt grew up in the coalfields of Ayrshire and lost his father in the First World War. Alex came from the tough ship-building school of Govan in Glasgow. Both of them brought the distinguishing marks of all the great managers – before they won or lost a game in the football big-time, they knew, as did Bill Shankly, Jock Stein and Don Revie, the unforgiving hardness of life off the field.

At vital stages in the development of United, over an astonishing period of twenty-five years, Busby worked against tremendous odds. Unlike Alf, Matt had to live with players week in and week out. He knew their strengths and weaknesses, and always had to ask the questions, is this lad the best available to me now, and is he going to help me and the people who pay my wages win the big trophies? Of course, he didn't have the luxury of picking those he considered the best, or most suitable, players in the land, plonking them in an England shirt and watching them develop, or not, over a few games. Alf could discard a player, make a clean break, say thanks but no thanks and get on with the job. Matt had to weigh things in a different way; when you're a running a club, you sometimes have to make the best of a difficult situation, even if you do have great resources, and when you do cut away players, you are not just denying them the honour of playing for their country. You are maybe taking away their living or, as eventually happened to me, requiring them to uproot themselves and move their families to another part of the country, one they don't know and really don't want to know. They don't have after-care for old professional footballers who come to the end of the line still dreaming their dreams.

I'm saying this now because it may just help to provide some understanding of the fresh joy and then the pain that came to me in the years following the World Cup when, suddenly and in my own way, I was one of the kings of Old Trafford. After that, I had injuries and learned that in football, at least in my day, however well you thought you were doing – I got a very nice £60-a-week rise, which took me up to £130 – there was no guarantee of a soft landing. In life, you have to die. In football, you have to face the day when you are done, knackered, and you don't really have any-thing left but an uncertain future. This isn't to moan about the old footballer's life; it is just to say how it was, and how, in its basics, it will always be.

Before I got to know all that, I had a wonderful extension of the glory that came with England at Wembley. For a few more brilliant years I knew how it really felt to be one of the élite, one of those untouchable first-teamers who drew my envy and awe when I was a kid fresh from Collyhurst and they worked at the Cliff and on the concrete outside Old Trafford. I might not have had the glamour of Bobby or George or Denis, but I knew I was an integral part of the reborn club as we swept to a second cham-pionship in 1967, and put ourselves in a position to move on the dream that had been snatched away from Busby at Munich ten years earlier.

My understanding with Bill Foulkes had become tight and instinctive and there was a great balance in the team. Best, Law and Charlton provided the glamour and the goals; Foulkesy and me in the centre, Tony Dunne and Shay Brennan on the flanks, shut down the opposition, and with big Alex Stepney in goal we knew we had a defence that could fight and contain the best that Europe could offer. We also knew that in Matt Busby we had a manager who had one supreme strength – he knew players and, when they had passed their tests, he trusted them.

His style of discipline had seeped into our blood. He didn't shout; he didn't rave. He waited for something to happen that he could act upon, that he could react to with all the authority that he had refined over the years, and once again you saw his force in a new and dramatic light. Once, when he became concerned that our card-playing had reached a level where it might cause problems to the spirit and unity of the team, he didn't give us a big lecture on the perils of gambling. He just came up in the middle of a session, picked up the cards and threw them out of the window of the team bus. No one said a word.

One of the greatest memories of the Busby style is of the time we lost 7–2 to Sheffield Wednesday in that period when I was first making my way in the team. We lost the game at Old Trafford. United didn't lose by that margin to anyone, anywhere, and for it to have happened in front of our fans had sent pain and anger into the boss's bones. That was clear enough, soon enough, but not too soon. He gave us a little time to grasp fully what had happened. When we came into the dressing room from the field he was standing at the treatment table, a big man immaculately dressed and with his face turned to stone. We sat on our benches, heads down, without anyone uttering a peep.

A few days earlier we had produced a great result at Wednesday's Hillsborough ground. It was a 2–2 draw and fiercely fought. I remember it well for two main reasons. My future brother-in-law had a tremendous game, and I had a real battle with one of the toughest midfielders in the game, Tony Kay. Kay, who later went to prison after being convicted of taking bribes, was extremely talented as well as being very hard. All that Saturday afternoon we kicked lumps out of each other and as I walked off the field I said to him, 'Hey, I'll see you at Old Trafford on Wednesday night. There will be sixty-five thousand in the ground, and I'll be on the field. Don't forget.'

'Some fucking threat, that was,' I said to myself, as I stared down at my boots. Wednesday cut us to pieces and Kay played particularly well. Finally, after what seemed like an age had passed, Busby moved away from the treatment table and came to each of us in turn. He just looked into our eyes, one by one, for about a minute. He didn't say a word. His eyes just bored into us. You could, I thought, have heard a sparrow cough back in Collyhurst. When he had completed his circle of the dressing room he walked to the door, turned and issued his famous, deadly phrase. 'That is not Manchester United,' he said before going out and quietly shutting the door behind him. We hardly moved or spoke for another ten minutes.

Above everything else, Busby had instinct. He could get to the heart of a player and bring the best out of him. In that, he was very similar to Alf. Ramsey put a lot more detail into his work, and was particularly keen on working on corners and free kicks, but Busby did not neglect the essentials. On Fridays he would get out the blackboard and tell us what was expected, and not always in the broadest terms, although he knew that all the ground would be covered by the great organiser Jimmy Murphy. Busby had a nose for possibilities, a hunch before vital games. In the run-in to the 1967 title, when we got a little jaded with the pressure of games, he injected me into the forward line for two games against Fulham. I scored on both occasions, which was a big lift towards our title win.

In 1968 Busby was consumed by his desire to win the

European Cup. He had been shattered by the semi-final defeat by Partizan Belgrade in 1966 after George Best fell injured after devastating Benfica in Lisbon, and although we were again among the title contenders going into the spring, there was no doubt about the boss's priority. He had lost his brilliant young Babes pursuing the European dream, and he knew that there might never again be a chance as strong as this. His will to succeed in this ambition was extraordinary, and sometimes I felt that part of the fuel for it was the pain he felt every day of his life after Munich – physical and mental pain. Every day he would go into the treatment room and have Ted Dalton work on his body. Dalton would work him hard and then there would be a crack and you would hear Busby groan. Every day he needed that work from the physiotherapist and when it was happening his face would turn grey. Every day Dalton had to re-align the boss's body.

Perhaps because of the intensity of his feelings, the fact that to him the European Cup had become as much a crusade as a football tournament, he did get more anxious than I'd ever seen him when we travelled to the frozen coalfields of Silesia in Poland for the quarter-final against Gornik in Chorzow. There may be tougher places than Chorzow to play an away game, but I will take a lot of convincing. Bestie had given us a one-goal lead from the first leg at Old Trafford and we all agreed that we could have done with at least one more. We respected the Poles a lot. They were a coming force in the game and they played with wonderful heart and determination. They also had pace and skill.

Busby was especially concerned about the strength, pace and quality of Gornik's star striker Lubanski. He was a brilliant figure, proud and positive in everything he did; he was the kind of opponent whom you admired, even loved, as you tried all you knew to stop him any way you could. Sometime later it was devastating to hear that Lubanski had lost a son in a car accident.

I made my first overhead kick in the street in Collyhurst with my friend Tony Lucas. Now I do it in World Cup action against French defender Robert Budzinksi.

Geoff Hurst breaks Argentina with a superb header past Antonio Roma. It was a moment of destiny made in West Ham – Martin Peters delivered the cross.

Martin Peters heads for goal against France – a stylish effort from a class player.

Bobby Moore and I embrace aft the semi-final defeat of Portugal My mission had been to take Eusebio out of the game.

Battling with Eusebio – the biggest challenge of my career.

bby Moore offers the World Cup for Alf to kiss and I tell him he should take his
ute. But he said, 'You players won it – you take the cheers.'

e job is done. Martin Peters and I share a joke. Bobby Charlton (*extreme right*)
s his own thoughts.

The Playboy Club said we should wait for a picture shoot. Danny La Rue's club w[...] more hospitable. John and Sandra Connelly (*left*), Kay and I, Lesley and Alan Bal[...] and Judith and Geoff Hurst enjoy the night of triumph.

The European Cup is ours – ten years after I wept for the Babes, I hold up the trophy. Shay Brennan, Alex Stepney and Paddy Crerand also show how they feel.

The Stiles at play. John (*left*) and Peter take over the slide. Robert is not overly impressed.

go back to Old Trafford with Middlesbrough the FA Cup, and the welcome is warm. We rced a draw, but lost the replay 3–0.

After the game at Old Trafford I get a hug from the Lawman, but the good days are stretching thin.

I lead Middlesbrough against Bobby Moore's England Select for Harold Shepherdson's testimonial – Harold (*left*) and Sir Alf watch as referee Pat Partridge waits for the drop of the coin.

The Preston team fighting to revive a great old club. *Left to right*: Harry Hubbick (trainer), Bobby Charlton (manager), Peter Robinson (chief scout), Matt Woods (trainer) and Jack Crompton (assistant manager).

Sir Matt Busby, flanked by George Best and Francis Burns, is back with his boys – twenty-five years after winning the European Cup.

John Stiles – he had a touch of elegance I never had, but he also had the burden of being the son of a famous player.

John Mulligan, my first football coach, tells the 'This is Your Life' audience that they don't make players like Nobby Stiles any more. I say that must be because he is retired.

Me and the MBE – it was nice to get hold of it thirty-four years after winning the World Cup.

The gang of grandchildren made me count my blessings. *At the front*: Caitlin and Harry. *Behind, from left to right*: Megan, Chris, Alex, Emma and Cameron.

Lubanski was by far the greatest threat to us, and one reason why Paddy Crerand argued that we should insist on playing the tie despite terrible conditions of freezing snow. It was true that we liked to play open football and the pitch would not be suitable for such an approach, but Paddy said that, apart from anything else, the hard, slippery surface would work against the danger man Lubanski. In the end, Busby decided to go with Paddy's instinct and although we could probably have had the game postponed, we said it should go ahead. We kept our lead in a ferocious battle in the biting cold.

Although the action could not have been harder, or more tense, the memory of the game is overwhelmingly warm. The Poles were poor but fiercely proud, and extremely friendly. In the cold, they passed warm vodka to our fans, and when I think of that and then consider all the horrors on the terraces that ate into football in the late sixties and seventies and are still with us today, I feel a terrible sadness. The game was annexed by those who didn't really love it, but latched on to the violence that admittedly did happen on the field. There, it was part of something far wider and deeper than mere aggression, and waged, in most cases, with great respect between even the hardest of players. A brilliant example of how things could be, even in the most competitive of atmospheres, is provided by that frozen night in Chorzow. We went back to our hotel muffled against the cold but warmed by what we had seen and heard – and achieved. Busby sat up in the front of the bus and any eye contact was the kind you could bear.

That was something I couldn't say about our visit to the concentration camp of Auschwitz, which was just a short drive from our hotel. Even though we had been warned about the bleakness of the place, the absence of birdsong and the terrible sense of what had happened there, we were not prepared for the experience. I saw everything, the cells, the gas chambers, the rooms where experiments were carried out, the wall where so many were lined up and shot, the piles of children's shoes, the pictures of the kids on the walls, and the little offices at the corners of the blocks, which still had the old telephones and the notepads for compiling the lists of execution squads. You could look out of a window of a room where so many had faced death and you could see the railway sidings where thousands were unloaded in what would be the last days of their lives. It was all the more haunting because it was a beautiful, clear winter's day.

You wanted to get out of there and hug your children. For a long time afterwards I had bad dreams of Auschwitz, and for a little while at least the business of winning or losing a football game didn't seem to be a matter that totally occupied the centre of the world. But football was my life, and still my future, and now that included the possibility of adding a European Cup winner's medal to the one they gave me for winning the World Cup.

We drew Real Madrid in the semi-final and when Busby heard the news his expression tightened a little. As a football team, we had been handed a great challenge. As a man, Busby was invited to go back to the most emotional phase of his long career. He had to battle with the club that had set him his greatest football goal, and laid down the standards that his brilliant young team had been striving to meet when they were cut out of the sky.

Again, we could take only a single-goal lead to a foreign field, and for much of the drama played out in front of the crowd of more than 100,000 at the Bernabeu stadium, it didn't seem to us nearly big enough.

The match was a special challenge for me because it was one of the few occasions, under both Busby and Ramsey, when I was given specific marking instructions. My man was Amaro Amancio, a player who had a lot of Gento's speed and rather more subtlety.

He did the thing players least like – he ran at them, offered them the ball and then struck very quickly.

The first half was a disaster for all of us. They scored the goal that put them level early and the crowd went mad. By half-time it looked as if another European mission would end in disappointment. They were winning 3–0 in the game, 3–1 on aggregate, and the fact that their failure to score at Old Trafford was a disadvantage under the away goals rule seemed quite irrelevant. I was particularly distressed because Amancio had scored one goal, a toe-poke from close in, and had left me with a tightening thigh which required heat treatment at the interval. I'd chased him down the line on the right, forcing him on to his weaker left peg, and the ball had run out for a goal-kick. As Alex Stepney prepared to take the kick and we trotted into position, Amancio suddenly whacked me. He gave me a tremendous kick on the thigh, and right away I feared that I wouldn't last the game. Apart from his involvement in the goal, Amancio didn't have a lot to show for his first-half work, as he didn't at Old Trafford, but he had done something off the ball that had created the possibility of him causing mayhem against a half-crippled marker.

Despite my own fears during the break, I noticed that Busby was at his most brilliant. His voice was calm, and if someone had arrived from another planet he would never have guessed that he was looking at a man whose greatest ambition was just one more Madrid goal away from completely unravelling.

'Now come on, boys,' said Busby, 'you're still in the game. Just play your football, believe in yourselves.' There was no desperation in his voice. He just went around spreading a bit of calmness and belief. This was the best of Matt, the man who made you want to run through a brick wall if it meant that you didn't have to look at him and see reproach in his eyes.

My own conviction was that one way or the other I had to do

Amancio. Even though they'd put the heat into my leg, it was still tightening and I realised he was going to get away from me, and if that happened we could forget about getting to the final. But suddenly we were back in the game and the great noise from the vast terracing went quiet. David Sadler, a very underrated player who could both defend and attack, scored early in the second half – and, off the ball, so did I.

The build-up was the same as before. I shadowed Amancio down the line, straining to keep up with him, and the ball ran out of the play. This time I had my eyes on him as Stepney prepared to kick. When the ball was in the air, I ran beside Amancio and said, 'Oi,' and when he turned I gave him a good smack. He went down and the Spanish fans went crazy. Despite the din I heard one of my team-mates shout, 'Fucking hell, Nob.'

It was a desperate thing to do, and it could easily have thrown the game because if I'd been sent off, our chances of holding a very quick Real team who already had the lead were pretty slim. But fortunately, neither the referee nor the linesman saw the incident. I ran up to the referee, pointed to Amancio sprawled on the field and said, 'He's injured, ref,' which was a perfectly accurate statement. Amancio stayed on the field but no longer to any damaging effect.

Like the Simon incident at Wembley, hitting Amancio could have brought a terrible shadow to my career, and later I shuddered just imagining a typical headline – 'Stiles sent off in Night of Shame'. But if Busby saw what happened, he didn't mention it, and soon enough it was in the margins not of a 'Night of Shame' but a 'Night of Glory' – a night when, in our different ways, we all delivered for Busby.

Had the boss questioned me, my reply would have been different from the one I gave Ramsey when he asked me about the tackle on Simon. When Alf asked if I meant it, I could have sworn my answer on oath. No, I didn't mean it. In the case of Amancio, there could be no excuses or pleas of mitigation. It was a brutally simple matter. My leg was tightening all the time, I couldn't sprint flat out and I just thought, 'Bollocks, I've got to do something – the bastard attacked me and maybe ruined our chances.' So I whacked him. He disappeared as a threat and I tucked in alongside Bill Foulkes and did the job that had become my trademark. There was still so much to do, however. At half-time we were 3–1 down in the game, and 3–2 on aggregate. David Sadler's goal early in the second half put us level and with the away goals advantage. But we knew we couldn't sit back and let Real come to us.

When we needed to take the game to our opponents, I tended to go forward, but Foulkes kept yelling in my ear, 'Stay back, we can't give anything away, keep it tight, keep it fucking tight.' And then Bill Foulkes, who usually went upfield only when we won a corner, did something extraordinary. George Best went on a run and pulled the ball back and there, running on to it, was our big, stopper central defender, crashing it into the top of the net. I forgot my injury and ran the length of the field and threw myself on to the back of the big man, who turned to me and said, 'What did I tell, you little bastard – get back.' Real needed two goals now. We had ten minutes to survive, and we did it with a lot of scampering and a lot of covering. Our nerve held, and I noted with satisfaction, as the crowd roared its team on, that Amancio, who had been such a threat, was scarcely visible.

I suppose the Amancio incident poses a few questions about what kind of player I was. Well, there was no question that I played hard but I also tried to operate on some kind of rough sense of justice. In my defence, I have to say it is necessary to understand the climate of the game back then in the sixties. In English football there were no divers and it would have been unthinkable to try to get an opponent sent off unfairly. There were various illegal ways of doing that, but conning the referee into a wrong decision was not included. You may say this was selective morality and you would be right. In the case of Amancio, he got away with something that wasn't right, and was potentially devastating to my team. The match officials had completely missed it. So I took the football law into my own hands. I do not congratulate myself. I knew at the time that I'd taken a risk that could have backfired horribly, but the decision had come in a flash, and when I hit Amancio I wasn't just getting back at him for his attack on me; I was doing what I thought was right for the team.

My game was hard and, like those of Tommy Smith and Norman Hunter, the tough men in the trenches of Liverpool and Leeds, it wasn't about the cloak and dagger approach. You tackled, you went for the ball, and if in the process you shook up an opponent, told him you were there, well, that was a bonus, and in that sense I was only fulfilling Matt Busby's order. 'Show him you are there, Norrie, in the first ten minutes,' he used to say.

There is a difference between a dirty player and someone whose job was to tackle hard and up front, and I always argue that when everything was equal, I stayed on the right side of that line. The job Matt Busby, and Alf Ramsey, expected me to do was well enough defined. I was a reader of the game and a tackler. I had to tackle, tackle and do some more tackling. I had to sort people out. I had to win the ball because without it, the greatest talent in the world couldn't begin to operate.

I had also seen very good players have their careers threatened by one bad tackle. John Giles was nearly ruined by a tackle by Johnny Watts of Birmingham. After the game I went with him to the hospital. He was told that he just had bad bruising, but he was in agony, and the following day they took him to a specialist in St John's Street. There, he was X-rayed and it turned out that he had a broken leg, a hair-line fracture, and his ankle was out of its socket. John quickly acquired the reputation of being a hard man, but I know that after the Watts tackle, when he feared that his career might be over, he vowed to look after himself on the field very carefully. If that required a pre-emptive strike he would do it. Well, he had a young family at home who needed looking after. He would do the kind of thing I did in the Bernabeu stadium. He would do what he could to survive, and have his team succeed.

Rightly or wrongly, I had done something quite vital to an achievement that amounted to far more than survival in Madrid. I had helped carry United to what Busby always believed was the club's destiny – a European Cup final. Our opponents were Benfica and, encouragingly for Bobby Charlton and me so soon after our triumph with England, it was to be played at Wembley stadium. My task, with the help of David Sadler, was also familiar. I had to stop Eusebio, again.

Eusebio, a great player, was frustrated once more but this time, because of United's way of playing, the job had to be tackled differently, and in the end the margin was much finer than it had been in the World Cup semi-final. For one vital thing, Alex Stepney had to pull off a big, unforgettable save.

I played in front of the back four for England, and in the centre of it for United, so when we dropped deep, out of necessity, Sadler was required to pick up Eusebio. We spent the night swapping him over. It worked well enough until the last minutes before we went into extra time locked at 1–1. I had to make a decision, one of thousands that face a professional in the course of his career, but on this one, Matt Busby's European destiny might just have hung. Antonio Simoes broke quickly with the ball after Shay Brennan had gone forward in an attack. I was tracking Eusebio, with Bill Foulkes behind me guarding José Torres. Shay was making his ground back and Tony Dunne was out on the left. We were paying the price of our big commitment to going forward, but as Simoes played the ball in front of him, I made my decision to go for it, to break up the attack at source. I felt that Simoes was pushing the ball too far forward, and if I moved forward I could get there and shut down the danger. I was reassured that the ever-dependable Foulkesy was behind me. What I didn't know was that just as I set off, Torres made a run that dragged Bill out wide. So there was no one behind me, and before I could get in the block, Simoes knocked it by me. As I turned, I was horrified to see Eusebio bearing down on Stepney's goal.

Alex stood his ground and made a terrific save. He could easily have sold himself, made it easy for Eusebio by diving one way or another, but he just stood there making himself big and when the shot came his reflexes were perfect. Eusebio said, 'Good save,' and my inclination was to kiss the big Londoner pretty much as I had George Cohen, but there was still a lot of work to do. Later, after Bobby Charlton and George Best and the boy from down the road in Collyhurst, Brian Kidd, who had taken over from the injured Denis Law, had knocked in the extra-time goals, I could think only of the fine line that separates glory and disaster.

The phrase 'what if . . .' keeps leaping into your mind so often that you have to make a conscious effort to turn it away, but of course it keeps pounding on. What if Alex Stepney had blinked, what if Eusebio had really kept his head and approached the goal a little more in the fashion of Jimmy Greaves and been a lot more clinical in his finish? Eusebio was a great person and an extremely talented player but my suspicion is that the blood ran to his head, and instead of placing the shot he decided to blast his way to glory. These questions were easier to put aside when we reached the lobby of our hotel in Russell Square, where the champagne corks were popping and Matt Busby stood in the centre of a great crowd of well wishers.

There was a different feel to our celebration from the one that followed England's World Cup win. For Kiddo and me and for John Aston Junior, the son of the coach, who had played so well along the left, there had to be a special intensity all of our own. We were the only Mancunians in the team, and in some ways it was not so much a triumph for our football club as the blood of our lives. We were kids when the Busby Babes were wiped out and we had felt the sorrow of the streets of our city.

Two men in our midst had most reason to feel that a great journey had been finished – Matt, soon to be Sir Matt, Busby and Bobby Charlton. Bobby was knighted many years later and when it happened, I thought that sounds right, Sir Bobby.

Matt was as dignified as ever but you could see in his eyes what this night meant to him. And Bobby? You couldn't really know, no more than you could his innermost thoughts on that long flight across the Pacific. As John Connelly, Shay Brennan and I went with our wives to our old haunt, Danny La Rue's, Bobby went up to his room. He said his stomach hurt. My guess was that his feelings ran just too deep for any public inspection.

15

DIE, EL BANDIDO

FOOTBALL, like life, gives and takes away. It gave us victory over Benfica in the European Cup final, but it also gave us Estudiantes de la Plata of Argentina in the World Club Championship in the following autumn. When Bobby Charlton and I realised where we would be going and who we would be playing we just looked at each other and rolled our eyes.

Of all the games I played at every level of my career, the ties against Estudiantes, the first in Buenos Aires in September and the second at Old Trafford the following month, had only one rival in meanness and danger and the number of times they provoked the overwhelming question, what has this got to do with football? That was the quarter-final of the World Cup at Wembley when we were bathed in spit and would have been happy if the security guards had turned a blind eye to the efforts of the Argentinians to get into our dressing room after the game – and Alf was so appalled he dismissed all Argentinian footballers as 'animals'.

I knew I wasn't going to file away the new experience in the folder of great and happy trips when we arrived in Buenos Aires. There was a big crowd at the airport brandishing placards and banners. One said Bobby Charlton, El Campione, the Champion. Another said Denis Law, El Rey, the King. Still another said

George Best, El Beatle. The fourth said Nobby Stiles, El Bandido, the Bandit. I said, 'Fucking charming.'

No, the signals were not good right from the start. Our motor-cycle outriders had to swerve around a dead horse parked in the middle of the road and when we got to our digs the first bad impression was confirmed. Sir Matt told us we would be staying at a luxurious country club, but it was a classic case of not believing all you read in a brochure. It was a very primitive golf club and we appeared to be in the servants' quarters. There were no wardrobes. We had to put our clothes on the floor because the metal lockers attached to the walls were all being used by members. The training pitch nearby was bumpy and had the consistency of concrete. The stadium where we would play the game had high wire fences around the pitch. Not so long ago I came in late after a sports dinner and couldn't sleep. So I made myself a cup of tea, turned on the television and flicked through the channels. There on the screen was that old ground with those same fences and the same screaming crowd; one of the sports channels was running an Argentinian league game. It felt like I was being returned to an old nightmare.

Inevitably, I suppose, I was a target after the World Cup quarter-final and I did feel a lot of personal hostility. Sometime later I was told by somebody quite high up at the FA that the word on the grapevine was that there was no way I was going to finish the game. One way or another, they were going to get me off the field. I never found out whether this was true, but it did seem like a legitimate suspicion. Certainly I had never felt a more menacing atmosphere. At dinner in the golf club we would sit around the table and there would be a crowd five-deep watching us, pointing at various members of the team. It might have been feeding time at the zoo, and it seemed that I had been voted the monkey.

By the time we got to the ground we were all on edge, and by

the kick-off there wasn't any doubt that Bobby and I were revis-
iting the spirit of the match against Antonio Rattin and his boys.
The spitting started immediately. You would go up to head a
corner and when you landed your face was covered with gobs of
spittle. The football was terrible. You just couldn't believe that
such a gifted football nation would willingly drag itself down to
this level. I couldn't help wondering what Alfredo Di Stefano
would have made of this approach to the game. The man who lec-
tured Puskas on the need to play the game honestly at all times
could only have been disgusted.

One of the Argentinian defenders was particularly keen to do
some damage. I forget his name but we christened him Dracula.
He came up for a corner and on the way back did Bobby Charlton,
leaving him with a big cut on his ankle. I had my own war with
Carlos Bilardo, who later coached Argentina to victory in the
1986 World Cup on the back of Diego Maradona's brilliance. We
had quite a number of skirmishes and in one of them he butted
me. This, I felt, entitled me to crack him one, which I did, after
checking that the referee was looking in another direction.

At half-time Sir Matt operated on a business-like footing. We still
had a game to win but why we were bothering seemed a bit of a
mystery to most of us. In view of the legacy of the World Cup game,
and Celtic's war with Racing Club of Buenos Aires the previous
autumn, after they became the first British club to win the European Cup by beating Inter Milan in Lisbon, it seemed like official
negligence that our games were played at all. No one would have
been surprised if Matt had said, 'OK boys, get dressed – this match
is doing nobody any good, and least of all the game of football.'
Instead, Busby suggested we should work on beating Estudiantes'
offside trap, which had ruined any possibility of an open, exciting
game. They sprang it and we fell for it, monotonously.

Busby's plan for the second half was that when they pushed up we would come back with them, and Paddy Crerand would look for me on a break. As he did from time to time, Matt had me playing at inside-right for this game. The move worked beautifully early in the second half. Paddy collected the ball and sent through one of his brilliantly weighted long passes. I was on my bike and clean through and I could see that the linesman's flag was down, but the referee blew anyway, and I was incensed. I pointed to the linesman and the referee just waved me away. Bobby was standing nearby and I turned to him and said, 'Bob, there's just nowt down for us tonight.' Bobby asked why and I replied, 'Because the referee's blind.' The referee ran up and asked what I had said, so I turned to Bobby again and said, 'He's fucking deaf as well.'

I was sent off immediately — which, when you considered all the skulduggery that had been going on, gave credence to that rumour about my certain fate at the hands of officials. It also made me wonder about a conversation Jock Stein, the great Celtic manager, apparently had with Matt before we flew off to South America. According to the story, Jock told Matt that when Celtic played Racing Club, he was asked to pick out of a hat the name of one of three referees for the game. Stein said that he was later told the same name had been written on all three pieces of paper.

Altogether, it was a dreadful, high-risk experience and there were times in Argentina when you had to wonder why on earth Matt had exposed us to the dangers. He knew that Celtic had been drawn into a full-scale battle on the field. He knew the feelings that had been aroused among our hosts by the World Cup defeat and the Rattin affair. But that, I realised when I thought about it, was Matt's style. He defied the Football League when he first took United into the European Cup, and even after the terrible experience in Munich, he never lost his belief that football was the great world game and that its beauty and its brilliance would ultimately triumph over all difficulties.

I know how appalled he was by the growth of hooliganism through the sixties and seventies, and I was reminded of this when reading about Thierry Henry's reaction to being hit by a coin thrown from the Chelsea terraces. The Arsenal star was indignant, understandably, after leaving the Stamford Bridge pitch with blood on his face, and his manager Arsene Wenger was insisting on a thorough investigation of the incident. I couldn't help comparing Wenger's reaction with Matt's when I was involved in a similar incident. In fact, it was rather more serious. A dart landed in my arm. I went to the touchline and had it removed and at half-time I was given an injection. The incident had been missed by the referee and the linesmen, and Matt's decision was that we shouldn't draw any attention to it. It would be bad for football and the club and it might encourage such behaviour. I could only speculate how bad it would have been for the game if the dart had landed in my eye rather than my arm. I knew it would have been quite bad for me.

In the end, though, you had to admire Busby's basic feeling for the game and his determination that we should play in Europe and elsewhere, and face all our tests. His belief in the future of football was unshakeable, and as I look back now and think of all the trips to such places as Budapest, Prague and Argentina, and that freezing night in Poland, I know how much I benefited from my time under his wing. Yes, the Argentina trip was in many ways a disaster, and didn't bring anyone benefit, but it was part of Busby's belief that football was a world-wide game, and basically strong enough to prosper wherever its flag was raised.

For a little while after we left the dressing room in Buenos Aires for the team bus, I feared a rather more serious fate. As we turned down a dark corridor, I felt something hard being pushed into my back and heard a voice close to my ear saying, 'I'm going to kill you, you little English bastard bandido.' My blood ran cold until

I whipped round to face a grinning Brian Kidd. It was Collyhurst humour of the worst kind.

Down to ten men, United lost the game 1–0 and could only draw 1–1 at Old Trafford. To complete the misadventure, we were banned from European competition for a year because of crowd incidents, no doubt provoked by more battles on the field, one of which involved Georgie Best having a go at an Estudiantes defender who had been kicking lumps out of him all night. I was out of the game because of my sending off in Buenos Aires and I watched from the stands feeling completely miserable.

When George was dismissed just seconds before the final whistle, I saw the big Argentinian goalkeeper racing off the field in his direction and I immediately jumped up from my seat and rushed down to the dressing room. When I got there the goalie was manhandling George but before I could do anything Paddy Crerand, who had also anticipated the trouble, suddenly appeared. He got hold of the goalkeeper and hammered him – three times. Paddy had always acted as George's minder and on this occasion I suspected he was expressing, very physically indeed, all the frustrations that had been building up in all of us since we had first stepped down from the plane in Buenos Aires. Paddy, as I said before, came from a hard school – a fact that the battered and whimpering goalkeeper would no doubt have been the first to confirm. Fortunately for him, Matt had arrived and he stepped in and said, 'That's enough of that, Paddy.' On this occasion, however, he did not announce that it was behaviour unbefitting a Manchester United player. I could only imagine he was also feeling quite frustrated.

The vital goal for Estudiantes had been scored by a skilful but quite ruthless player, known back home as 'The Witch'. He was Ramon Veron, the father of Juan Sebastian, who may not have entirely fulfilled all of the hopes Sir Alex Ferguson had for him when he signed him from Lazio, but on many occasions has thrilled Old Trafford with the sheer quality of his skill. Juan Sebastian, I'm told, was nearly throttled by Roy Keane at training on the Monday morning after he had made a mistake against Middlesbrough which the club captain felt had cost United the championship in 2002. Veron's defensive qualities are not the kind that would probably ever impress Keane, but I can understand easily enough why Fergie saw in the Argentinian a possible new dimension for his team. There are times when his passing has been quite beautiful, and when I see him control the ball so easily and cut through a defence with a moment of brilliance, I can only be bewildered all over again by the refusal of his father's generation to play the football of which they were so obviously capable.

Both the Argentina and Estudiantes team had a wonderful ability to make the game look easy. When they weren't spitting and spoiling, they could light up the sky with their touch and their vision. It was all such a waste and, looking back now, I see it as a time when a potentially great football nation seemed determined to betray itself. The other sadness for me, as I look back at that time, is that I can see so clearly now that for me, as a player at the top of the game, it was the beginning of the end.

Some critics seemed inclined to signal my decline even before a series of knee injuries forced me out of the England side and began to endanger my place in the United first team. One of them was the leading football commentator Barry Davies, who was at the airport with a camera crew when we came home from the Estudiantes game. As you might imagine, I wasn't in the best of moods. Apart from being scared out of my wits by Kiddo, I was still raging over the treatment we had received generally and, especially in my case, from the referee. I was in the middle of a tirade when I saw Davies summoning me to be interviewed. He just flourished his hand in my direction and I'm afraid my response was not the kind that is likely to endear you to a television star. I told him precisely where he could put his microphone. Quite soon afterwards, as the cameras played on me yelling at one of my team-mates in 'Match of the Day', Davies said I was a player who liked to shout a lot, and perhaps if I played as well as I shouted I might be considered a good player. Some of my friends thought that was quite a harsh judgement on somebody who had helped to win both the World Cup and the European Cup, but then I had rather heavier problems on my mind.

More serious damage to my career was being inflicted by the wear and tear on my knee joints. I had two cartilage operations between 1967 and 1969, the first coming after I turned sharply in a game against Sheffield United, and fresh damage had threatened my place in the European Cup final. I played that game with my knee strapped, and in an earlier round, against Sarajevo, I had lost my place to an up-and-coming young challenger, John Fitzpatrick.

The pressure builds on a player in this situation and in my case there was from time to time a touch of panic. As a kid, you live to play the game, and when you can do it professionally, it is perfection. But the dream comes at a price and as I moved into my late twenties, I was discovering how high it can be. You think of your wife and your kids and wonder how you are going to look after them when you lose the only job you can do – the only one you ever wanted to do.

As always, my brother-in-law, who knew all about the stresses that come with serious injury to a footballer, provided some valuable advice. He had seen how I kept rushing back into the team without giving myself sufficient time for a full recovery, and he told me, 'Look, Nobby, you're not doing yourself any good. You have to give it time. You have to recognise that it's better to miss even a full season, with something still left of your career. Resign yourself to being out for a year. Then if you get back in any time under that, you have a bonus. The way it's going, you're just going to ruin your knee.'

I took his advice. I said I would try the long course, but it was very hard. I was getting treatment at the ground and did strengthening exercises in a little gym in Stretford that they opened up for me at 7 a.m. But all the time I was seeing the other players – especially John Fitzpatrick – running around, and it was destroying my head. I knew, deep down, it was always going to be a struggle from then on, that the old confidence in my indestructibility, which I think you have to have if you are going to tough it out all the way to the top from somewhere like the Red Rec, would never be quite the same. You cannot admit to such fears in public or on the field, you go about your business, but you get some long, sleepless nights, and once again I was learning the value of a good, strong wife.

I made my comeback, after being out for a total of eight months, in the FA Cup semi-final replay against Leeds at Villa Park – the night Georgie Best went on the field after being caught with a girl in his room in the team hotel. Wilf McGuinness, who by now had taken charge of the team with Sir Matt as general manager, had a tremendous bust-up with George, whose off-field activities were becoming almost a staple of tabloid front pages. The word had got out to Leeds before the game and several of their players, including John, put plenty of pressure on George. They said things like, 'Call yourself a professional when you're shagging a bird before a big game?' It was the kind of provocation that was regularly forthcoming during a game, but this time it had a particularly raw edge. George was a great lad, one of the greatest talents the game has ever seen, but this was one he hadn't thought his way through. Leeds knew that, in any circumstances, George could be devastating, so they played every card available to them. It might not have been nice, but it was the way it was in the professional game, and always will be.

I had my own problems that night at Villa Park and for some terrible moments I thought they had come to a head in the cruellest way. I went into a tackle with John, the man who had been such a friend, the brother of my wife, and somebody who had patiently talked me through months of disappointment and fear, and I came out of it with a sharp pain in my knee. I thought that John, of all people, had delivered, accidentally, the blow that might end my career. As I sprawled on the pitch, John stood over me with great concern on his face, and I saw the beginnings of tears in his eyes. Thankfully, the pain died and I was able to play on, although at what cost to my chances of stretching out my career with United I couldn't know.

Apart from surviving that crisis, I had another piece of good fortune that night. It was that Eddie Gray, a brilliant winger, didn't seem to realise he had me at his mercy. I had been brought back into the team at right-back and Eddie, whose ability to destroy defences with his wonderful skill on the ball was blossoming that season, would have been a severe test for a top regular full-back whose head wasn't filled with demons because his knee was decorated with scar tissue. He had lovely balance and timing and his left foot was a superb weapon. If he had taken me on, he would have killed me. I never knew why he didn't, then or after we had played our way to a second replay at Bolton. He was still a kid, and maybe my reputation as a destroyer loomed in his mind. Whatever the reason for Eddie's caution, the extent of my good luck was clear soon enough when he ran riot against Chelsea's Dave Webb at Wembley after my friend Billy Bremner scored the goal that put us out of the Cup at Burnden Park.

Surviving Eddie, piecing together some of my old presence on the field – you don't forget how to read the play, or make a tackle

– brought a result that I could hardly have dreamed of through all those months of slapping poultices on my injured knee. I got a call from an old friend – Alf Ramsey. He wanted me back in the England team. With my struggle for fitness, my increasing sense that I was fighting an uphill battle to hang on at Old Trafford, thoughts of reviving my England career had been pushed into the margins. But Alf was keeping faith with me, and in the insecure life of a footballer, that is a vital gift. I even thought I might get my confidence back; maybe I could play through the crisis – maybe I wasn't finished after all.

My return was against Northern Ireland in the old home inter-national series at Wembley and I received a warm welcome back from a 75,000 crowd. When my name was announced there was a great cheer, which was very encouraging. However, when George Best's name was read out in the Irish team there was a completely different reaction. There was heavy booing.

George had scarcely been out of the papers since he had been caught with the girl in the hotel room. He'd also been involved with an actress and a Miss World, and after he went missing for a few days Sir Matt suspended him and fined him two weeks' wages. Before the game against England he had been training on his own. At that time, the regular life of a professional footballer must have seemed very remote to a player who was increasingly having to get by on his natural talent. Very few players in the history of the game had had such talent, but there are limits to which you can stretch any asset, and the feeling that was expressed so loudly by the Wembley crowd was that George's career was in ruins and the destruction was by his own hand.

Despite all that, I was a worried man. The cheers may have lifted my spirits but they didn't change reality. Put the challenge to Georgie and, I knew well enough, he could still produce some-thing quite extraordinary. He still had the natural ability to destroy a defence, and players of the greatest dedication would have to spend their lives envying it. The point of worry for me was that the Irish were playing George in the striking role and Alf had me in my club position in the centre of defence.

George wasn't hugely in the picture in the first half and we came in at the interval a goal up. Then, early in the second half, I learned the extent of George Best's greatness at a time when he was supposed to be heading for the gutter. Of course, I knew all about his brilliance. I'd seen him destroy Benfica in Lisbon's Stadium of Light. I'd seen him score goals after which you had to rub your eyes. I'd seen his talent erupt so many times in so many places, but never before had I been on the receiving end of the extraordinary action he could produce from, it seemed, nowhere.

The Irish played a long ball over my head and as I turned to go for it, I was three or four yards ahead of George, but as we got to the edge of the box, George was a yard in front of me. He was bearing down on the goal and Banksy was making himself as big as he could. But I knew Bestie so well, I could read clearly what he was going to do. He was going to fake a blasting shot and then drag it inside the goalkeeper, very tightly. So I had to make my tackle and I had to make it one of the best I had ever delivered. I went straight through the ball, and straight through George, but without the result I was looking for. I finished up on my back on the dead-ball line, looking back at George. He moved to his left past Banksy, and put the ball in the bottom of the net. Seventy-five thousand fans who had an hour earlier booed and jeered the mere mention of his name filled the old stadium with cheers. As I got to my feet I thought, 'What a player!'

Afterwards I shook his hand and said, 'Well done, George – only you could have done that. I'll never forget that goal.' To me it summed up the career of Georgie Best. There he was, with the world falling in on his head, drinking, losing touch with what had made his name so brilliantly, but still able to produce something that made the little hairs on the back of your neck stand up.

It was supposed to be my night of triumph. The World Cup glory was still fresh enough in everyone's minds. Everyone knew me from my victory dance on this same Wembley field. But it was George's night. You could look back and say there was some player indeed; there was someone who as a kid had something people in the game call the bounce, something mysterious, but real in its effect. It's as though the ball knows something the rest of us don't and it bounces kindly for the greatest players. Irrational? No doubt. The great players make their positions; they have a genius for knowing where to be at any given moment. But sometimes it seems they have something more, something that you just can't fathom.

What was tangible enough was George's amazing strength. He was a skinny kid when he arrived at Old Trafford and he never got to have much flesh on him. The strength sprang from deep inside him. He was a phenomenal trainer, and that was true whatever the situation. He could arrive unshaved and smelling of booze, but he was still brilliant when the work started.

I never got to know him deeply. He was a lovely lad, there was no edge to him. It was just that in a dressing room, players tend to drift naturally into their own little groups. George would mix with Denis Law and Paddy Crerand while I usually found myself in the company of Bobby Charlton and Shay Brennan. But we all mixed well enough together, and when we played we were a genuine team and respected what we each brought to the table.

There was never any doubt about George's contribution. His awareness of his team-mates on the field wasn't always the best – when the ball was passed to him there was never any guarantee that it would be returned, however well a position had been taken up – but there was never much delay in forgiveness. That was because you always had to believe in George's capacity to do anything he wanted on the football field, and when the criticism of him mounted, when the general view was that he had let down his club and his game, I could never judge him just on those areas where he had, for one reason or another, gone wrong. I always thought you had to take in the whole picture. You had to see where he had come from. He was a kid from a tough area of Belfast who came into a new and overwhelming world. You had to think how the world took him up, ran after him and made him feel that he was someone quite different from everyone else. George made his mistakes, like everyone else, but in his day there were no minders or publicists to screen a kid from some of the consequences. There was no celebrity industry in football then. George was a new and unique sensation in the game, and when you look back at what he went through, and how little preparation there was, or protection offered, it shouldn't really be any surprise that he ran off the rails.

George has sometimes said to me that he was disappointed United didn't push on after winning the European Cup in 1968. He had a feeling that a goal had been accomplished, and while he was part of it, he wanted more. He felt that more should have been done at that time to drive the club forward. Maybe a little bit of a void did come after the great European Cup win. Maybe George felt a little let down, and I know that he felt he should have received more financial reward for what he had achieved, and what, in other circumstances, he might well have gone on achieving. Such questions can never be black and white, but about one thing we can be sure. George Best never owed anything to football. If he sold anyone short, it was himself – and there were times, I learned that night at Wembley, when you really couldn't pin down his huge value to the game he briefly, but quite unforgettably, graced. Unlike Eddie Gray, Georgie Best didn't hesitate to put me to the sword.

Fortunately, the blow wasn't fatal. A few days after George had turned me inside out while scoring that amazing goal, Alf was back on the phone. He was going to take me to the 1970 World Cup in Mexico.

━━━ 16 ━━━

MEXICAN SUNSET

EXICO! Maybe it would happen in Mexico. Maybe in the white sunlight and the thin air the months of career crisis would fade like an old nightmare, and in its place there would be the warm, familiar dream of the World Cup. But then perhaps we would also see pigs flying over the Sierra. Unfortunately, I was not a player in Mexico; I was a piece of psychological warfare waged by Alf, and, sadly, quite a small one.

The nearest I got to the action was sitting on the bench as a substitute for the magnificent group game with Brazil in Guadalajara. I think Alf had the idea that if the game went a certain way, if we found ourselves really up against it, my experience – and my reputation – might just be a factor. If I went on the field at a certain point, maybe the Brazilians would remember my 'Bandido' status in South America, and that might give them reason to pause.

But in that broiling heat, England needed more than memories of when the World Cup had been won. England needed Gordon Banks to be at his best, and he was. When he saved from Pele – more brilliantly, it seemed, than any goalkeeper had ever saved before – we leapt up from the bench and shook our heads in wonderment. Banksy, in his rather dour way, said that he didn't really know what all the fuss was about. He was merely doing his job and, if anyone cared to remember, he had made equally good saves back at home in bread-and-butter league games. But goalies are like that; some of them would complain about living conditions in the Garden of Eden, and we refused to tone down our praise.

The fact was that Banksy had stood alone against a sensational outpouring of Brazilian brilliance. Carlos Alberto, a superb captain and right-back, had fed Jairzinho with a pass that left Terry Cooper for dead, and when Pele rose above Tommy Wright, our goal was at his mercy. The way Banksy turned himself around and tipped the ball over the bar was simply out of this world.

We felt the same about Mooro's performance that day, and if there was ever a perfect picture of what football represented at its best, at its purest, it was the one taken of him and Pele embracing and exchanging their shirts at the end of Brazil's 1–0 win. Both had battled to their limits, and what limits they were. They stretched to all the greatest attributes a player could have – strength, timing, skill, a constant sense that however important their role, they were part of a team, and an absolute refusal to settle for being second best.

In the end, Mooro had to accept the brilliance of Pele's new team in which Tostao, Jairzinho and Gerson, who was missing in Guadalajara through injury, were outstanding, but this was no surrender of the World Cup. England, after wins over Romania and Czechoslovakia, went through to the quarter-finals as second-placed qualifiers, and still a team that would not be ruled out as a significant force. Indeed, some argued that the team of 1970 had a greater range of individual talent than the one that had won in '66. Certainly Francis Lee, Alan Mullery, who had taken my place, and Terry Cooper were impressive representatives of a new generation of England players. Everton's polished centre-half Brian

Labone had succeeded big Jack. From time to time, big Jack and I growled out displeasure at the passing of the years, but we were professionals and although we ached to be part of the action, we accepted that we had enjoyed our own run at the glory and now was the time for stand-by duty. It didn't make it any easier, however, when you were stuck on the bench and you could hear the roar of the crowd and smell the grass. Even so, I have no illusions about the extent of the challenge I would have faced, with my dodgy knee and dwindling belief in my own physical powers, had I been called into action against Brazil.

That day in Guadalajara I finally saw why so many good football judges had come to believe that Pele was the greatest player of all time. The most striking impression was of Pele's immense strength. I had played against Eusebio twice, and I would always remember his power. Pele was on a different level.

If I had been playing against Pele, I would have been doing Mullery's main job of stifling the great man. Mullery was much more strongly built than I was, and although that isn't always the decisive factor when it comes to the winning of tackles, it was nothing less than daunting to see the ease with which Pele held off his marker. Repeatedly, Mullers tried to hustle Pele off the ball. Repeatedly, he failed. He just couldn't get close enough, and at throw-ins and corners Pele exerted tremendous leverage with his strong arms.

When Brazil scored their winning goal, we saw another vital aspect of Pele's game – humility. It was best expressed in his understanding of the needs of the team. Pele cut out two England defenders with the simple pass that played in Jairzinho. That was pure Pele. As a teenager in the 1958 World Cup final in Stockholm, and on countless other occasions, Pele showed just how spectacular he could be, but when you looked at him in his maturity – and his performances in Mexico surely represented his prime – you saw a talent that he had honed down to all the essentials of winning football. If a simple pass would work best for the team, he would play it. It was only if he was under pressure and lacking other options that he would launch some outrageous initiative. He was both the engine and the heart of Brazil, as well as being the ultimate example of that nation's superb feeling for the game.

Mooro's contribution to England was different but in its way equally huge. More than anything, he gave calm – endless calm. It was staggering that he should provide such leadership when you considered what he had gone through in Bogota just a few days earlier. The story is known well enough. He was accused of stealing an emerald bracelet from Fuego Verde (Green Fire), a jewellery shop in the lobby of our team hotel, the Tequendama. We were hanging around the hotel, killing time, as professional footballers are so often obliged to do on the road, before we played Colombia in a warm-up game, which we won 4–0. Mooro and Bobby Charlton mooched around the shop for a few minutes before the owner made his charge. Bobby Charlton was shocked and there were tears, mostly of rage, pouring down his face when he told us what had happened. Mooro had been taken away by police and security guards.

Alf seemed to smooth away the difficulty quickly enough, however, and the captain was able to join us for our final preparation game in Ecuador. The trouble was that when we returned to the Tequendama on a one-night stop-over en route to Mexico, the shop owner struck again. He claimed he had a witness who saw Mooro take the bracelet. Mooro wasn't on the plane when we flew to Mexico the following day. He was under 'house arrest' at the British embassy, where he stayed for four days before a judge threw out the charges on the grounds of insufficient evidence. In Mexico, Alf had told us that of course the captain was completely innocent and the matter would be resolved satisfactorily. 'Don't worry about Bobby,' he said. 'Most certainly, he will be leading us into the World Cup.'

Bobby Charlton, who was the first to be accused, was convinced that it was a set-up, and it emerged that it was indeed part of the Fuego Verde's operating strategy. The owner, who soon afterwards was forced to close the shop, claimed £6,000 damages for a bracelet that was valued at £600. Some, though, thought that it might have been something more than a cheap scam and that the real motive was to upset the reigning world champions who were still deeply resented in Latin America after Alf's 'animals' outburst at the end of the previous World Cup. Certainly we felt hostility in the air when we got to Mexico. One inconvenience was that Mexican fans gathered around our hotel at night, sounding their car horns and beating drums.

But under Bobby Moore's leadership, we were strong enough to withstand the effects of a bit of noise, and this was confirmed when he returned to the team after Alf had met him with an embrace at the airport in Mexico City. 'Forget about what happened in Bogota,' said Mooro. 'I'm fine and if we all stick together, this can make us stronger.'

So it was until Alf made the decision that some would always say broke his aura as the man who had led England to unprecedented heights. Sixty-nine minutes into the quarter-final against Germany in Leon, we were coasting to a semi-final against Italy. We were looking like world champions. Bobby Charlton, with Franz Beckenbauer again in attendance, was running the show from midfield. We led 2–1 through goals from Mullery and Martin Peters, Beckenbauer pegging one back in the sixty-seventh minute, when Peter Bonetti – replacing Banks who had suddenly been hit by a stomach bug – was slow to get down a low shot. I sat next to big Jack in the stand, and in the tremendous heat –

players were losing as much as 10lbs a match – we marvelled at the composure and the rhythm of the England performance. Despite Beckenbauer's goal, England still had a clear edge.

Then Alf changed the team, and put a noose around his neck. It would take another three years to tighten, when England failed to qualify for the 1974 World Cup in West Germany, but from that hot day in Mexico there was no doubt that Alf was a marked man at the Football Association. He had gone his way, quite brilliantly, but in the process he had upset quite a few of the FA councillors; before his arrival, they had always been the lords of all they surveyed. In their eyes, Alf had rudely intruded into their empire and had never shown them enough respect. He was just a little too independent for a lot of the official blood, and he had also made some enemies in the press. Pay-back time dawned in the sweat and the pain of Leon.

In the wake of the Beckenbauer goal, Alf brought off Bobby Charlton, deciding that he would conserve his energy for the semi-final, which was due to be played at an altitude of 7,000ft in Mexico City in just three days' time. Despite the heavy criticism at the time, which has lingered so strongly down all the years, I still do not see that Alf was wrong. Bobby had put in a tremendous effort controlling the midfield, with excellent support from Mullers, and inevitably he was feeling the heat. With the adrenaline flowing, a player can resist the worst effects of fatigue but Alf had to consider quite how much his most important player had left in his tank. Could it be replenished in time for another major performance in the semi-final?

It wasn't as though Alf lacked impressive back-up. When Bobby came off, he was able to send on Colin Bell, a powerful, gifted player and a cornerstone of the rise of Manchester City. Malcolm Allison had christened him Nijinsky – after the great racehorse, not the dancer. There was nothing airy-fairy about Bell – or

Norman Hunter, who replaced Peters along the left with the purpose of shoring up his tiring Leeds team-mate Terry Cooper in the battle to contain the fresh legs of Jurgen Grabowski along the German right.

Ramsey was slaughtered when Uwe Seeler got the equaliser eight minutes from the end, and then the new scoring sensation of world football, Gerd 'Der Bomber' Muller, knocked in the winner in extra time. It was terrible to see the game, and the World Cup, sliding away from England and big Jack couldn't bear it. As Beckenbauer took control of the game, Jack walked away, cursing. He couldn't accept that Alf's World Cup was going to end this way and he went into the shade beneath the big stand, listening to the roar of the crowd and fearing the worst. I stayed in my seat, watching with the gut certainty that the moment had been lost and, also, reflecting all over again on the greatness of Bobby Charlton. When he left the field, Beckenbauer was suddenly huge and it made you consider the extent of the talent that had, over most of two massive games – the World Cup final of '66 and this one – forced the the Kaiser into such a subdued role.

There was no doubt as we headed home that Alf's spell had been broken. He was accused of making a catastrophic decision, but it was not as simple as that. Football never is. The truth is that even the greatest of managers and coaches is ultimately at the mercy of the performance of his players. The reality of it had to include a harsh judgement on the fine goalkeeper Peter Bonetti. He was at fault in all of the goals, and if that hadn't been so, if Gordon Banks hadn't woken up as a victim of Montezuma's revenge, if a brilliant header by Geoff Hurst hadn't missed a post by a fraction instead of bouncing out to the lurking Francis Lee, the chances were that Alf would have returned to England as, once again, a confirmed hero. He had prepared another excellent World Cup team. They had fought an unforgettable battle with the eventual champions Brazil, who were widely considered the greatest winners in the history of the tournament. He had seen the team outplay Germany for most of a taut game played in conditions that were almost impossible for players from northern Europe. He had guided us through the Bobby Moore storm. He had the respect of all his players. But he flew home under a shadow that would never lift. For quite a while, I knew how he felt.

The shadow over me had nothing to do with my professional reputation. That had taken me to Mexico, but one of the first things you learn in the game is that you cannot live on past achievements for more than a few games. Reputation couldn't get me a game for England at that point in my career and when I came home the question uppermost in my mind was whether I could keep my place in the United team.

Ironically, for once I had plenty of time to think about the challenge of a new season. Unlike today, England players in my time were not given any special dispensation when they returned from World Cup service. I was amused to read in 1998 that United had given Gary Neville three weeks off after the World Cup in France, when England played four games. No doubt there was a little bitterness, too. After helping to win the World Cup, Bobby Charlton and I had three days off. Then we had to report for training before going on a pre-season tour that took in Glasgow, Munich and Vienna. It was a catastrophe for the club, and for me. We lost all the games, conceded thirteen goals, and I got sent off in the last game against Vienna Austria after getting myself drawn into a battle with a very large forward.

It was remarkable that we managed to pull ourselves together in time to win the championship that season. I felt absolutely knackered, which wasn't too surprising when I reviewed that 1965–66 season. The explanation for Gary's extra break was that he had had a gruelling year. Well, I worked out that I had played around sixty-six games before embarking on that pre-season tour. I'd played forty-one league games, missed just one game in the European Cup campaign that took us to the semi-finals against Partizan Belgrade, played in the FA Cup to the semi-final stage, appeared for the Under-23s, the Football League, the full England team, and played in the six matches in the World Cup. A few years later they made the film 'They Shoot Horses, Don't They?' about a marathon dance contest. Watching a terrific portrayal of one of the contestants by Jane Fonda, I thought, 'I know how you feel, love.'

But when I had the time to recover from the disappointments and the dramas of Mexico and prepare for the new season, which was looming so large in my mind, there was really only the worry that my knees just wouldn't stand up to the new campaign. I fretted morning and night and for once even Kay couldn't reassure me. The miracle of recovery hadn't happened in Mexico and when I reported back to Old Trafford, thirteen years after I'd arrived as the hopeful, eager kid from Collyhurst, I had an unshakeable feeling that this was the end of my road as an inheritor of the dream of Coly and Duncan and all the other Babes.

It was made official that I had come full circle when Matt listed the squad to travel to Dublin to play Shamrock Rovers in another pre-season game, and I wasn't in it. I wouldn't be going back to the city I knew so well, and where I had played at Tolka Park as an eighteen year old impressively enough for Dickie Giles, the knowledgeable football man, to swear that I would play for England. No, I would be staying at home with the kids fighting for promotion to the reserves and, ultimately, the first team. Something inside me went dead, and when I got home to Stretford I said to Kay, 'It's really happened – I'm finished with United.'

I knew it was only a matter of time before I was on my way and

I told Kay that I would have great difficulty in running out the string and waiting for the club to grant me a testimonial. That would have been a great benefit to us at a time when we were struggling to look after young kids and pay the mortgage, and it would have made a lot of sense to push for it. I knew I was very popular with the Old Trafford fans, who recognised and identified with my passion for the club, and I reckoned that a benefit match would do well. It was also true that, despite my reputation in the game, I had no guarantee of making a sweet deal with any club that might come for me. My struggles with injury were well known. I was damaged goods.

Eventually, Stan Anderson of Middlesbrough came in. The club where Brian Clough had made his name, and Wilf Mannion had been a great star, had fallen on difficult days and were becalmed in the Second Division. Stan knew about my knee problems but he calculated that my experience and attitude to the game might help to give his team a bit of iron and edge. He was taking a gamble but he reckoned it was worth £25,000 of his club's money. Neither Kay nor I really fancied the move. It was a major uprooting for the kids and we were unsure about how we would settle into a new life so far away from our roots. But shaping everything was the question of pride. I had to ask myself if I could kick my heels behind the lines while my old team-mates and my replacement, who would be drawn from candidates including John Fitzpatrick and Martin Buchan, went off to fight the big battles.

Shay Brennan was ahead of me in the queue for a testimonial. He had been at the club two years longer than I had but when he was offered the job of player-manager of Waterford back in the League of Ireland, he took that and settled for a small pension from United. It seemed like the likeliest development for me and when I met Stan Anderson I hoped that I could negotiate a deal that, in all the other uncertainties of our future, would at least give us some kind of financial boost.

In this hope, I was thrown something of a lifeline by Stan. When we met he said that if I could persuade United to take less than £25,000 for me, say £20,000, Middlesbrough would give me the spare £5,000. In 1971 that was a lot of money. It was the price of a nice house clear of a mortgage, which would have been something to take from all the years of glory, and compensate a little for the wrecked knees and the growing doubts about what the future would bring. As I looked at it from my perspective, I was quite hopeful before my scheduled meeting with Matt.

The more I thought about it, the more reasonable Anderson's proposition seemed. The club had got me for nothing as a fifteen year old at a time when Bolton Wanderers were ready to hand my parents £3,000. At the time negotiations with Middlesbrough opened, I had given fourteen years' service. My knees were shot through, and what faced me now was not a natural extension of my career – even a return to the England team if I could put some decent form together – but a desperate eking out of the last of my physical resources. I would have to play out of instinct and knowledge and stretch my body to its last limits. I would have to disguise the extent of my decline as best I could – and from time to time remember, with a terrible yearning, how it was to run out on to the field convinced that you were strong enough to beat the world, and that in doing it you had the capacity to run and tackle and pass for ever.

Unfortunately, Matt didn't see it my way. He said, 'Norrie, I'm sorry, I can't even put this proposal to the board. It would not be considered. You know, Middlesbrough are getting you for nothing, and you have to remember you have always been paid well here.'

To say that I was gutted would be an understatement, and my

mood wasn't improved when I heard that Dave Mackay had been able to make a brilliant deal with Brian Clough at Derby County when he was released, with thanks, by Tottenham Hotspur. Mackay had given the London club brilliant service, but then I thought, as I massaged the hurt, I hadn't done too badly for United.

Many years later, I noted that Ryan Giggs, a great lad, a brilliant player and a fine servant of the club, drew a benefit pay-out of more than £1 million; and David Beckham, another brilliant contributor to the United cause, negotiated a deal of £100,000 a week. I would be lying if I said I didn't feel an old surge of resentment that times could change so dramatically, but bitterness never did anyone any good. I have always known that. If some hard times did follow my last official meeting with Matt, I'm pleased to say, with my hand on my heart, that I never regretted a second of my time at Old Trafford, or my association with one of the greatest of all football managers. It was something that could never be accurately measured against the small pension I was eventually granted by the club. Matt, as I said earlier, was a man of his football times. He was shaped by the way the game had always been run, and by the hard times of his youth back home in the coalfields of Ayrshire. It was also true that when he was buried in Manchester, on a rainy day as it was when some of his Babes went to their graves, he didn't depart this life a rich man. In the end, his financial rewards were also quite modest.

These were reflections for later days, not for when Kay and I packed our bags and sold our little house in Stretford. We sold it for £5,500, a profit of £2,000. It was all the money we had in the world as we travelled up to the north east and took a mortgage on a nice house in the countryside in a charming little village called Yarm. In the morning you could hear birdsong rather than traffic noise. When you walked in the garden, everything seemed very still, and I thought of how different it was from the sensation I'd felt as a boy going into the little backyard of our house and hearing the steam engines going through the tunnel from Exchange and Victoria stations. You could hear a pin drop here in this lovely little village where we were surrounded by wonderfully kind people who seemed so anxious to make us feel at home. The birds sang and the cows in the neighbouring fields did what cows do.

For many people, even some townies like the Dubliner Kay and me the Manc, I'm sure Yarm would have been a place to embrace for the kind people and the soft, beautiful countryside, but we knew right away it wasn't for us. In fact, it was doing our heads in.

THE WAY I COULD
NEVER BE

THERE were some good players at Middlesbrough, boys such as Eric McMordie, a clever Irishman, and Alan Foggon, a winger, and a couple of effective forwards, John Hickton and David Mills. It would have been nice to take them by the hand and lead them into the big-time, but you have to be on top of everything to do something like that.

You have to believe in yourself and what you can still do, and if you can't convince yourself, how can you get it across to kids who play alongside you and do not see some World Cup star but just another player scuffling to stay in the game. For me it was over, all but a bit of shouting and play-acting a part from the past, and I knew it in my heart. If I had not, reality would have come quickly enough. In my first game for Middlesbrough against Hibernian, the old Celtic star Bertie Auld kicked me on the knee. I went down. It was the start of a long count. Middlesbrough wouldn't be going anywhere until my old mate big Jack arrived to take them back to the First Division, and by then I was gone.

Wherever this old club was going, I knew I couldn't really be part of the journey. I lasted two years – two years of trying to do the best I could, of living with the fact that now it was somebody else tending to nick the ball from me rather than the other way around. I saw clearly that my ambition to win back my England place had become a fantasy. The real challenge was justifying my status as a professional in the Second Division. To do that, I had to nurse and protect a knackered knee. It was no kind of base on which to re-make your football empire.

My stock-in-trade, my sharpness in winning the ball and the sense of being on top of everything, was badly frayed, and it didn't help that I was no longer operating in the zone of comfort I had made for myself at the centre of the defence. Middlesbrough wanted me to play in midfield where they thought I could exert maximum influence, which was an extra problem because I was no longer in the glory business. I could still read the game well enough. I could still identify a point of weakness in our defence. I could still see opportunities opening up in the other team's half, but reading and doing are two radically different things. The job was survival, and when I got home to Yarm in the afternoon I could see that even Kay's brilliant ability to lift my spirits, and to persuade me that I should take the world as it was rather than how I wished it to be, was under a bit of pressure. We were learning that nothing was simple, and certainly not the life of a fading football star. We had to take the best of what football still offered and live, as optimistically as we could, with what was left.

A little relief came when I was invited to join Dave Mackay and Cliff Jones in a veterans team for a five-a-side exhibition series in Rotterdam which was running alongside a tennis tournament. Kay came along and, like me, welcomed the chance to get away for a few days. We were offered a fee of £200 and expenses, and Mackay was determined that we should stretch our allowances as far as they would go. The first thing he did when we arrived at the hotel in Rotterdam was to order large gin-and-tonics all round. Our dedication to the tournament was not, I have to confess, absolute, and the shameful truth was that we lost every game. One clear memory – there weren't so many after some heavy nights in the bar orchestrated by Dave – is the sound of Kay's hoots of laughter in the stands as she watched our futile efforts.

On the eve of our departure the organiser of the tournament said that we should pack up the kit, including tracksuits, we had been given and leave them in a bag at the hotel. He would be around in the morning to pay us our money and take us to the airport. Dave was particularly sceptical and said that we should keep the gear and at least have something for our efforts, such as they were, apart from hangovers. Dave's suspicion was proved correct. The organiser failed to appear in the morning and we left for the airport with our thick heads and new tracksuits, but minus Cliff Jones. He too had gone missing. He had made his own way to the airport after discovering that Dave had been charging all the drinks to his room.

It had been, I realised clearly and sadly enough, a faint echo of the carefree days of a football professional when you lived in a cocoon that separated you from real life. You worked hard when you had to and you enjoyed yourself whenever you could when your club or your country took you on the road. You were insulated from realities that touched most other walks of life. You were ferried from airports to hotels to stadiums. There was always somebody to take care of you and hand you your passport or your hotel room key. It wasn't, when you thought about it, always the best training for real life.

At Middlesbrough we made good friends but couldn't get any sense of permanence. Kay hankered to be back in Manchester in the life that had seemed so fixed and secure and had given me such professional satisfaction. Inevitably, my thoughts frequently returned to Old Trafford. At Middlesbrough I had Harold Shepherdson, my old England trainer, but there were many days when I longed to be surrounded by the men I knew so well, particularly Bobby Charlton, whose days at United were drawing to a close with the arrival of Tommy Docherty as manager, and Shay Brennan, who was enjoying a happier new life in Waterford and the gentler world of Irish football.

I recalled with special fondness the long trip through North America, New Zealand and Australia that we made in the summer of 1967, when Bobby and I seemed to be walking on air. There were no smudges on our horizons then. The memories of World Cup triumph were still fresh. We had just regained the league championship and we faced a winter during which we would tackle the great goal of the European Cup with better resources and greater confidence than ever before.

We played games in San Francisco and Los Angeles before arriving in Auckland to be greeted by the Haka war dance and New Zealand Sunday licensing laws. It was hard to say whose face showed more shock, Matt's when he saw the Maoris prancing in their war paint or Georgie Best's when he realised he had to go looking for take-away booze.

The Australian leg of the marathon trip was a special challenge for me. I had to find long-lost relatives and, as I learned soon enough, Australia is rather a big place. I also had to lug not just my own suitcase and bags through the various airports but also those of Bobby and Shay. We had a rule that losers in our regular card games had to pay certain penalties. One of them was to become a beast of burden when we hit the road.

There was no sign of my relatives – the family of my father's sister Liz, who had gone out to Australia in 1949 – in Sydney or Melbourne but the missing link was re-forged in Brisbane, where I immediately recognized my cousins Edmund and Leon McGrath when I walked down from the plane. I knew they were my blood as soon as I saw them. They both had auburn hair, as I did in my youth, and pale skin. They took me to see my Aunt

Lizzie, and millions of kangaroos, which until then had not been sighted by any of the team.

It was fascinating to hear the story Aunt Lizzie and my cousins told. In the end, they made a good living in the new vast land, but only after some desperate early days. The word back home was that Lizzie and her husband Edmund had landed on their feet on the other side of the world but the reality was much different. After paying their £10 assisted passage, they found themselves in a camp that was very basic indeed. Aunt Lizzie said that in some respects it resembled a concentration camp. Sanitation was poor and the overcrowding was terrible. Although I would soon enough have the perspective of a visit to Auschwitz, there was no doubt that my Australian cousins had been born into a tough world. It was good to see how they had prospered and had such good, full lives, and I told Aunt Lizzie I could go home and tell my dad that his little sister had certainly conquered her new frontier.

I'd like to say my duties as baggage master were quite as successful but it would be a lie. It was always a tough job for somebody who carried the nickname Clouseau, and when Bobby and Shay complained about my inefficiency I said it was their fault. It wasn't me who dragged out the card games so interminably. It wasn't me who laid down the rules and certainly not me who kept extending the games from best of three to five, seven and onwards into the small hours of the morning. So when the disaster came, as it did while we waited at the airport for the plane that would fly us home to England, my defence was that I was a victim of circumstances.

Bobby was the aggrieved party. Throughout the trip, he had been an enthusiastic photographer. He had pictures of almost everything except the, for him, elusive kangaroos. He had wombats, Sydney Bridge, koala bears, billabongs, Ned Kelly statues, the Opera House and the Great Barrier reef. He had Melbourne Cricket Ground and Sydney Cricket Ground, Bondi Beach, various China towns and Ayer's Rock. He had sun-ups and sun-downs, eucalyptus trees and hats with corks hanging from them. They were on the rolls of film in the bag that also contained his camera. He gave me the bag and told me to look after it while he went to buy something from the airport shop. Unfortunately, I knocked over a bag containing duty-free booze, the bottles smashed and spilled liquor into Bobby's bag. When we all reported back to Old Trafford, I asked him how the photographs had turned out. He said that all but one of them, which happened to be out of focus, had been completely ruined. I apologised profusely. He looked at me quite coldly and said, 'Don't worry, I should have known better.'

His rage lasted a few years only, and when my time at Middlesbrough had so clearly run its course, Bobby threw me a lifeline. He invited me to join him at Preston North End, where he had moved in 1973 after playing his final game for United, appropriately enough, in the beautiful Italian town of Verona, Shakespeare's city of gentlemen.

The new Middlesbrough manager, big Jack, understood my situation well enough, and it may have suited him that I left. He said he couldn't really make me much of an offer to stay, and he understood why I wanted to join his brother in Preston. He knew that Kay and I hadn't settled in his native north east and it was also true that he needed to build a new, strong young team, which he promptly did with great success.

Kay was delighted by the development. In her trips back to Manchester, she had fallen in love with a house in Sale – a nice big house with a good garden and the space to make a games room for our growing family. The deal with Preston was made quickly. I would take a drop in wages, around £50 a week, but it was not so big that we couldn't cover the mortgage on the house in Sale. I would commute to Preston, an hour's drive along the M6, which was still relatively free of traffic jams.

There was an additional bonus for someone who felt so lost for two years. Apart from Bobby, I would be rejoining David Sadler and Francis Burns, two great lads and very good players. I've spoken of the respect I had for Saddy, a player who could perform at both ends of the pitch and who had been such a vital factor in the European Cup win. Franny would probably have been involved in that triumph but for what Matt judged to be a critical lack of pace. On the ball, Franny was a fine, cultured player, but the boss had worried that he might be exposed against the pace of the veteran Gento for Real in the semi-final and then the quick Benfica wingers Simoes and Augusto.

It seemed to me that we had an excellent chance of staying in the Second Division, and with Bobby's name, and maybe mine, attracting attention and local talent to the once famous club served so brilliantly by Tom Finney, I thought the long-term prospects were also bright. But we failed to beat the drop into the Third Division and I continued to struggle on the field. It was terribly frustrating. There was every incentive to do well. There was the love of Bobby, and of Kay who, after terribly hard days in Yarm when I feared that she might be in danger, along with me, of suffering a nervous breakdown, was enjoying the house in Sale and the company of her old friends. But sometimes the more you want something, the more elusive it is. This is especially so if you happen to be a professional footballer with a basically broken body.

Bobby survived that season as manager, and I did as a player, but only just. I realised that if I wanted to stay in the game for any length of time, and I couldn't imagine doing anything else, I had to get some coaching qualifications. The great men of the game, the Ramseys, the Revies, the Busbys and the Shanklys had learnt the game on the factory floor. They understood the way players were and they were also aware that it was knowledge that could never be translated into a manual or written on a blackboard, but there were new trends in the game and coaching badges were becoming an increasingly influential currency in the football job market.

So I went to Lilleshall, the place where my international career had taken off, where I had smelled the grass as though it was a key ingredient in some ancient warrior's potion, and enrolled on a coaching course. The idea was to arm myself with the means to make a career in football and to look after my family. I knew the game well enough – I had no doubt about that. My instincts were good and my teachers had been superb, all the way from Sister Veronica and John Mulligan to Sir Matt Busby and Sir Alf Ramsey, but you needed papers now. You needed some former school-teacher to give you a stamp of approval. I went to Lilleshall with the old, much-travelled professional Ray Treacy. We braced ourselves for a hard summer of football learning, but soon enough we discovered that we would be spending most of our time with tears in our eyes – tears of laughter – and, from time to time, rage.

It was the second kind I found prickling my eyes when one classroom session was taken by the great man Charles Hughes, the Football Association's director of coaching and a former school-teacher who prided himself on rarely attending a professional game. He later announced that the Brazilians had got it all wrong. A common practice at Lilleshall was to show film of the 1966 World Cup, even though we were six years on, and ask for comments on what had just been shown. Hughes ran a clip covering Germany's late equaliser and then asked, 'Can anyone tell me what was wrong with this situation?' When no one answered, he asked again, and after being greeted with another silence, he answered his own question. He said, 'It was because there were too many men in the wall.'

It had, of course, been my job to line up that wall. Ramsey had given me that responsibility, and with only one proviso. I had to check with the goalkeeper to see if he was happy with his sight-line. I shot up my hand, but Treacy, who was sitting next to me, gave me a dig in the ribs and said, 'Get your fucking hand down if you want to get your coaching badge.' Later, I was told that the previous year one of the lads had argued with Hughes on the theory of the game, and although he obviously knew what he had been talking about, he had failed his badge. Treacy said he was back this year, keeping his trap shut.

Ray's warning had been well timed because I had been on the point of blasting Hughes. What he didn't know was how much work had gone into the preparation of defensive walls in the few days before the World Cup final, work directed by me and supervised by Alf. The possibility of conceding free kicks around our goal area was of special concern to the manager. He noted Emmerich's ability to bend a shot around a wall with his left peg and also Held's dangerous work with his right foot. We worked all one afternoon on potential situations, and each time I consulted with Gordon. In the end, he said he wanted an extra man in the wall and we would have have two players outside the line of the kicker and the goal. That way, he reckoned, even with bend, if the shot went outside the line of the wall, it would not directly threaten the goal. Banks, the world's best goalkeeper, reckoned he could deal with the other possibilities. So we had eight men in the wall. It was all done and negotiated and what actually happened was that Emmerich clattered the ball against the wall, it took a freak deflection and fell into the path of Wolfgang Weber. These things can happen in football and, as I was about to say to Mr Hughes before Treacy intervened, 'No coach in the world, not a combination of Helenio Herrera, the black magician of Inter Milan, Jock Stein, Matt Busby and Alf Ramsey, and certainly not some shithead who has got the game from a book, is going to be able to tell you precisely what the ball is going to do when it hits someone at a particular angle on his fucking arse.'

There were other tragi-comic moments, and it seemed that the great challenge of the course was not to master the technicalities of coaching but to stop yourself laughing out loud.

It was particularly hard to do that during one exercise when the supervising coach realised he hadn't got enough men to form a wall, so he improvised. Some workers were digging drains next to the pitch. He went over to them, borrowed a couple of lengths of drain-piping and stuck them up in the wall of players defending the goal. The professional whose job was to beat the wall simply smacked it over the drain-pipes and into the top corner. The coach said, 'No, you can't do that. It went over the wall. The wall didn't move.' Another day we saw a coach barking out instructions after looking at the back of his hand where he had it all written out.

Most of the demonstration work was done by the professionals because, unlike most of the coaches, they had sufficient technical skill. So we had the crazy situation of coaches telling profession-als to do things they were incapable of doing themselves. This produced a most bizarre result when the coach in charge of one session put me in a twenty-yard grid and asked a group of four or five to run the ball past me. My job was to stop them. It was some-thing I had quite a bit of experience of doing, marking players such as Eusebio. To cut short the story of a long, hot and crazy afternoon, I have to say that no one, not once, got the ball past me. Finally, the coach came into the grid and told me I was doing it all wrong.

'I thought you wanted me to win the tackle, and win the ball?' I said.

'Yes,' he replied, 'but you're not doing it right. I want you to explode into the tackle.'

Richie Barker, an experienced player, had been watching all this and suddenly he stepped forward.

'This is a complete load of fucking bollocks,' he said. 'This guy has played in a World Cup final and you're telling him he's doing it all wrong. He's winning the ball every time. For God's sake, look at what he's doing.'

The truth was that nearly twenty years earlier my dad had given me the essentials of tackling. I always remembered him saying, 'You can have your Eddie Colman and your Stanley Matthews and they can play all kinds of tricks, they can do this and that putting their feet over the ball, but we can be completely certain that the one thing that won't happen is that the ball will move without them touching it.' That was my dad who wouldn't know a coaching badge from a Guinness label. I listened to him and absorbed what he said and as a result I had won the ball in a hell of a lot of places before I arrived as a beat-up old professional at a coaching session in Shropshire.

Although you had to laugh hard and often, if with your hand wisely covering your mouth, the situation in terms of the development of English football was quite horrific. The game was being taken over by people who simply didn't know what they were talking about. The disease was spreading throughout the game. More and more jobs were going to these new technocrats of football. Later in my stay at Preston, we played against a club where they placed towels and sand near the corner flags. The idea was that they would play for throw-ins and their players could dry the ball and their hands before making the big throws into the penalty area.

We were entering the age of Charlie Hughes's favourite tactic, POMO – position of maximum opportunity. That meant you skipped the midfield play of a Bobby Charlton or a Johnny Haynes or a John Giles. You got the ball into the box by the most direct route. You humped it in and hoped some big lad would get on the end of it, knock it in or knock it down or knock it about the box, and that something would happen. Howard Wilkinson believed in that philosophy, he was a disciple of Hughes, and until he went to manage Sunderland, he was the FA's technical director. Graham Taylor was another long-ball merchant and we saw what happened to England under his management. Today English football lovers can only thank God that the wheel has turned and that the most successful teams, Manchester United and Arsenal, are playing the game as it was meant to be played, with enough imagination and skill to make a real challenge for properly trained, serious defenders.

Apart from winning all those tackles, I remembered to do that rather more vital chore of keeping my mouth shut while I was at Lilleshall. So I got my badge and returned to Preston, sunburned and with cracked lips, as a sometime player and a full-time apprentice coach. I was so scorched from the sun that my son Robert was alarmed when I tried to give him a hug. There wasn't much more encouragement on the field. I continued to struggle and after a poor season in the Third Division Bobby Charlton left by, as they say, mutual agreement.

The Preston board immediately offered me the job, but although it would have meant more money I told them there was no way I could take it. I would never have felt comfortable walking in my friend's shoes. So the job went to a very big man in the game, Harry Catterick, and I faced a very uncertain future. When fitness allowed, and Bobby needed me, I had played in the Preston first team but with ever-dwindling impact. It was only a matter of time before I was consigned to the scrapheap of old players, most of whom would find it hard even to imagine a life beyond the game. In this I was certainly no exception and I was greatly relieved when the new manager called me at home and invited me to be his coach. I'd hated Lilleshall and so much of what it stood for, but I enjoyed the real work of coaching. I loved it out on the training field, bringing on the kids and reminding some of the old pros about the basics of the game.

Harry Catterick was an imposing figure, representing a whole way of life. He was not one of the new, voguish tracksuited breed glamorised by Big Mal Allison and his many imitators. Harry wore camel-haired coats and impeccably tailored suits, but behind the dandy image was a tough professional whose achievements represented an extremely solid body of work. He had brought the championship and the FA Cup to Goodison Park following a great tradition of cultured football built around the magnificent midfield axis of Bally, Colin Harvey and Howard Kendall. He had also brought on the great folk hero Alex 'Golden Vision' Young, and single-handedly revived the great years of Dixie Dean and Joe Mercer. In his rather dated way, he was still suave and he certainly made a big and, when I thought about it later, rather hilarious impression on me and my assistant Alan Kelly, the goalkeeper who had recently done in his shoulder and, like me, was grateful for the opportunity to coach.

At our first meeting, Harry said he wanted me to write down my full pre-season training programme, morning and afternoon sessions, and have it on his desk in twenty-four hours. It was a nightmare assignment because I hated to put down anything in writing. I was a football man and I did what I did instinctively. But with Kay's help, I put all my plans on paper. I scoured my memory for all that I had learned from Busby and Ramsey and their assistants Jack Crompton and John Aston, and Les Cocker and Harold Shepherdson, and there were a few ideas of my own. They all went down and I left the paper with Harry's secretary. A day or so later when Alan and I returned after training to our little office at the Deepdale ground, there was a neatly written note from Harry, and two bottles of beer. He said he was delighted with our work and that we should enjoy the beer. It had been well deserved.

That made for an unusually relaxed weekend, but the effect was rather spoiled on the following Monday morning when he delivered a tremendous bollocking to both Alan and me. He picked holes in our work and suggested we were very much on trial. A little shaken at first, Alan and I eventually agreed that the best policy was to keep our heads down and get on with our work. Harry's management policy seemed clear enough. It was to keep us on our toes, one way or another.

Alan and I survived. Harry, after two indifferent seasons in the Third Division, didn't. Again the board came to me with the manager's job and this time I felt able to accept. I could scarcely have had a better start. We went straight up to the Second Division. Franny Burns was still playing for the club and he brought a touch of class as captain. We had a little development going. Micky Robinson, a big strong lad from Blackpool who had been playing somewhere in Sweden, had been signed by Catterick on the recommendation of Alan and me, and he was knocking in goals all over the place. A great atmosphere, after years of struggling, was created very quickly. Sometimes it happens like that at a football club. After years of battling against the odds, suddenly things fall into place. The breaks that went against you start to fall in your favour. The players start showing up with eager faces. There is laughter at training rather than moans and groans.

In that changing of mood our veteran trainer Harry Hubbick was a great help. He was a classic old football man, a gnarled little character, and, I reckoned, ten years older than he claimed to be. In his day he had played against some of the great ones, including Stanley Matthews, and sometimes I would say to him, 'Harry, tell the lads how you found it marking Stan,' and he would just grunt and say, 'Matthews, fucking Matthews – I had him just like that,' and flick his fingers. Sometimes I ran him home after a game and he was always beautifully mannered and well spoken in front of Kay, but the moment he stepped out of the car I knew he would be swearing like a trooper.

A young groundsman used to get agitated when the players scuffed up his carefully prepared playing surface as they ran around the pitch. One day, Harry and the groundsman, Brian, had a bit of slanging match after the latter had thrown his fork into the ground in anger. The result was, for some strange reason, a challenge race between the two of them. Everyone wanted to have a bet on the outcome after the groundsman, who was a good forty years younger than Harry, agreed to give the old man a start of fully a quarter of the length of the race, which was to be around the touchlines of the pitch starting and finishing at the halfway line.

All the lads were in the stand cheering for Harry, and there was a great roar when he jumped the gun, limping away at a tremendous pace, with the groundsman shouting, 'Oi, you old bastard.' It was a hot afternoon and the groundsman had arranged for one of his mates to leap out and throw a bucket of cold water over him at the halfway mark. The young man picked up speed after being doused with cold water and was gaining on the old man, but Harry just managed to stagger over the line in front by a few inches. There was a great rush down on to the field and Harry, grinning his crooked old grin, was carried shoulder-high around the ground.

You cannot make things like that happen. If you are lucky, they just do, and I had a good run of breaks on the way to promotion. In the end, it came down to a match at Wrexham between the home team, who were already champions of the Third Division, and Peterborough, who were managed by the excellent former

Nottingham Forest player John Barnwell. If Wrexham won, we would also be promoted. A great crowd from Preston travelled down for the game, and beforehand I talked with Arfon Griffiths, the Wrexham manager. As a small but highly skilled inside-forward, he had played with such brilliance for his home-town club that he found himself transferred to Arsenal. Arfon told me he had five or six injuries, but assured me that his team would be playing hard.

The team were as good as their manager's word and, thanks to a great save in the last minute by the Welsh international goal-keeper Dai Davies, we got the result we wanted. After some lean years, it was a wonderful night, crowned by a call of congratulation from Shay Brennan. It took three years for the shine to wear off and for us to go back to where we started, in the Third Division. We had gone up by the narrowest of margins, goal average, and we went down by the same fine measurement, but for much of the time in between there was plenty of promise around the place. Micky Robinson, who is now a big-name in Spain as a television commentator after a spell as a player there, continued to demolish defences and inevitably he attracted the attention of the big clubs.

The most persistent were Manchester City. Big Mal's first offer was for £150,000 and the board were very impressed. The direc-tors wanted to sell him at that point, but I said that there would be better offers down the road. The kid was young and strong and full of ambition and it was just bad business to take the first bid that came along. I won the argument, and another one when Mal moved the offer up to £300,000; but when City came again with a then massive £600,000, even I didn't see the point of further resistance. Micky was hugely important to the club but he had now seen his name linked with a top team over a period of time and it was natural that he would become impatient. I said it was time to profit from one of Preston's best investments and when the big money was deposited in our bank, I was given less than a sixth of it to repair the loss. I got £90,000 to spend on Stevie Elliot, a fringe player at Nottingham Forest. It was the way of life in the lower divisions.

If I blamed myself for anything it was my failure to understand, before it was too late, a crucial difference between First and Third Division players. Until the season of relegation, I had hammered home all my demands of the players throughout the season. I'd told them what to do at corners and throw-ins and free kicks. I'd never ceased to state the obvious and then, maybe because of echoes from my past at Manchester United, I simply stopped doing it. I assumed the message had got home, that you could say certain things only so many times before the value wore away. I remembered something Jimmy Murphy had said. 'I'll tell a player something three times,' he told me, 'but no more. If he hasn't got the point by then, he's never going to.' But Jimmy had always worked with the cream of the game. He never had to draw pictures for Duncan Edwards or Eddie Colman or Bobby Charlton. At Preston, we had good and in some cases talented lads, but they did not operate at that level. One of them, Gordon Colman, came to me at the end of the bad season and said, 'Boss, why did you stop talking to us? Why did you stop telling us what we needed to do?' I told Gordon that I thought I had done all the talking that was necessary, but he shook his head and said, 'No, Boss, you didn't.'

The axe fell swiftly after relegation and although it hurt I had reason to believe that in some ways it was something not to regret too deeply. I had come to suspect that I simply wasn't hard enough to be a manager. When I told a kid he was finished I felt his pain. I couldn't put enough distance between me the player, the hopeful lad and the scarred old pro, and me the manager who, in his own way, had to play God. I couldn't turn off. I took my worries home to Kay. Shortly before I was sacked, Kay knew better than I did that I was slipping into trouble, and dangerously so.

We were sliding towards relegation and one night after a board meeting, which had not gone well, I arrived home very late. I couldn't get to sleep. I had terrible pain in my stomach, which I couldn't do anything about. I sat on the stairs most of the night, groaning as quietly as I could. When in the early morning Kay saw the state I was in, she said, 'I think I'd better call the doctor.' He came around to the house, asked me how I was feeling, took my blood pressure and did a few more tests. He then asked me, 'Do you have to go in to work today?' When I thought about it for a moment, I realised it wasn't so necessary. It was a Friday morning, a time of short, sharp training, a little tuning. Alan Kelly could handle things easily enough. I told the doctor I thought I could take the day off. The doctor said, 'That's good, I'll give you something to settle your stomach so you can get some rest.'

So I went to bed and I woke up at 11.30 a.m. the following day. I'd slept for twenty-seven hours. I shouted to Kay, 'Jesus, I've got to get to Preston.'

'It's OK, Nobby,' she said. 'I've got all your stuff ready. Just relax. I'll bring you some tea and a bit of toast.'

I had the tea and the toast, and the next thing I knew it was Sunday morning. I'd slept for another twenty-four hours. Kay had slipped me something she had been given by the doctor. He had told her my blood pressure was going through the roof. I was thirty-nine years old. When the sack came, right after relegation, I realised it was probably not the worst thing that could have happened.

18

LIFE OR DEATH ON THE M6

THE worst thing that could have happened would have occurred on a spring afternoon in 1989, eight years after I was sacked by Preston, on the M6 somewhere between West Bromwich Albion football ground and my home in Sale. It would have happened if I had gone through with a plan that suddenly leapt into my mind. It was to drive my car at maximum speed and end my life.

The depression that brought that idea to mind hadn't come in a rush. It accumulated over a number of years in little spurts. A pattern had become familiar, of hope and then disappointment, hard, sharp disappointment. Part of it, I knew, was as much to do with my own nature as the vagaries and the cruelties of football, which, at the professional level, would always lurk at the edges of the joy.

Perhaps, for the sake of my story, I should retrace my steps from that bleak moment when the Preston chairman took me on one side and told me that the directors thought it was time for a change in the manager's office. I had hoped for a little more patience. He thanked me for my efforts, he recognised how hard I had worked. Almost every football man, at some stage of his career, comes to hear those words.

I knew that my love of the game, whatever happened, would remain intense. On the field, I had been well equipped for high-level competition until my knees gave out. I loved the battle. Tell me to mark Eusebio or some young, hard Slav or a Russian with thighs like sides of beef or some jet-heeled, tricky little South American or an Italian with long hair and a little beard who looks as if he's just stepped off the set of 'La Dolce Vita', and I would roll up my sleeves and say, 'Just bring the bastard on.'

Off the field, however, it didn't seem to come so easy. I loved working with the lads and I especially liked helping the young kids. Maybe that was something I picked up right at the start at St Pat's, when I saw how much someone like John Mulligan could help a young player to understand the game and whatever talent he might have. But dealing with directors and handling the politics of the game that go on in and out of the boardroom and around the manager's office and in the dressing room, that was a different matter. I didn't play that game so well.

While I was mulling over that reality in the wake of my departure from Preston – and considering the strong advice of my doctor that I should be careful never to pile such pressure on myself ever again – John Giles called to invite me on a working holiday to Vancouver in British Columbia, where he was coaching the Whitecaps in the North American Soccer League (NASL). He knew I was down after the Preston experience, and he thought the trip would give me a lift. He was right. Vancouver has to be one of the most beautiful cities in the world, and at that time when the NASL had still to learn the folly of trying to run before you can properly walk, there was tremendous optimism in the air that tasted like a mixture of champagne and pine. The stint went well, I got on with the eager Canadian kids who were hungry to learn the game, and when John suggested that I come out the following spring with Kay and take a coaching job, I was delighted.

We let out the house in Sale and rented a pleasant, roomy condo in the hills in North Vancouver above the Pacific. We were excited by this chance to start afresh in a lovely environment, but we had hardly had a chance to settle in before it became apparent to me that the NASL was showing clear signs of going arse upwards. Some of the clubs had over-committed themselves critically. Television earnings were disappointing, much less than projected when the New York Cosmos were signing Pele and Beckenbauer, and my mate Bestie was becoming a bit of a cult figure in the Silicon Valley with San Jose Earthquakes. The Whitecaps had invested in the talent of Bally and the Dutch superstar Rudi Krol as well as the knowledge of my brother-in-law.

The league was contracting fast and in the course of our two years in Vancouver it was stripped down to skeletal levels. In 1981 when we went on a road trip, the destinations would include New York, Dallas, Chicago and Los Angeles, but the game was dwindling in the big market and Phil Woosnam, the former Welsh international who had become commissioner of the NASL, was living to regret his claim that within a decade his league would be challenging the super powers of the National Football League, major league baseball and the National Basketball Association.

Just to darken our prospects further, John had fallen foul of Bob Carter, the new, publicity-hungry owner of the Whitecaps, a former policeman who had made a lot of quick money in the offshore oil business. In an effort to shave the wages bill, Carter made unsubstantiated and, in the end, utterly discredited charges that John had been guilty of a conflict of interest when the club had signed Pierce O'Leary, David's brother, from his former club Shamrock Rovers. John immediately resigned and made a nonsense of the claims of the man who, in a few years' time, would have more than enough of his own problems after being convicted on sex charges and seeing his business empire crumble.

John won his public battle, and kept his reputation, but none of this helped lay down a future for the Stiles family on football's new frontier. By 1984 John was the new manager of West Bromwich and I joined him, along with Norman Hunter, as one of his coaches.

John had had great success with West Brom in the mid seventies when he moved there from Leeds United as player-manager. He immediately won promotion to the First Division and steered the club to a high position before deciding that football management in England was too much at the mercy of amateur directors, and moving first to Dublin, then Vancouver. Now back again, he realised soon enough that he had made a mistake in retracing old ground and after a year, and relegation, he handed in his resignation, saying that he had had enough of the game – a vow that still stands today. John began to work for Irish television and newspapers, and landed a contract with the *Daily Express*.

I was required to battle on at West Brom in various capacities, including chief scout, various coaching appointments and just for a month, as manager. I served under first Ron Saunders, who was in charge for two years after stints at Norwich, where he made his name, Manchester City and Aston Villa, and then, briefly, Ron Atkinson and Brian Talbot, the former Ipswich player. I got on well enough with Saunders, hugely enjoyed big Ron's passing sojourn between Manchester United and Sheffield Wednesday, and then faced the most discouraging time of my career. Talbot didn't seem to like me and the feeling was solidly mutual. So it goes in football and it was just a matter of time before I was gone.

My most enjoyable period at the Hawthorns in terms of work satisfaction was when John Giles appointed me youth coach. My greatest success was in bringing in the big, raw-boned striker Steve Bull. John had signed him, on my recommendation. When the signing was proposed, the chairman Syd Lucas said, 'We'll sign him but I don't know why we're doing it.' I said he would regret it if he didn't take the boy and the big lad gloriously confirmed my judgement. At one stage, Steve's progress levelled off but I discovered he was also playing Sunday League football. He was running himself into the ground on Saturday afternoon and then turning out for a pub team on Sunday morning. I told him he had to conserve his energy and think like a professional. Lucas was never convinced and sold him to Wolves with another of our signings, Andy Thomson, for £65,000. Steve played for Wolves for ten years and became a huge favourite of the Molineux crowd as he hustled his way to twenty-one hat-tricks. He also played for England. If Lucas noticed the boy's progress, he never mentioned it.

There were other good lads at West Brom. When you look back on your time at a football club, you don't remember so much the politics and the stress, but those young boys fighting to make their way in the game. They become part of you because you can identify so easily with their ambitions and, so often, their absolute desperation to succeed. So when I think of West Brom now, I don't think so much of Syd Lucas's attitude or all the frustrations, but the efforts of David Burrows and Carlton Palmer. You look out for them and hope they do well. Carlton had a rough time when he took over Stockport County, and whenever he got a bad result, I felt a little bit of his pain. He was a quirky kind of lad, not everybody's favourite, but what registered with me was how much he wanted to succeed.

I wasn't quite so impressed with Garth Crooks, who went on to make a career for himself in television, and I like to think that this isn't a delayed judgement shaped by the fact that he was awarded an MBE quite some time before Bally, George Cohen, Ray Wilson, Roger Hunt and me.

Crooks was involved when I gave Steve Bull some advice that I thought was crucial. When I had Steve in the A team he was knocking in goals all over the place, but then in a reserve match, when youngsters were mixed in with some first-teamers recovering from injury or trying to find a bit of form, he made no kind of impact. Whenever he got into a decent position he laid the ball off. At half-time I said, 'What are you doing passing the ball away, why don't you go for a goal?' He told me that Garth Crooks, who had a bit of a name in the game after his stint at Spurs, kept calling for the ball. I gave him some basic advice. I said, 'Forget Garth Crooks, you're there to score goals. He can look after himself.'

You think of the lads who fought their way through and, sometimes with a sigh, the good ones who for one reason or another didn't make it. One of them was a smashing little player I encountered on my first working day back from Canada. I thought he had it all, pace and vision, plenty of skill and an excellent heart. I recall asking him for his name and he said, 'Why?' I said, 'Why what?' He said, 'Why do you want to know my name?' I said, 'Because I'm your boss and I want to know your name. I also think you might be a good player, you cheeky little bastard.' His name was Wayne Dobbins. Unfortunately he got a boot in the rib and suffered a damaged pancreas. He was never the same after that. It's sad to think of the casualty rate in football. So many kids just don't make it to the starting line.

But however much I felt for a Wayne Dobbins, and imagined how I would have been affected if I had been cut down like that as a boy, it was hard to look beyond my own situation. The great beauty of football for me had always been its power to release you from all your worries and fears. I remember once reading a comment by Mal Allison that when he ran on to the football field he suddenly felt relaxed and reassured. It was as if he was on an island where nothing could touch him. It was his place where he felt utterly secure, the only place in the whole world where he got that feeling. When I read that, I nodded, and said, 'Spot on, Malcolm.' But in the late eighties, even that last comfort seemed to be breaking down.

Sometimes I had to drive the motorway seven days a week. I ran my own car, without expenses, and when it broke down it was a crisis. We were broke. My only assets apart from the mortgaged house in Sale – the payments on which were increasingly hard to find – were my World Cup and European Cup medals and championship medals, and I couldn't bear to think of selling them. If I did that, what else would I have to show for the football career that had filled me with such pride?

Sometimes I would say to myself on the motorway, 'What the fuck am I doing? What use am I to anybody, what life can I give Kay who has been so good all these years? What can I do for my boys?' My eldest boy John was starting his own hopeful journey in football at Leeds United, but he was on very little money. At Christmas time, he would come home with his wife and baby, and Kay and I would do what we could, but it was very hard. You had your pride, you bought the presents you could and later I was very touched when one of the boys told me that Kay had said the Christmas present I had bought her that year, a hardback biography of a Hollywood actress, was a possession she would always treasure most of all because she knew how desperate I was about how little money we had. It was certainly true that I was worn down and feeling, more than at any time in my life, beaten.

One day I put my bank card into a hole in the wall – I needed petrol money for the journey to West Bromwich – and I got the message back 'insufficient funds'. I stood mesmerised by the blinking screen. It felt as though someone had stuck a knife in me. There were people behind me in a queue but I don't know if they saw what happened or noticed who I was. I didn't know because I couldn't bear to risk catching anyone's eye. I walked away with my head down, went back home and scratched around for the price of a few gallons of petrol that would get me to the work that was no longer enabling me to pay my way.

It was around this time that I had to fight hard against the feeling of futility that came to me so strongly I thought of shutting my eyes and putting my foot down flat on the accelerator. The bad thought wouldn't go away. I felt the dream had gone, finally, and could never be recovered. I'd tried everything I could since the knees started going bad. I'd coached, scouted, managed, flown over the Rockies with my wife and kids, hoping for some deliverance in the game that had become my life, but here I was driving up and down the motorway with no money – no money for petrol, for a packet of cigarettes, for a night out with my wife. When I didn't feel suicidal, I felt tired, bone-tired.

Something had to give way; mentally and physically I was at the point of breakdown, and when it happened I was on the outside lane of the M6 going north near Shugborough, travelling at around 70 m.p.h. I don't know for how long I had my eyes closed, probably for a second or so, but when they snapped open I could see that the outside lane was coned off, and automatically I turned into the inside lane, where there was a big lorry alongside me, and I glanced along the side of it.

It was as if we were locked together and although the whole incident was never much more than a blur in my mind, I had the sense that the lorry driver was brilliant. He held me on my line as I started braking. He took me into the bollards before I pulled away and parked as soon as I could. I was still in the outside lane. When the motorway cleared, I was able to drive the car, which was battered all along the left side, on to the hard shoulder behind the lorry. A traffic policeman was on the scene. I said to the lorry driver, 'I'm sorry, mate,' and he said, 'Don't worry, Nobby, how are you feeling, are you all right?' I said I was fine, and that I didn't really know what happened. I explained that I had been working and driving quite a lot. While I was talking to the lorry driver and the policeman, somebody pulled up, got out of his car and started pointing his finger in my face.

'Typical, typical,' he shouted. 'Instead of getting in fucking line you're going on the outside and trying to get back in. Typical. Typical. Who do you think you are?' I tried to explain I hadn't been trying to steal a few places on the motorway but I gave up and said to myself, 'What the fuck is this all about?'

I drove home very slowly. I didn't worry about where I was going to get the money to repair the car. I didn't think how it would look driving a battered old wreck up to the club and parking it somewhere near the Jaguars and Mercedes of Syd Lucas and Sir Bert Millichip, the chairman of the Football Association, who had been knighted for his services to the game. I just wanted to get home to Kay.

When I got into the house, Kay was on the phone to the Brennans in Waterford, and she handed me the phone.

'How are you?' asked Shay.

'Fucking skint,' I blurted out.

When Kay took back the phone, she said, 'I don't know what he's on about. We're always skint.' I wondered all over again what I would do without her. When I told her what had happened on the motorway, and how terribly low I felt, she said, 'Come on, fella, we're going for a walk.'

It was a lovely evening and we talked about everything – my feelings of failure and desperation, how much she meant to me, and how sad I was that I couldn't provide her with a better life and all the nice things I wanted her to have and which other women, who wouldn't know how to begin to support a man in the way she did, took for granted. She listened to me at some length and then patted me on the arm, and said, 'Now, now,

Nobby, stop all that – for God's sake, don't you know I'd be happy to live in a tent if it was the only way I could be with you.'

It was around the time she was saying this that we passed an off-licence and by some miracle she was able to find in her pocket the price of a bottle of brandy. We took it home and drank every last drop, and in the morning, when I awoke with what felt like a tomahawk stuck in the middle of my head, the phone was ringing. I stumbled down the stairs to take the call. It was from Alex Ferguson. He wondered if I would be interested in coming back to Manchester United to coach the kids.

19

THE END OF THE AFFAIR

FERGIE asked me to go down to the Cliff training ground. When the gates of the old place opened up for me and I drove through in my ageing Ford, my heart leapt up in my chest. I was invaded by a thousand memories. I'd been away for eighteen years but it was as though I'd just stepped back a day.

I saw them all in my mind's eye – Coly, Dunc, the young Bobby, the Lawman, Georgie with his six o'clock shadow. I heard David Gaskell shouting 'bar' and standing there with his arms down as the ball sailed towards the back of the net. I heard the jeers and the shouts. I saw Matt walking down to the training field, immaculately suited and silver-haired, checking on his empire, saying little, seeing everything.

Now I was sitting across a desk from the man who had vowed to make the Busby tradition live again. I had come back home from a discouraging place and for the first time in so long I, too, felt alive again. I'd met Fergie just once before, at West Bromwich when he attended a meeting of managers and coaches, and we had just said hello. Now he was friendly but businesslike. He didn't seem like a man who wanted to waste too much time on small talk.

'I hear you've finished at West Brom,' he said. 'How would you like to come back here and do the training with the School of Excellence?'

I said I would like that very much. I tried, but probably failed, to keep the excitement out of my voice. I wondered if Fergie realised he wasn't so much offering me a job but returning me from exile.

Ferguson had still to make his breakthrough with the first team, still to lift the burden of a more than twenty-two-year wait to follow up the championship win of 1967, but it was clear to me straightaway that he had already done vital work to open the supply lines of young talent. He had confronted the fact that life had changed, and that football in schools was no longer a great force that threw up genuine contenders as a matter of course, and wrapped them up before delivery to the doors of Old Trafford. There were no more John Mulligans tearing around the school-yard or the Red Rec with whistles in their mouths and United blood in their veins. Fergie was cute when he came down from Aberdeen; he recruited Brian Kidd to work his roots. The legendary scouting system, which under Joe Armstrong had plucked Duncan Edwards from Worcestershire, Bobby Charlton from the shadow of the pit in the north east and Eddie Colman from around the corner in Salford, had run down to just two scouts when Ferguson arrived. He would buy his Keanes and his Cantonas, but he would lock up the locality. He would get Ryan Giggs, Paul Scholes, Nicky Butt and the Neville boys and he would raid Essex and pick up David Beckham.

I would work under Eric Harrison at the School of Excellence, sifting through the Under-10s, 11s and 12s, and I would also get to coach with Kiddo the next wave of United, the best group of young players at the club since the birth of the Babes. I had that old feeling when I drove home to tell Kay all about it. I had that sense that had become so unfamiliar it might have belonged to another life. I felt like bursting.

Ferguson had pulled in Kiddo and given him a budget. He'd won a vital battle with the board, convincing the directors that you couldn't make a great club without investment, real seed money. So Kidd was given the tools and he did the job. He winkled Giggsy out of the Manchester City system, and the others followed. United hadn't been good at spending money, and the basis of Ferguson's triumph was to shine a light on that policy and turn it around. Everything had a price, especially success, and if you didn't pay for it, you didn't get it.

Ferguson knew that well enough after taking on Celtic and Rangers in Scotland and winning. He knew what it took to change the balance of power and it just wasn't enough to have good intentions. Alex introduced a system of incentives for the scouts, even though most of them would have done it for nothing. He wanted to bring an edge to their work. If a scout found somebody the club signed as a schoolboy, he would get a bonus of £100. If the boy went on to play for the first team, there would be another payment of £200, and still another if he made the England team. It was sound economics. The club began to sign players who, in a year or two, they wouldn't have been able to buy for multi-millions.

The great bonus for me, on top of the coaching with the School of Excellence, was that I got to work with what would prove to be the nucleus of Ferguson's all-conquering team – Scholes, Beckham, the Nevilles and Nicky Butt. Giggs had gone through the system the year before I arrived.

In my first two years, 1989 and 1990, I went with the youth team to the Milk Cup tournament in Ireland as assistant to Kiddo, and in the third year I was given control of the team. We had done well in the previous tournaments but had missed out on the trophy, going out in the quarter-final and semi-final stages.

In 1991, the boys were more physically mature, and we won

the tournament, beating Liverpool 5–1 on the way to the final with Hearts. Keith Gillespie was the star of the game against Liverpool, scoring a hat-trick. I remember that game mainly for what it told me about the quality of the boys coming through the club, and also because we scored something of a psychological victory before the game started. Phil Thompson, the former England defender, was running the Liverpool team and we got into a dispute over which side would wear the red shirts. It got quite heated. Liverpool are Liverpool and they play in red, said Thompson. I said that was precisely our position, but as we got deeper into the stalemate I turned to one of the Irish officials and asked him what our options were. He said we could play in green. There was a big crowd, many of whom were already likely to support us because the game was in Port Stewart, Harry Gregg country, and it seemed to me that if we just happened to be playing in the green of Ireland, but with our United socks, we were guaranteed even warmer encouragement.

We took the green shirts and we slaughtered Liverpool, who had Robbie Fowler and Steve McManaman in their side. That wasn't, however, the most significant match of my brief reign over the bunch of kids who would dominate English football for the best part of ten years. For me, the important game was a scuffling quarter-final, penalty shoot-out win over Motherwell. It was the match during which I learned most about the players. I had to lecture Gary Neville and Nicky Butt on the need for self-discipline, and tell David Beckham that he had been behaving like a spoiled brat.

Neville and Butt had been lured into over-reaction to some needle by the Scottish lads, and it was something on which I felt I could hammer home the point with some authority. I loved the attitude of both kids, but they were at the stage of their development where bad habits had to be killed stone dead before they took hold. I took the main culprit, Gary, aside and asked him if he had looked back on a goal that could have put us out of the tournament. I asked him, 'How did we lose that goal, Gary?' He said nothing. I said it was because he had got involved unnecessarily with an opponent and conceded a free kick. The Scots had exploited it with a big high cross that put pressure on our goalkeeper, who was roughed up before the ball was knocked into the net. I told Gary he had taken the bait, which was the last thing a good defender should do. I said I could tell him this because someone had to tell me at his age, someone like Matt Busby.

David Beckham was my captain and central midfielder, which because of the natural creativity of his passing is the position in which I would play him for England today. But he wasn't in England form that day in Ireland. He couldn't get truly involved in the game, and to make matters worse, when we won a penalty near the end of the match, he claimed it and missed it, which meant that we had to go into extra time. I wanted more bite down the middle of the pitch, something David just hadn't been providing, so I pushed him out wide right and brought Paul Scholes inside.

Scholes got on with the business, as he seems to have been doing ever since, but Beckham put on a massive sulk. It was infuriating to see such a talented player letting himself down like that, but when extra time was over and we were still level and had to go to penalties, I saw something in him that I liked very much and almost made me forget what had gone before. Gary Neville claimed the first penalty, but Beckham, who had missed from the spot earlier, did not hesitate to follow him. He smashed the ball into the back of the net with great power and, I thought, quite a bit of anger.

Before the next game, I told him I was putting him back into the centre of midfield, but at no stage did I want to see any signs that he might get another 'cob' on if the game didn't quite go how he wanted. I told him he had behaved like a naughty boy who had had a sweet taken away. You didn't win matches, you didn't become a big player, like that. Now when I see him play, I sometimes like to think that the old message is still firmly implanted at the back of his brain. On other occasions, I think that I was totally wasting my time, but usually the moment I think that, he does something that takes my breath away.

A David Beckham will always have an old football man like me in two minds, partly because he represents a world with which we can never really be familiar. You have to love his talent, and if occasionally he reminds me of the petulant kid I had to deal with all those years ago, there are just as many times when he recalls for me that occasion when he so willingly stepped up to take a penalty despite the fact that he was in the middle of a nightmare. That particular quality shone at Old Trafford in the World Cup qualifying game against Greece, when the entire England team looked as if they were playing from a faulty memory. He had misfired on so many free kicks in that game but he kept believing in his ability to put one away.

For Ferguson, another old football man, the dilemma presented by the boy always ran deep. He detested the publicity that surrounds him. He loves the simplicities of a Scholes or a Keane or a Butt. He likes to know what he is getting. But he also knew that with Beckham he had to take the rest along with the best. It is a necessity of modern football and the modern world, and that was the main reason I was so happy working with the kids when they were at the age when their love of the game was as innocent and natural as taking a breath.

The triumph in Ireland was satisfying and I liked to think that I had imparted something of value to some superb young players as they made their inevitable way to the top. However, I did not expect or want it to change my situation. I was working hard for not a lot more money, but I was probably happier than at any point since I had been obliged to stop playing. I no longer drove on a grim automatic pilot past Stoke, Stafford and Cannock to the Albion ground. I didn't get home only to slump into a chair before dragging myself to bed. I didn't have the drain of daily petrol money. We were able to put a few quid aside. Kay was, naturally, a lot happier, too. She was no longer sharing a house with a lost soul.

I worked with the kids through the week, took the B team on Saturdays and I did a bit of scouting. I was content to let the days roll by. Inevitably, there were a few irritants. I didn't get on well with Les Kershaw, the chief scout, and some of the assignments he handed me did not smack me in the eye with their relevance; but in all the circumstances, I was happy to go about my business. For the first time in a long time I felt like a round peg in a round hole. Unfortunately, the decision of Archie Knox, Fergie's first-team coach and number two, to resign and return to Scotland, squared my circle.

Ferguson asked my opinion about the best candidate to succeed Archie and, without hesitation, I nominated Brian Kidd. I said that the coach Brian Whitehouse, who was ahead of Kiddo in the Old Trafford pecking order, was a good football man, but I just felt that Brian's experience as a player at Old Trafford, and the easy way he moved around the new breed of professionals, made him the likelier nomination. I didn't think much about the implications of Brian moving on from his role as Youth Development Officer and head of the School of Excellence. Had I done so, I might have spoken a little more carefully, but when you are asked for an opinion by your boss, and in this case one who had helped turn your life around, I think you are obliged to give an honest answer, and this is no doubt especially so if you had wanted the best for the club since early boyhood. The fact was, though, I had a tremendous working relationship with Kiddo and I realised soon enough that I had unwittingly endangered my own recently renewed existence at Old Trafford.

Ferguson quickly decided to promote Brian and gave me his old job. Later, in his autobiography, Ferguson wrote that he had been impressed with my work as a youth coach and felt that my status as an old player of some fame would prove valuable in attracting young local players. Whatever my value to the club in the new role, the re-shuffle was a personal disaster. I hated the new job. The club gave me my own secretary, and she was a lovely, competent girl. The problem was me. I hated the paperwork, I hated dealing with parents and always having to say the right thing. I hated having to tell kids that they would be better off finding a good apprenticeship away from football and seeing their faces crumple. It just wasn't my kind of work.

It was something you had to do with a good sense of the wider picture and the interests of the club. I was no good at any of it. I loved working with kids, passing on tips, telling them how it was as a professional, and getting them to improve their games. For me, there was nothing like seeing a boy come on, watching Paul Scholes hit all of his targets in life, knowing that you helped someone as honest as Stevie Bull make his mark. I had conditioned myself to seeing a lot of that in the years that would take me to retirement. I saw myself in a role that might have been made for me – someone in the background, working with the kids, who could be consulted from time to time. I had been consulted, along with the others, by Fergie when he was concerned about the mood of the first team after defeat by Sheffield Wednesday in the League Cup. When we all flew to Rotterdam for the European Cup-Winners' final the coaching staff were asked to look at the first team up close and get a sense of what they were thinking and feeling.

Fergie's style when his trusty lieutenant Knox headed home smacked a little of Busby. He was picking people's brains and getting a consensus view before the team went in against Barcelona at the Feyenoord Stadium for a taste of high-level European action. The general view was that the atmosphere had improved a lot, and so it was proved as Mark Hughes scored a brilliant goal from an acute angle and, it seemed, we had left a calling card in the big theatre. But if the show was promising, my role in the cast was not.

I lasted twelve months shuffling papers, trying to be diplomatic, and quite often failing. I had an anger in me that, I suppose now, was fuelled by terrible disappointment. I had been going well, and enjoying every moment of what I had been doing, and then suddenly nothing was working for me. I had a row with Kershaw, with whom I couldn't establish any real relationship. One day he was talking about Europe and I said it was bollocks, we would never win the European Cup playing the way he suggested. I then committed a cardinal sin – I said it was something I knew about.

When Fergie gave me the sack, he said he regretted it but didn't we both agree the new job wasn't suitable for me and the old one, the one I adored, had been filled. The sense I got, as I felt as though my stomach was being cut away, was that I was simply another casualty of a hard business. It reminded me a little of my conversation with Matt when I passed on Stan Anderson's proposal, and it occurred to me that right here was the reason I would never make a manager and the man who was giving me the hard news, like Busby before him, was plainly a great one.

Someone quite high up at the FA later told me that there had been knives out for me at Old Trafford, and while this didn't totally surprise me, I still felt I had probably played a part in my own downfall. With hindsight I should have gone to Fergie and talked it over with him when the re-shuffle happened. I should have given him my real feelings, and maybe he would have accepted that I did have something to pass on, in the flesh on the training field rather than on a piece of paper.

As it was, the manager gave a small sigh, expressed his regrets, and got on with the business of running a great football club – quite brilliantly, as it turned out. My business, because I was lost in an office and found it hard to tell a kid that he wasn't going to survive in the game that he loved as I had done at his age, was to try to re-make the rest of my life. I could complain as long as I liked, but it was the way it all worked.

I couldn't go home to Kay immediately. I needed a little buffer zone. I went to Longford Park, where in the old days I played on the putting green with John Giles. When I eventually got home, Kay made me a cup of tea and said, as she always said, that something would turn up. Later, she told one of the boys that when she saw my face that afternoon she feared I had suffered a heart-attack. I suppose, in a way, I had.

EPILOGUE

O NE day, in the aftermath of the real heart-attack, which came like a steel fist smashing into my back in the early summer of 2002, nine years after I had retreated to Longford Park not knowing what I could do with the rest of my life, I got up from the hospital bed where I had been drifting between sleep and watching the World Cup from Japan and Korea on television.

Showing un-Clouseau-like care with the drip leads and the attachment to the monitoring machine sending out the wavy lines I didn't want to understand, I looked out of the window and saw a group of people who had worry and love on their faces, and although I had a wound, and quite a bit of fear, I also had, in a way I had never known before, a certain sense of the wholeness of my life. The gathering below the window told me that. It was my family – my wife, three sons and their wives and partner, and six grandchildren. Suddenly, I had the feeling that they knew what I knew. It was that I loved them as they loved me, and if there had been a few scrapes and a lot of worry, particularly over the last few days, it was not as though I hadn't done my best for them in the only way I could.

The doctor had just told me that the heart-attack, which had come as a nasty little joke in the middle of my contribution to an anti-cholesterol campaign, appeared not to have done too much serious damage. If I was sensible, and if I cut down on the after-dinner speaking schedule, which had been my principal means of earning a living after the axe fell at Old Trafford, there was no reason why I shouldn't see quite a bit more of the growth of those grandkids being fussed over by Kay down in the hospital car park.

John, my eldest, who gave it all he had as a professional with Leeds United and Doncaster Rovers and now juggles a hundred different projects as he criss-crosses the country as a comedian and an impersonator, had Christopher and Emma with his first wife, and now has Harry with his partner Sinead – and her son, Cameron. John takes a tilt at life and when I ask him what makes him run so hard, he says, 'You tell me, Dad – I suppose, like you did, I just want to make some kind of mark.'

Peter, who teaches in Bolton, is married to Andrea, who is also a teacher. Peter is a runner. They have Alex. Robert, the passion-ate Preston fan until they gave me the chop, always had a ball between his feet as a kid. He's married to Mary and they have Megan and Caitlin. He was a chef but now he's studying the Russian revolution.

I looked down at them all, with Kay the mother hen clucking away, and I felt a burst of shame about those dark thoughts on the motorway which had, for a little while, pushed me away from that basic belief that you can never let your problems get on top of you. You have to tackle the fucking life out of them.

When I got back into my bed, miraculously without hitting some knob that would have put the entire hospital on red alert, I ran through my head some after-dinner material that could be worked around the convenience of lying up in hospital in front of a television set with an entire World Cup stretching out before you and no nagging wife to stir you from the sofa, just a nurse from the 'Carry on' series serving endless cups of tea.

When my mother Kitty sang her little ditty about Norbert Peter Patrick Paul going off down Livesey Street to play football and beat them all, she could not have imagined that one day I would be talking for my supper from such places as the captain's table on the *Queen Elizabeth II*, and in the Savoy in London – and nor could I have done so unless Wilf McGuinness and Murray Bernie, a vice-president of Lancashire Cricket Club, had talked me into it in those days that opened up like an abyss when my career in football ended at Old Trafford. Wilf said I had an asset I could use – I had memories of the greatest day in English sport, a day on which I had danced my way into the ken of a large part of the nation. Murray organised my debut gig, at Old Trafford Cricket Ground. My mouth was dry and my hands were shaking when I went into that big room. I remembered what the Lawman had said after his first engagement – 'Never again, that's just too hard,' and he is one of the greatest natural showmen football has ever seen.

But with Kay (my scriptwriter and ideas woman) at my side I got it done, and it was never so hard after that first time when my shirt was soaked with sweat and I knew terror that I hadn't experienced since Brian Kidd impersonated a gunman in a dark corridor in Buenos Aires. My life reeled back before my eyes before I went out to take that first bow, and I gained strength from that, too. I thought of my great friend Shay, who had died too early, and how when I heard the news it was the saddest day of my life. I recalled his dry reaction when I sat next to him with my head streaming blood as the team bus drove away from the Bernabeu Stadium after our European Cup semi-final triumph. I had been hit by a bottle thrown by a fan. I said to Shay, 'I'm going to charge thirty pounds for a new shirt.' He said, 'What are you talking about – the suit didn't cost that.' I remembered how I had auditioned for the role of Al Jolson at the boy's club when I couldn't sing a note or dance a step. I thought of how I'd come to win a World Cup and a European Cup medal even though I was born a half-blind dwarf who was bombed by the Germans and run over by a trolley bus before he was one. I wasn't going to be talking about nuclear research. I was going to speak on a subject close to so many people's hearts. How close? I recalled my brother, a responsible married man and father, telling me how he had had to fight in the street after I had scored an own goal against Manchester City at Maine Road.

Why do we care so much about the games we play? Why did I sit up in my hospital bed and shout, against doctor's orders, 'Go on you little bastard Butty,' when one of those boys I coached, Nicky Butt, clattered an Argentinian in the World Cup game? Because it is in our blood. We are English – and we take a bit of knocking down.

INDEX